PROPHETS

Words of Fire

Megan McKenna

ORBIS BOOKS

Maryknoll, New York 10545

The Catholic Foreign Mission Society of America (Maryknoll) recruits and trains people for overseas missionary service. Through Orbis Books, Maryknoll aims to foster the international dialogue that is essential to mission. The books published, however, reflect the opinions of their authors and are not meant to represent the official position of the Society. To obtain more information about Maryknoll or Orbis Books, please visit our website at http://www.maryknoll.org.

Copyright © 2001 by Megan McKenna

Published by Orbis Books, Maryknoll, New York, U.S.A.

Published by Orbis Books, Maryknoll, NY 10545-0308
Manufactured in the United States of America

Unless otherwise indicated, scripture quotations are from the Christian Community Bible, copyright © 1991 by Bernardo Hurault (17th edition).

Library of Congress Cataloging-in-Publication Data

McKenna, Megan.
    Prophets : words of fire / Megan McKenna.
       p. cm.
    Includes bibliographical references.
    ISBN 1-57075-364-4 (pbk.)
    1. Prophets. 2. Bible. O.T. Prophets –Theology. I. Title.

BS1505.55 .M35 2001
224'.06 – dc21

                                00-052375

PROPHETS

For JB and Jeffrey Briggs

For all my black fire ... you are white fire.

With gratitude and unwordable love.

Contents

Introduction

It's not the earthquake that controls the advent of a different life
But storms of generosity and visions of incandescent souls.
—BORIS PASTERNAK

This book, of necessity, covers an enormous amount of material, in terms of historical time, the large number of prophets, and their varied messages. There is a succinct story told by Jewish rabbis and teachers, this by David Wolpe, that should be kept in mind when reading this book:

> Once upon a time a man approached the rabbi who was learned and wise, saying: "Rabbi, I don't want to boast but I consider myself a devout and learned Jew. I have been through the Talmud three times in my studies!" The Rabbi smiled back at him, nodding, and said: "Admirable. Admirable. But my friend, I have a question for you. How much of the Talmud has been through you?"[1]

Prophets are difficult to talk about because they are not like us at all. They suffer terribly. They live on the outskirts. They live as strangers even to those they love most dearly. They cause dissension. They are intent on making us see the truth about ourselves, which can result in our feeling humiliated and shamed. We slink away from such a glaring eye or are enraged beyond words, thinking only how to silence that person forever.

Their styles are unique and diversified, yet they all attack with a similar intensity. They never let up until we change, or until we make a choice, or until we attack back, or until what they say comes to pass on us — or until they disappear or die. When they denounce, they go after everyone indiscriminately, but especially governments, the economy,

1

the military, leaders, priests, other prophets, other countries. Then they turn on us as a people and on each of us as individuals — there is no escape or rationalizing. Their words sting us — as individuals and a people — into a recognition that we are the absolute worst of the lot and should know better. They remind us over and over again by their presence that their prophetic word comes out of our sin, our evil, our injustice, our collusion with systems and authority that do harm, our insensitivities, our absorption with ourselves. They lay our lives bare, down to bone, marrow, and soul. They try to break through our well-planned and smoothly functioning worlds to say that we are the problem. We're the product of our systems. We're immersed in their values. We typify the systems that grind down the majority of the world. We are self-righteous and without religious sensibility, either in relation to God or morally in relation to one another, especially those who are brutalized by our injustice and lack of concern.

Prophets don't just go after the system or the politicians or the rich and powerful — they go after us all. Either we are among the poor — those who, while money is being wasted, cry out, are hungry for food, decency, and shelter, who are caught in cycles of violence, and who suffer for lack of medicine — or we are among those who are profiting from the system and the labor and suffering of the poor. The problem is not the government or the church — it's us! And one is only a prophet when one is cast off, outside the system, hidden among the voices of the silent, the mute, and those stunned by evil. Many of us in the church today would be seen and revealed as armchair critics, whiners, individuals and groups set on bettering our own positions in society and church, who are paid for praying, teaching, going on retreats, seeking spiritual direction, theologizing, and so on, making sure the system continues to function and making sure that knowledge and information do not convert, cut to the heart, and move us out of our safe positions to stand over there — there where every word burns, where every word tells the truth, and where every word puts us further outside what is acceptable and allowable. Yet the Jewish tradition that birthed prophets as wild offspring would say that life is never so full as when you stake your life on it, even if you lose your life doing it.

The prophets ached over injustice and were torn to shreds by it. They had *no* life but God's honor — which was the only hope of the poor. They were reminders in the flesh of that honor — painful, angry truth-tellers who knew what was wrong. They made people nervous, sick to their stomachs, vicious, and self-righteous. Or worse, after all the reactions, the prophets were ignored — the people didn't change, didn't convert. And then the prophets' words came to pass: the warnings, the threats, and the punishments that were the natural consequences of people's behavior came about. The prophets were, after all was said and done, people who knew the truth, who spoke it, and who effected it in their worlds. They had to speak, whether people responded to them or not. An old Zen story puts it clearly:

> Once upon a time an old Buddhist monk went to the town square every day to cry out for peace with justice and for an end to hostility and anger. His cries went unheeded and unheard and had absolutely no effect on his country's war-making or his own neighbors' hatred and petty selfish lives. After awhile even his own monks were embarrassed for him and sent a delegation pleading with him to stop, saying that he was having no effect and that people thought him senile or crazy. They did not want to be associated with him anymore. They begged, pleaded, and rationalized with him to stop. They told him, "No one cares what you say. They don't even listen to you anymore. Everyone in the country has gone insane with fear and war, selfishness, greed and killing. Why go on?" His answer was given directly, looking his own monks right in the eye: "I cry out for peace and justice so that I will not go insane!"

This too is the prophet. The prophets' vocation is to cry out — to God, to the air, to any open heart; they cry out on behalf of God and on behalf of the poor because no one is listening except God. They cry out for those no one heeds, except maybe in passing in lip service. There have always been three kinds of prophets: the individual chosen, sent, and compelled to speak; the scripture that is the word of God; and the poor. In contemporary theology one of the people who made this most clear was Ignacio Ellacuría, a theologian and prophet of El Salvador who both lived and ministered with the poorest and was also an articulate spokesman on human rights, a professor at a university, a Jesuit, and, in the end, a martyred prophet. He wrote:

> Among so many signs that always exist, some calling for attention and others barely perceptible, there is in every time one which is the principal one, by whose light the others should

be discerned and interpreted. This sign is always the histori-
cally *crucified* people, which joins to its permanence the always
distinctive historical form of its crucifixion.[2]

This book is about prophets, the prophets of the Jewish tradition,
and it will be quickly apparent that The Prophet, Jesus of Nazareth,
seems to be missing. In Luke's resurrection account, simply referred
to as the Emmaus story, we overhear a conversation between two disciples running away from Jerusalem who are intercepted by Jesus,
although they do not recognize him. They describe what their exalted notions of Jesus had been before those ideas were dashed by his
bloody crucifixion and death: "Jesus of Nazareth. He was a prophet,
you know, mighty in word and in deed before God and the people. But
the chief priests and our rulers sentenced him to death. They handed
him over and he was crucified. Yet we had hoped that he would redeem
Israel" (Luke 24:19b–21). In older translations that last line read: "Oh,
we had so hoped that he would be the one who set Israel free!" And
they go on, talking about what happened around the empty tomb, and
then they fall silent, in their dashed dreams and lost hopes, in their
despair. And then it is Jesus' turn. We can almost see him take a deep
breath — he has had to do this many times before, and they never hear.
They do not see. They do not listen or obey or remember. The story
tells us:

> "How dull you are, how slow of understanding! You fail to be-
> lieve the message of the prophets. Is it not written that the Christ
> should suffer all this and then enter his glory?" Then start-
> ing with Moses and going through the prophets, he explained
> to them everything in the Scripture concerning himself. (Luke
> 24:25–27)

The present book, after a first chapter on the nature of a prophet,
begins with Moses and continues through all the Old Testament
prophets. It is meant to be read backwards — from where we stand
now back through the person of Jesus Christ, the prophet of Nazareth,
the crucified and risen one, back through the history of Christianity and of Israel, our ancestor. And it's meant to be read forward —
through the history of those called the chosen people of God, through
those called to the Kingdom of God, as the brothers and sisters of the

prophet Jesus up through our own day — and on into our as yet unknown futures. So in a sense this is a book about Jesus as the word of God made flesh, the passion of God made manifest beyond anything the prophets could have imagined, though Jesus is only mentioned by name a few times.

In conjunction with the words above of Ignacio Ellacuría, it is also a book about the crucified one, the Body of Christ, the crucified people of the world, the poor, and it should be heard and read while standing with them. Ellacuría wrote about Jesus the Christ with a vitally new and demanding perspective that I have sought to incorporate throughout this book. He turned to the figure of the Suffering Servant from Second Isaiah "on which the primitive Christian community fastened in order to understand Jesus' death."[3] And then he argues that "this entitles us to use the image to offer a christological interpretation not only of 'the death of Jesus,' but of the 'crucified people,' " which he defines as that "vast portion of humankind which is literally and actually crucified by natural,...historical, and personal oppressions." Ellacuría also reminds us of the disturbing fact that the ongoing crucifixion of the poor and oppressed has been a defining aspect of "the reality of the world in which the church has existed for almost two thousand years, [literally] since Jesus announced the approach of the Reign of God."[4]

In a sense, from the very beginning of time, every prophet stood at the foot of the cross, watching those crucified and crying out on their behalf; they spoke and wept and raged in its shadow. Ellacuría's good friend Jon Sobrino adds to this image of Christ what this means for the majority of the world's people and for the rest of us today: "The crucified peoples — shows us what we are; we tend to ignore it, cover it up, or distort it, because it simply terrifies us."[5] Today the prophets speak on behalf of hundreds of millions of people, rather than just a small, insignificant nation centuries before the coming of Christ. If these people are, as the theologians of the Third World call them, "the presence of the crucified in history," then all theology is radically altered by positing them at the center of reflection, of interpretation of the scriptures, and of moral responses within the parameters of worshiping as a community of believers. We are to become a single people, universally the people of God, who worship in truth and who live in justice and peace — a clarion call and a light to the nations of the sanctity of God's name for all the earth.

Today, if the poor of the world are prophets by their lives and their dying, then there are far more prophets than we have previously imagined. Leonardo Boff has written that there is a significant analogy between the innocent death of these crucified people and the martyrdom of Jesus. Just as Jesus was a martyr for the Kingdom of God, so these people are martyrs of the kingdom, prophets by their presence and their lives and their deaths. Sobrino builds on this idea, extending who these prophets and martyrs of today are to all those who "lay down their lives for love." Not only are they the outspoken ones — catechists, priests, religious community members, peasants, journalists, students, delegates of the word, doctors, and lawyers who were hunted down because of their service to the people — but the people themselves are prophets, witnesses, and martyrs to the truth:

> Finally, there are the masses who are innocently and anonymously murdered, even though they have not used any explicit form of violence, even verbal. They do not actively lay down their lives to defend the faith, or even, directly, to defend God's Kingdom. They are the peasants, children, women, and old people, above all who died slowly day after day, and die violently with incredible cruelty and totally unprotected.[6]

These are the people who seek justice and peace for themselves and their communities — what the prophets of old cried out for as central to the worship of Yahweh, the God of those who cried out from Egypt's bondage. They struggle simply to live, and their suffering reveals the presence of Jesus who, in the tradition of the Suffering Servant, was "crushed by sin." They bear the burden of all the world's actions, and — even if they are unaware of their religious meaning — they seek to break the hold of injustice and proclaim once again that those who seek the truth become the light to the nations. Their presence in the world reveals the lie that is the life we lead, the lie the world seeks to conceal. All theology, all spirituality, all ethics, all prayer, and all ritual must be done at the foot of the cross, at the foot of their cross, with them as prophets and with all the prophets who have gone before us in faith:

> At the hour of truth, unless we profoundly accept the truth of the crucified peoples and the fundamental responsibility of successive empires for their crucifixion, we will miss the main fact.

That is, that in this world there is still enormous sin. Sin is what killed the servant — the Son of God — and sin is what continues to kill God's children. And this sin is inflicted by some upon others.[7]

There are few enough individual prophets in every generation. Fortunately, the poor and the crucified of the world confront us with truth, holding up a mirror to our lives and values, our sin, and our collusion with the systems of the world that destroy other human beings as a matter of course. Their existence, their shortened lives, their sufferings, and their premature and violent deaths cry out for mercy and for people to join their struggle. The spirituality of the prophets, if you can speak of such a thing, is based on three principles: *prophecy* — the message and the honor of the name of God through justice and peace; *their presence as God's witnesses* in the world for truth and against those who disobey the word of God; and *pity* — the overflowing of compassion and mercy.

To borrow the words of Abraham Joshua Heschel, prophets are "the voice that God has lent to the silent agony, a voice to the plundered poor."[8] And "the prophet's ear ... is attuned to the cry imperceptible to others" (7). "Reading the words of the prophets is a strain on the emotions, wrenching one's conscience from the state of suspended animation" (7), and they serve as "witnesses" who must "bear testimony" in such a way that they "reveal" God (21). Their words reveal or uncover God, and in their words "the invisible God becomes audible" (22). They are about the business of and the hard work of the "exegesis of existence" from the singular eye of God (xiv). And the prophet speaks, acts, lives, and breathes from inside — inside God and inside the people's pain, knowing both "divine pathos" and intimacy with God as well as involvement with the people" (26). I am especially grateful to a photographer, Mev Puleo, who with her camera and words bound together what the prophets have done with their poetry, their persuasive symbolic actions, and their persecution borne with the people.[9] Centuries after Moses or Isaiah or Jesus of Nazareth, there are prophets who sing, take pictures, cry out, prepare reports on human rights abuses, and preach hope in slums and villages. And some of those pay the ultimate price for the truth by the witness of their deaths.

The prophets can seem harsh, unbending in their righteousness, te-

dious in their repetitions, and scurrilous in their denunciations, but
we must remember that their words and actions are born of God's
pity, God's compassion, and God's truthfulness. Their very existence
is birthed in God's horror at what we do and in God's terrible dis-
may at our refusal to be made in the divine image — God's people
of justice and peace. A story about Elijah told by Rabbi Jose (ca. 135
C.E.) reminds us poignantly of how closely God is bound through the
prophets not only to Israel's existence and future but over time to all
the peoples of the world:

> Once I was walking through the city of Jerusalem at the time of
> evening prayer. I slipped off the main street and into a side street
> that held ruins of the devastated city. I entered one of the ruins,
> leaned against a crumbling wall, and prayed, quietly chanting
> the old words. As I prayed I sensed the presence of another and
> turned to see the prophet Elijah standing close by the wall. He
> waited until I finished and he greeted me with peace, bowing
> with extended hands. I returned his greeting, wondering why he
> had once again come to visit me. It was he who asked the ques-
> tions: "My child, what are you doing here?" I thought, wasn't it
> obvious that I was praying?
>
> I answered, "I came inside to pray."
>
> "But why inside?" he asked. "Couldn't you pray on the streets
> as easily?"
>
> "No, I was sure to be distracted, or interrupted." He looked
> at me intently and asked another question: "What was it like
> to pray among the ruins? Was there anything different than
> the usual? Did you hear or sense anything? Did your prayer
> change?"
>
> I was surprised but remembered Elijah's role of teacher, the
> one who reminds and enlightens, and so I answered him truth-
> fully. "Yes, my master and teacher, it was different. It was hard.
> It was lonely. It was like praying and having an echo of sor-
> row come back upon me. And I kept hearing something — the
> cry, the call, the moan of a dove, but it was not of this world.
> I thought it kept trying to say something to me. It too was
> praying."
>
> Elijah pushed me, his hands on my shoulders: "Remember!
> Think! What was it saying?"

I closed my eyes and the cry came back, so full of sadness and loss: "My children, my temple, my people, my land... all is broken, all is in ruins, and my children are in exile, scattered like seed on the wind among the nations.... My children, my children, my children..."

"Yes" was the prophet's response. "That lament, that prayer, rises three times a day from everywhere in what was God's city, God's dwelling place among the people, but so few, so few, have ears or hearts to hear."

Woven throughout the tradition of the prophets, and of the rabbis of Israel, is the idea that God mourns, that God shares the sufferings of the people, that God is so wed to those he has chosen that his faithfulness brings him intensely close to those who suffer, even when their sin and injustice bring terrible ruin upon them. It is this God who searches out the prophets and seizes their hearts, their words, and drives them unceasingly into the midst of the people, hoping that this time the people will hear, will heed and come home to obedience and to justice, and so to peace with their God.

Interlaced in the long prophetic tradition is the move from God's concern with one people to concern for other nations and tribes, even the enemies of Israel, and then in the later prophets to all the nations, all the earth, and the promise, the hope, and the demand that Jerusalem be the city for all and that God's name be known everywhere.

A story by Reb Zalman, a contemporary rabbi, contains a piece of another story in which the Reb asks Moses a burning question about the temple in Jerusalem and whether or not it will ever be built again. He describes it as the "question closest to his heart." He wants to know how this rebuilding of the temple will happen without destroying the mosque that is presently built on the Temple Mount. We are told that Moses smiles as he gives Reb Zalman the answer to his question. Moses says:

Even now the Temple is being restored far under the earth by the prayers and longings of Israel. Your own prayers, Reb Zalman, during the past forty days, have gone very far in restoring the Holy of Holies itself, the place of the Ark of the Covenant. And when the Temple has been completely restored this way, then the time of the Messiah will have arrived, and the Temple will rise up out of the earth, in all its glory, for the whole world to see.

And as it rises up there will be a wing of the Temple for each nation of the world, and that is why it is written "My house shall be called the House of Prayer for all nations."

Moses leaves, and the Reb has his answer.[10]

We move backward and forward in time, for all is present for the Holy One. After the disciples on the road recognize Jesus the prophet, the crucified and risen one, in the breaking of the bread, they remember. They remember and exclaim to one another, "Were not our hearts filled with ardent yearning when he was talking to us on the road and explaining the Scriptures?" (Luke 24:32). Again an older translation is better, more poetic, and more to the point: "Were not our hearts burning... or on fire as he opened our minds to the Scriptures?"

The word of God in the scriptures, in the mouth of a prophet, in the crucified peoples of the world, or in the person of Jesus the crucified one risen and among us, sets our hearts on fire and instills in us those seeds of fire that can be stirred into flame again and again — the flame of hope, of justice, of zeal for the honor of God, and of righteous rage against evil, insensitivity to others' pain, and the hypocrisy of religious people.

The Jewish rabbis teach that the Torah, the words of God, are "black fire written on white fire." The words of the prophets, on the page and in our covenant written on our hearts and on the faces of our brothers and sisters, are "black fire on white fire." May these words on this paper make our hearts burn as the scriptures are opened to us and the message of the prophets echoes in our minds and ears. May we remember that these words are born in the furnace of God's heart and that these words of fire are but breaths and intimations of God's own love for all of us. We end with selections from a fourth-century prayer composed by St. Ephrem, a member of the Syriac Christian community. The prayer is called "Blessed Is the One Whom the Prophets Portrayed":

In scripture he is written; in nature he is engraved.
His diadem is portrayed by kings, and by prophets his truth....

He is in the rod of Moses and in the hyssop of Aaron and in the
    diadem of David.
The prophets have his likeness, but the apostles have his gospel.

In the beginning again upon the wood alighted the weary dove
On you, the tree of life, came, took refuge, and alighted the
weary testament.
Revelations gazed at you; similes awaited you; symbols
expected you;
likenesses longed for you; parables took refuge in you....

By his healthy meal he weaned [and] took away the milk.
By his baptism were abolished the bathing and sprinkling that
the elders taught....
In the genuineness of his truth and the power of his light
he showed his beauty [to] his own.
His adornments came [and] were beautiful on him;
his sufferings came [and] were completed in him.[11]

There is now one word of fire, one word, one prophet, one hope, one people, and one God. A Hindu saying repeats the theme: "Call God what you will, God's name is Truth." May this book make us all words of truth, words that honor the name of the Holy One, words that lift the burden from the poor and crucified of the earth, and words that set afire a new creation, a new century with people who "do justice, love with mercy, and walk humbly with one another and with their God of peace on earth." May it be so. Amen. Amen. Amen.

❦ ONE ❦

The Prophet

What in the world is a prophet? What manner of beast? Often the prophet is imaged as a ragged creature, disheveled, living in wild places, apart from humankind and civilization, fanatical in dress and behavior, threatening and uncouth in ways and words. Jewish scholar Rabbi Abraham Joshua Heschel begins *The Prophets: An Introduction* with the words: "This book is about some of the most disturbing people who have ever lived: the men whose inspiration brought the Bible into being — the men whose image is our refuge in distress, and whose voice and vision sustain our faith."[1] These men and women capture our imagination at the same time that they repulse us. There is something about them that we sense as radical, as disruptive, as too intense for more than a few moments of conversation or meeting. A short dose of their presence seems to be more than enough, thank you!

A Jewish story can perhaps bring us to the heart of what it means to be a prophet. I have seen a one-line version of this tale attributed to Rabbi Nachman in a collection of his sayings called *The Empty Chair,* but this is the way I heard it once and the way I tell it.

Once upon a time there was a great rabbi who had many disciples. Parents would go hungry and endure hardships to save money so that their children could go and sit at the master teacher's feet for even a few months, or a year or two. His wisdom was very highly valued and his mere presence led to changes and transformations. One day the rabbi was working on his Torah portion, pouring over his books and praying, and the other students were gathered at another table, supposedly engaged in the same work.

They were studying the Torah portion and doing some research, but they were also talking about what was going on in

13

their own lives in between more serious appropriation of the
text. One of them said, "I just can't concentrate. You don't know
how bad my life has been. I just can't pay attention to these read-
ings. My mother is visiting and my wife — she is fine when my
mother is not around. But my mother's very presence does terrible things to my wife and my life is so bad, I just don't know
what to do."

Another of the students looked up from the Torah portion and
said: "You think you have troubles! I have visitors, so many of
my relatives I don't know what to do. There are maybe eight or
nine of them, and we are trying to feed them on what we usually
have to stretch just for ourselves. I'm frantic and exhausted. I
don't know what to do next."

Another chimed in before the other had barely finished with
his tale of woe: "You haven't seen anything like what I'm going
through — I have all these relatives visiting me, but they're all
sick! I don't want to leave the study house. I'm more than happy
just to stay here and study the Torah. I dread having to go home.
It is so bad."

Everyone had something to say about their particular troubles, putting in their two cents. It seemed that everyone's life
was bad. Another interrupted with the words: "Bad! You haven't
heard bad! Wait until you hear my life!"

Suddenly, the rabbi slammed his fist down on the table, sending the books scattering. He stood up and looked at his students
hard and shouted at them: "Stop! Be careful! The Almighty,
the Holy One, listens to every word you say! And he, Blessed
be his Name, has been listening to you in your conversation,
and he is sitting back there thinking: 'Bad! Bad! I'll show
you bad!'"

The rabbi went on: "But God also listens if you say: 'Morning! Ah, blessed be the God of Heaven. God is good. Earth is
good! I heard the birds awake the morning. Life is so good!'
And God would have heard you just now if you'd said: 'My
children wrapped their arms around my legs this morning and
wouldn't let me go off to the study house! Life is good.' God
would have sat back and said quietly: 'Good! Good! Now I'll
show you good!' So be careful! God is listening to every word
you say! And the future is yours!"

The reaction to the rabbi's words is a gasp, a murmur that runs through the group. The seemingly simple story has massive insights, insights that are devastating for believers. The story, like a prophet, affords an insight, a momentary glimpse into the mind of God, as it were, altering reality forever after.

The story rattles attitudes we have toward life, toward church, toward people, toward good and evil. Our attitudes have power, and God, it seems, takes personally even our attitudes! The story posits that God, the Holy, is intimate with each one of us, with each situation of our lives. The creation that develops between God and us is an ongoing work. Often people don't like the story once they begin to talk about it. They derogatorily label it as "Old Testament," meaning that *our* God doesn't act like that — *our* God is interested in showing us love, not the "bad." That's the reaction until I change the words a bit and ask, What if the conversation were about politics and economics in the United States? What if God overheard our conversations about politics and money and our own self-serving ideas of justice? Mightn't God say: "You think you are one just nation under God? You think you know justice? I'll show you justice!" Do we think we know how to live the good life? "Hmmm," God might say, "so you think you understand what a good life is? Forget that and listen to me. I'll show you a good life." And suddenly, when I say these things, there is quiet in the room, a gulping kind of quiet followed by admissions of guilt, or at least a move to question our priorities and ways of living.

The story reveals that we see the world and one another the way we choose to see them, not the way God sees them. And so it hints that we might also see God the way we are and not the way God is. The prophet interrupts, intervenes, and jolts us into uncertainty or doubt and then turns and points directly at us and says: "What is wrong with the world is wrong with you!" Like the rabbi, the prophet is intent on stopping history — reality as it is — because the reality insults both human beings and God. This story is a prophetic moment that indicates what a prophet does and how it is done. This is the prophet's entire life — eating, sleeping, and drinking God's horror at what we are doing. The prophet is intent only on stopping us, if only momentarily, so that God's word can censure us, threaten us, and call us to repentance and transformation.

Often when I teach courses on the prophets, at the very beginning some participants state their interest in learning the spirituality of the prophets in order to incorporate into their own lives and ministries a specific manner of praying and relating to the realm of the Spirit. They will say that much is written about the prophets' methods or messages but little about their personal spirituality. In response I state that the spirituality of the prophet *is the message.* The prophets have no personal spirituality. They live for one thing: the word of God is in their mouths. And it is let loose whether they moan and groan, rant and rave. Their spiritualities are, in a certain sense, the very words that come out of their mouths. Each prophet becomes the message. They embody the word that is to be spoken to this people, at this time, in this place. Their very presence becomes a message in itself.

We have a tendency to think of a message as only words. And yet in Hebrew the term for "word" is *dabar,* which can mean word, gesture, action, presence, pattern of repetition, or liturgy. The prophet exists for one thing only — to tell God's truth, God's revelation to this people at this time. The Hebrew word for "prophet" is *navi* (in the plural, *n'vi-im*), which means "to speak for someone else." That is why the prophets' calling card, or their most often used expression to introduce a prophecy, is "Thus says the Lord." That is why they speak in the first person, using words such as "I the Lord, your God, say this . . . "

The validation of their words is utterly simple and undeniable. Those who listen to them either change in response to their pronouncements or resist them and attempt to kill them for their words. There is no middle ground. The prophets' presence is about choice, about standing in the right place, about commitment, and about obedience to God now. Those who listen must be converted, or else. As a result, prophets are very creative at capturing attention and keeping it while denouncing offensive behaviors and intentions. Those who are not converted will persecute the prophets relentlessly and without mercy and, in many cases, drive them into exile or kill them. For the prophets, the word of God is their spirituality. It defines both their response in life and their understanding of who God is. And so it should be for all of us, for the word of God reveals who we are and who God is and what constitutes the responsibilities and promises of that relationship.

At the beginning of this century and millennium we, the people of God, seem interested in every form of spirituality except the word of God. We seem to have forgotten that most of the ancient and more traditional spiritualities, though lived in a specific historical epoch, were originally derived from the scriptures. For instance, there is much interest in the spirituality of the medieval mystics such as Julian of Norwich. Yet Julian most likely lived sealed up in a wall of a church, studying the scriptures, while the world outside her anchorage was living and dying through the horror of the bubonic plague. The experiences that affected her most were isolation, visitations by strangers she never saw but only heard, and the backdrop of the black death that probably wiped out more than a third of the population of Europe. Julian's words were crafted and birthed out of terrible suffering and the contemporary experience of the crucified one in the people of God still crying out the ancient psalm: "My God, my God, why have you forsaken me?"

Or, if we look at the poems of mystical love and tenderness of John of the Cross, we often forget that they were written under excruciating circumstances, as John was locked in a closet, starved to death, tortured by his own brethren, and derided for his understanding of the religious community's call to imitate the crucified one in their vows, their way of living, and their prayers. These magnificent love songs, written under awful duress, were filtered through the word of God.

The word made flesh is the source of spirituality for believers. Our spirituality lies in the word that is the community of the Trinity, the word that is justice in practice, the word that is mercy for sinners, and the word that is transforming grace in the face of evil and sin. Our heritage is this word of the Lord in the mouths of our ancestors: Moses; Elijah and Elisha; Isaiah and the prophets of exile; John the Baptizer; and, finally, Jesus, the word of God made flesh that dwells among us now and always.

Another question students often ask deals with the methodology of the prophet. And, again, the method *is* the message. The clothing that is chosen, the gestures and dramas enacted, the rituals invoked, the words and tone chosen, the appearance and disappearance of the prophet — all are the message and the method. The prophet Elijah is testimony to this reality. Every time the king of Israel catches sight of Elijah approaching, he cringes and cries out: "You disturber of Israel, what do you want now?" The Christian Community Bible's translation reads: "On seeing Elijah, Ahab said to him, 'Is it you, the plague of Israel?' " (1 Kings 18:17). The very sight of the prophet can evoke the consciousness that all is not well in the world and that it is time for a reckoning, according to God's vantage point on history. This constant presence of the prophets as carriers of the message of God is backdrop for a line attributed to Francis of Assisi. "You must preach the gospel insistently, relentlessly, without rest, but only as a last resort use words." Our words must be backed up with our actions, and our flesh and blood must be revealed in what we stand for and against, in our ethical choices and moral decisions.

The prophet is a collaborator with the Divine. French novelist André Gide once said: "Art is a collaboration between God and the artist, and the less the artist does the better." This also describes the connection between the prophets and God. These are people gifted to save others at crucial moments in history, in the struggle between good and sin, when people have forgotten their covenants and have betrayed their relationship to God or mocked their call to holiness and imitation of God. Somehow the prophets know what God wills and hopes for the earth better than others do. They are people with an uncanny understanding of reality and human nature and with a strange ability to act on that knowledge. They have a drive so intense that it seems that nothing can withstand it. They reveal an absolute assurance of God's presence in history and God's attentiveness to what is happening among us. They are prepared to risk all in their courage to speak the truth and act with integrity. Truly, they are instruments of God's power and glory.

It seems that they are usually best known for what they resist, for what they stand against. They represent God's point of view in stark contrast to all other points of view. In this we share their stance, for our second baptismal promise is phrased: "Do you promise to resist evil and refuse to be mastered by any sin?" What we resist defines us as clearly as what we profess to stand for. The prophets resist evil and sin and their effects on individuals and society — they resist with all their hearts and minds and souls and strength, as creatively and imaginatively as they can, with the inspiration of God's Spirit.

And how they resist with style and panache! In addition to being prophets, they are poets, priests, shamans, actors, clowns and fools, hermits, exiles, and critics. They can hold their own with the best of the politicians, religious leaders, sociologists, anthropologists, psychologists, and economists. They are conscious tongues of fire and sword points aimed at the heart of public and private life, intent on exposing our motivations and the disastrous effects of our lives and insensitivities on others who suffer because of us. They are embodiments of consciousness-raising who often stand against us, resisting what we have become. Their resistance offers us another vision of humanity's destiny and vocation.

The prophets often see us as nearsighted, meaning we can only see what is immediately under our noses, connected to our own lives. We have lost sight of the vision of hope, of the future that God intends, while we have been concentrating with total self-absorption on our own immediate desires. We are like drivers lost in a fog of our own obsessions, unable to see the road clearly. And so we need the prophets, the far-seeing ones, the dreamers in broad daylight, the long-distance high beams that show us glimpses of where we are going and what the outcome of our choices and lifestyles will be. One way to define a prophet is a person who sees so clearly what is happening in the present moment that he or she can tell us what is going to happen if we don't change immediately and radically.

One of the harder aspects of the prophets and their messages is that they are almost always messages in the plural, messages directed to us as members of a people, of a group, of a community, and not as singular individuals. When a prophet seeks out an individual, it is always one who has a great deal of autonomous power, such as a king, a priest, or those who hold authority or power in a society, government, or institution. Otherwise, the message is directed to all, with no escape hatch. In our contemporary society this is perhaps the hardest aspect of prophecy to contend with, because we are intent on being seen and being related to primarily as individuals. When the prophet's message comes stinging home, we resist with, "Who are you to tell *me* what I'm doing or not doing? You don't know me at all," or "You don't know what I've done. . . . " And, frankly, the prophet doesn't care because the prophet sees as God sees: the prophet sees us as members of a people, of a community, of a church or organization or class, and contends with us together, not alone. In fact, if the prophet does attack an individual, it's even harder! In that case, the individual will be held accountable for the group and for his or her influence and ability to change or alter the outcome.

The prophet is a truth-teller, using the power of God to shatter the silence that surrounds injustice. Usually the very appearance of a prophet signals the end of Yahweh's patience with people and a judgment that must be brought to bear on those who have done wrong. The prophet's appearance is a signal of fire that the covenant of God

has been betrayed and that we, as the people of God, have been or
are unfaithful. When the prophet appears, it is time for us to be held
responsible for our actions and the state of our society and community.

Invariably, when I teach I begin with the insistent adage that I will
repeat over and over again in the course of the class: "Do not take
anything I say personally, but take it to heart." This is, in essence, how
the prophets went after the people, going for their hearts, their jugular
veins. They did not need to know the people individually. They knew
the people the way God knew the people, as chosen, as committed
to the covenant and the law, and as mindful of their history, of God's
saving grace and presence among them since their cry for freedom was
heard in Egypt. A prophet knows the nerves that are exposed, tender;
with just the right pressure the prophet goes for those. Every one of
us as human beings has nerves. Some of them aren't as sensitive as
others, but the prophet instinctively goes for the one that will cause
us to react strongly, even violently, as God infringes on our space and
life. The prophet is intent on crossing over our borders to expose us
for what we truly are as we stand before God. And just as the prophet
resists evil, we resist the prophet's truth, the word of God come upon
us to wreak havoc with our carefully constructed lives and religious
practices.

The prophet reveals and also conceals. This tension or balance is at
the core of the mystery. The actions and emotions of the prophet reveal
God and also conceal aspects of God. Every bit of knowledge about
God that we integrate or absorb reveals another level of knowledge
of God that is concealed from us. Our consciousness of God is like
an iceberg. The tiny bit that sticks up above the water line conceals
as much as eight times the weight and mass below the surface. The
prophet reveals that tiny bit of God that is apparent to all and yet, at
the same time, attempts to remind us of the enormity and massiveness
of what is hidden about God because of our sin, our evil, and our
evasion of God's presence. Prophets' presence and message are much
like radar: a blip on the screen that reveals a mystery far larger than
what we are used to.

Even in our own lives, we reveal portions of our past, our feelings,
our consciousness to certain people as we choose what is to be shared
and with whom. From many we consciously conceal even the core of
our identities while unconsciously hiding what we do not want others
to know. The prophet has the onerous task of revealing to each person

what is obvious to God but what we individually and collectively are intent on hiding from others, including ourselves. What we conceal most fervently from other people — the way we really are before our God — is what the prophet is intent on making public and making us accountable for. When we are deceitful, ignorant, sinful, blind, self-righteous, or dishonest and try to conceal it, the prophet comes to expose our failings. In so doing, the prophet reveals knowledge of God but also makes a definitive statement about the immensity and ultimate mystery of God.

At the same time, the prophet also reveals the ultimate reality that God loves us, but with a will to justice and integrity, with hope and demands that we become what we were created to be and not what we have become through sin and human design. God's love for us is a love that transforms, offers atonement and repentance, change, grace, and an alternative to what we have become. But it is all predicated upon "if" — if we take heed, if we change our hearts, if we turn from our evil ways, if we listen again to the voice of God, if we turn back to the covenant and heal the breach we have torn among ourselves, if we do penance, if we admit our guilt and reach again for God's mercy and tender hold on us. Again, this is always a collective turning and communal transformation that includes loving the people we have not loved or included in our lives, our laws, and our religion.

Every prophet is a mystery in which God uses a human being to reveal what we need right now. There is an immediacy, a relentlessness, and a fierce intensity that come, in the words of scripture, like a flash flood, a raging fire, or a hammer-shattering rock. The prophet reminds us that God rules intrusively, abrasively, and all-encompassingly. God is jealously intent on displacing any idolatrous order that has replaced the harmony and balance meant to benefit all peoples and creation. All the prophet's gifts, talents, emotions, and personality are used to express God's own "feelings" about us and what we have become in spite of grace and the abiding presence of the Spirit among us.

The message begins with denouncing of systems of power, greed, arrogance, violence, and hate, and it follows with announcing hope and life for the victims of our sin, evil, and injustice. It demands our response. As in the beginning of our history with God, God still hears the cry of the oppressed, the poor, the lost, and those we have been excluding from life, dignity, compassion, and a future. Study shows that the message has been very consistent across the generations of

prophets. It is a message based on who God is and what God wills
for all of us. It employs economics, politics, cultures — whatever is
at hand to declare the sovereignty of God. The prophet exhorts us to
put an end to any present government, idol, practice, law, situation,
or terrorism that harms human beings. At the same time the prophet
works for the emergence of a new community that will resist evil and
turn instead to praise and to the practice of justice and obedience. The
community must reject outright any world order or practice designed
apart from or against the rule of God. The prophet works with God
to continue the creation of a people who belong to God alone and
witness to the world of the presence of God among us. The presence
of God must be obvious to all in our own relations of justice and peace,
with special attention to the needs of the *anawim,* the privileged poor
of Yahweh, among us. The vision is one of hope, of God's creation
continuing in our time.

The prophet uses every resource at his or her disposal. Weeping, raging, crying out, criticism, blessings and curses, storytelling,
singing, dramas acted out, possessions and even cities destroyed, food
eaten or left to rot, ingenious set-ups and insults — all serve only one
purpose: the conversion of heart and the doing of restitution to rebal-
ance and heal the world again. However prophets may prophesy, their
integrity is shown by the way in which they give up their very lives as
testimony and witness as they side with the forgotten and the lost ones
and loudly proclaim that God, who is aware of their pain and feels
their suffering as his own, will not allow that pain and suffering to
continue. God is not indifferent to or far from anyone's life, but rather
draws near to those who know pain because of the sin and indifference
of others. The prophet loudly insists that God is not impartial and that
God will not allow anyone who professes belief in the Holy to harm
another. Often, the admonitions and instructions of the prophet concern what true worship of God should consist of, which is often a far
cry from what people think constitutes religion.

In the words of Abraham Joshua Heschel, listening to the message
of a prophet has an outcome:

> Thus in the course of listening to their words one cannot long re-
> tain the security of a prudent, impartial observer. The prophets
> do not offer reflections about ideas in general. Their words
> are onslaughts, scuttling illusions of false security, challenging

evasions, calling faith to account, questioning prudence and impartiality. One may be equally afraid to submit to their strange certainties and to resist their tremendous claims because of incredulity or impotence of spirit. Reflection about the prophets gives way to communion with the prophets.[2]

Heschel continues with an exhortation to honesty. If we are going to study the prophets, we must seek to ascertain their consciousness and what they intended to communicate. His words are indicative of how the words of the prophets are to be approached, the only way they are to be absorbed:

Pure reflection may be sufficient for the clarification of what the prophet's consciousness asserts — but not for understanding what his existence involves. For such understanding it is not enough to have the prophets in mind; we must think as if we were inside their minds. For them to be alive and present to us we must think, not *about* but *in* the prophets, with their concern and their heart. Their existence involves us. Unless their concern strikes us, pains us, exalts us, we do not really sense it. Such involvement requires accord, receptivity, hearing, sheer surrender to their impact. Its intellectual rewards include moments in which the mind peels off, as it were, its not-knowing. Thought is like touch, comprehending by being comprehended.[3]

Though the prophets came into history to demand that God once again be taken seriously and remembered as central to human existence, the prophets belong to all times and to all of us. Their consciousness of God is crucial to our becoming more human, to our survival as a people, and to our salvation and our freedom as compassionate and just people. We must not only acknowledge the world and existence of the prophets but move into their consciousness of God and their way of being in the world. Their sight, their feelings, their words, their fierce anger, their horror at what we do, and their compassion for the victims and for God's honor must become our own. We must be interested in "restoring the world of the prophets: terrifying in its absurdity and defiance of its Maker, tottering at the brink of disaster, with the voice of God imploring man to turn to Him. It is not a world devoid of meaning that evokes the prophet's consternation, but a world deaf to meaning."[4]

The study of the prophets is not one option among many others. It is the study of revelation as God grows desperate trying to get us to pay heed to life, to resist death, and to return to being human beings, instead of walking a razor's edge by courting violence, injustice, and meanness of spirit, all the while thinking we are good people. It is the study of divinity seizing hold of our human flesh in an attempt to touch us deeply and to walk among us, pleading and cajoling, threatening and crying out for a response that brings freedom to our very souls. Core to every generation and every community is the prophets' ultrasensitivity to evil, their depth of feeling for those in pain, their passionate devotion to God's honor, their consistent use of truthful words, their single-hearted and single-minded imagination devoted to raising the consciousness of people, and their faithfulness unto death.

And yet the word for prophets in Hebrew, *n'vi-im*, includes not just the prophets of Yahweh, whose word is true, reliable, life-giving, and life-shattering. It also includes false prophets, professional prophets, court prophets, and self-styled prophets. The prophet Jeremiah has something to say about these people: "I did not send these prophets, yet they went running; I did not speak, yet they prophesied!" (Jer. 23:21). From the beginning there have been debates over who is truly a prophet of God, sent by God to speak God's word. Even today there are many who purport to have the word of God at their disposal, to act on God's behalf, and to have access to God's inner court. But it seems that neither a commitment to justice nor a protest against injustice nor a firm desire to be prophetic accords one "prophet" status. A true prophet is called by God, a being sent, a being worded by God, and for the true prophet the experience of the word of God overpowers any personal desire or intent.

Kathleen O'Connor wrote:

> This brings us to the vexing problem of deciding who are true prophets. How do we know? To recognize that we have prophets among us is an act of hope, no more and no less. I mean a burning confidence that a certain word, a particular vision, accords with the very heart of biblical faith. Hope arises from prayerful attentiveness to both the vicious sufferings of our world and the freeing presence of God. Hope acts in the expectation that the justice of God will burst anew upon a people in darkness.[5]

Upon first reading that seems clear enough; yet hope is illusive, a gift in itself, a virtue, often rooted in a place or a people, that is to be practiced. Perhaps two criteria can be applied to help determine who is a true prophet and what is true prophecy. The first is the old adage, "By their fruits you will know them." A rule of thumb might be that any word or any prophet that makes a person feel more compassionate, more just, more truthful, more forgetful of self, and more attentive to others is a true word or a true prophet. That means, of course, that there are prophets both within and without our particular tradition and religious beliefs. Truth is universal as well as particular, and prophets are universally concerned with politics, economics, violence, and the victims of these realities. The prophet's message declares that justice is in short supply and that injustice is having its way in the world. A prophet arises as a statement that justice has departed from our midst, that simple human courtesy and kindness have disappeared as well, and that we are generally in a state of disrepair and disgrace.

The second criterion is more communal. The prophet takes sides, as does God, with the victims, those who know injustice and unnecessary pain, directed by and intended by one group, often religious people, against another. It is the victims who know who the prophets are, because the prophets are their voice, insistent reminders of their presence in a world that ignores them or blames them for its problems. It is usually this association with the lowly, the meek, the broken in spirit, the poor, the prisoner, and the outsider that elicits rage, resistance, or persecution in the life of the prophet. Witness the life, the words, and the person of Oscar Romero, the archbishop of El Salvador who was murdered because of his plea on behalf of the poor of his diocese and country. He became a prophet because of their need, their plight, because he saw their agony, as God saw it. But there were many anonymous prophets who taught him, everyone from his friend Rutillo Grande, S.J., to the many catechists and believers who stood up for their faith in the face of torture and demeaning poverty and cold-blooded opposition to the gospel. There were also the four women missionaries whose last witness was the laying down of their lives on behalf of the people. They became prophets of El Salvador when their blood cried out from the ground. And there were the Jesuits who were killed on the grounds of the University of San Salvador, along with their housekeeper and her daughter, because of their outspoken defense of human rights. One can become a prophet, a word of God spoken aloud, by one act that culminates a lifetime of faithfulness to the gospel. The prophet gives witness, as does the martyr, to the sovereignty of God in a world seemingly gone mad, gone deaf, and lost in its own destructive tendencies. The prophet is recognizable by word, by presence, and by the repetition of a message in season and out. In this book we will look at the traditional prophets of our own religion with its ancestry in the Israelite community, and we will also look at prophets from other religions, contemporary and ancient.

The Jewish tradition includes prophets of the oral word and those of the written word, many of whom are often referred to as the later prophets. One of them, Habakkuk (ca. 600 B.C.E.), models this kind of prophet:

> Then Yahweh answered me and said,
> "Write down the vision, inscribe it on tables so it can be easily read, since this is a vision for an appointed time; it will not fail but will be fulfilled in due time. If it delays, wait for it, for it will come and will not be deferred." (Hab. 2:2–3)

But always, besides the oral and written traditions, a third tradition holds precedence over the others. That is the living tradition, the person that embodies the word of God in flesh, in his or her life, and in the history of the people. These are also the prophets we will study, seeking to honor them, to incorporate them into our belief, and to pray that God sends more such prophets into the world today and that we heed the word of the Lord in their mouths. We will look at those who have gone before us in faith through the eyes and the words of Jesus, the prophet of God, the word made flesh among us. *And* we will look forward to the vision that is presented to us now in the word, the vision that must become true, or else all will perish from the earth. We end with a portion of a hymn popular in Latin America. It is called simply "The Prophet":

> Chorus:
>
> I have to shout,
> I have to take the risk,
> Woe to me if I do not!
> How can I escape you?
> How can I fail to speak?
> Your voice burns within me.

Do not be afraid to risk your life
For I will be with you.
Do not be afraid to proclaim my message
For through your voice I will speak.
Today I give you care of my people,
To uproot and tear down, to build and to plant.

Leave your brothers and sisters,
Your mother and father.
Leave your home, for the earth is crying out.
Take nothing with you for I will be at your side.
It is time for struggle
Because my people are suffering.

You will go where I send you;
You will speak what I command.
I set you apart.
I chose you to be my prophet to the nations.
GO!

❦ T W O ❦

Moses

The Prophet-Liberator

> Once upon a time a rabbi was lecturing on a point of the law
> and he noticed that a good number in the audience were falling
> asleep, nodding in their chairs. He was losing them! He had to
> rouse them, so he cried out: "Once upon a time a woman in
> Egypt gave birth to six thousand children all at once!" Immedi-
> ately the group stirred, and one of the students, Rabbi Ishmael
> ben Yose, asked him: "Who in the world could that be?" And the
> rabbi soberly answered: "It was Jochebed, when she gave birth
> to Moses, because he is equal to six thousand people!"
>
> From *Song of Songs Rabbah* 1.15 (paraphrase)

For many in the Christian community, the prophet par excellence is
Elijah, who disappeared in a fiery chariot and will return as forerunner to the presence of the Messiah among us. But for the Jewish
community, *the* prophet is Moses, the one who liberated Israel from
the bondage of Egypt and led them to freedom. He is the prophet of
memory: the memory of what Yahweh has done and is doing for his
people in the covenant and the law. The story of Moses and the law are
Israel's heritage. When the story is told and the law obeyed, the captivity and oppression of Egypt will never happen again. God's intent
is to prevent another Egypt.

The story of Moses is the story of the birth of Israel, the emergence
of a people dedicated to the worship and remembrance of God in the
world. Moses' message tells of power, where true power lies, how it is
used, and on whose behalf. In a sense, Moses introduces the people of
Israel to the reality of the one God. He singles out the most dramatic

28

and powerful of God's characteristics, that God is the champion of the losers, on the side of those imprisoned and oppressed by other forms of power that do not serve life. From the beginning this God is like no other on earth. Dorothee Sölle, a German peace activist and theologian, wrote about the unique character of the God of Moses:

> When our religions ask where God is to be found, they answer with many names. Some stress silence, the solitariness of the heart, the sinking into the collective unconsciousness.
>
> The biblical tradition has added another name to the names of God, a name that seldom appears in other faiths. This name is the name of *righteousness,* justice. It is the heart piece of our Jewish and Christian tradition. Without it, there can be no prayer, no incense, no mysticism or baptism. Without the poor, there is no closeness to God.
>
> We find our way to God by doing justice, for justice is God's will. Because it centers on justice, the Bible speaks incessantly of the poor. It warns us that the riches we heap up not only separate us from the poor but also disguise us from God and bar the way to God.
>
> And so God is always fundamentally involved with our economic order, and God's concern lies with the poor.[1]

God, Yahweh, the Holy One, will not allow history to continue to crush massive numbers of human beings without a reckoning. Moses' story and that of the people are told in Exodus, the "going-out" that begins brutally and cold-bloodedly with an assessment of power that uses people. A new king, the pharaoh, comes to power and sets "taskmasters over them [the Israelites] to oppress them with forced labor" (Exod. 1:11). The oppression and punishment are inhuman. "And [the Egyptians] became ruthless in making them work. They made life bitter for them in hard labor with bricks and mortar and with all kinds of work in the fields. In all their work the Egyptians treated them harshly" (Exod. 1:13–14).

Still the Israelites multiply, so the order is given to kill the male children as they are born. Genocide becomes the practice of the land. And in the midst of this slaughter, Moses is born. But his mother, Jochebed, and his sister Miriam do not obey the orders and hide him. Some readers have the impression that the women may have placed him in a specific place in the Nile so that the daughter of pharaoh would find him. In any case, she does find him and raises him as an Egyptian prince. As Moses grows up, he sees the heavy burden of his own people. When he reacts by killing, he must flee into the desert. He settles in Midian, marries, and begins a family of his own, naming his firstborn son Gershom as a reminder that he was "a guest in a strange land."

Now the story of Moses the prophet, the one called and sent to liberate the people, begins. We are told what precipitates God's singling out Moses as his servant: "The sons of Israel groaned under their slavery; they cried to God for help and from their bondage their cry ascended to God. God heard their sigh and remembered his covenant with Abraham, Isaac and Jacob. God looked upon the sons of Israel and revealed himself to them" (Exod. 2:23–25).

God has waited four hundred years to respond to that sigh. God waits until Moses is settled as a father and shepherd, living with a certain amount of security, insulated from the misfortunes of his people that once drove him to kill on their behalf. Chapter 3 of Exodus contains all the elements of the prophet's call: the command to obey, the message, the method, and the revelation of who is now wielding power.

While Moses pastures his sheep on a mountainside, he sees a burning bush. He draws near, and God calls out to him to remove his shoes because he is standing on holy ground. Moses is called by name and answers God, "Here I am." He is told to go no closer. God reveals who he is: "I am the God of your fathers, the God of Abraham, the God of Isaac and the God of Jacob" (Exod. 3:6). This is a God of history, of continuity, of memory, of connection, of the past infringing on the present, of generation, of story. Then God becomes very specific about the nature of his visit with Moses:

> I have seen the humiliation of my people in Egypt and I hear their cry when they are cruelly treated by their taskmasters. I know their suffering. I have come down to free them from the power of the Egyptians and to bring them up from that land to a beautiful spacious land, a land flowing with milk and honey. Go now! I am sending you to Pharaoh to bring my people, the sons of Israel, out of Egypt. (Exod. 3:7–10)

It is God who has spoken the words of liberation and freedom. The process has been set in motion, and history is being altered even as

Moses hears the word of God from the burning bush, with his eyes closed and his face hidden from the sight of God. The revelation of God is staggering. God is the God of freedom, of release of captives and prisoners, the patron of the poor and the oppressed. God hears the cries, prayers, and sighs of those reduced to misery and bondage and of those who are dehumanized by forced labor and cruelty. The verbs are in the present tense: even as the sighs are released, God is moving to release the people and envisioning a hope and future they cannot imagine.

There is a story told in the Jewish Midrash, in *Exodus Rabbah* (chapter 2, section 2) about how Yahweh tested Moses before appearing to him and choosing him. It reveals another aspect of this God of the burning bush who hears sighs and cannot help but respond to them:

> Once upon a time when Moses was tending the flock of his father-in-law, Jethro, a young kid escaped and ran away. It gamboled off, unaware of any danger until it stopped by a cool stream to drink and rest. Moses followed the kid most of the day until he discovered it by the waters. He knelt beside the lamb and whispered: "I didn't know that you were thirsty. That's why you ran off. Now you must be very tired." And with that, he picked up the kid and carried it on his shoulders back to the flock.
>
> And God murmured to himself: "Because you showed mercy among even animals, certainly you will show mercy when you tend and feed my flock, Israel."

The God of Israel and Moses is a God of tender regard, a God of mercy who carries the weak and goes out of his way for the wandering and the lost. Moses, his prophet, will carry many of the same characteristics.

A mountain, fire, and an angel are all present as God calls to Moses from the burning bush. When Moses responds, "Who am I that I should go?" he is assured that "I will be with you." Moses follows up with another question: "Who are you?" The answer of "I AM WHO I AM" is intentionally not easy to grasp. God further says that Moses should say to the people, "I AM sent me to you" (Exod. 3:14). Moses is exhorted to go and is given specific instructions on what to say to the Israelite elders and to pharaoh. Moses is also told what God will do, what will inevitably come to pass: the children of Israel will leave Egypt as a people that belongs to God and moves under God's power and protection. A sign is given. After the Israelites are led out they will come together and worship on the mountain. They will see God face-to-face and know God's will. This God wants to be worshiped and served by men and women who, in turn, will set others free. This free and just God seeks those who will live in freedom and justice as his own people.

God shares some of that power with Moses, his servant, to aid him in the task God has set for him. When Moses pleads for an interpreter, his brother Aaron is assigned to the task. Moses returns to Egypt, obeying the voice of the God of the mountain. Moses has become the prophet-liberator of God. From then on, Moses and God talk back and forth regarding every aspect of the power struggle between pharaoh and Yahweh. What ensues is the story of the plagues and the recalcitrant reactions of pharaoh to a God he does not believe in, and so dishonors and insults. The story culminates in the ritual of the Passover, ordered by God. It is the liturgy of the people who slaughter a lamb and eat it together, in haste, wasting none of it. It is the passing over of the Angel of Death and their own imminent passing over to life in freedom. On that night, death reigns for all who do not worship the God of life. As judgment is brought upon Egypt, the God of life passes over all those who announce that they belong to this true God by marking their doors with the blood of the lamb. They are told: "This is a day you are to remember and celebrate in honor of Yahweh. It is to be kept as a festival for all generations forever" (Exod. 12:14). The Israelites are allowed to depart, and from that time on all the firstborn of Israel are to be consecrated to God.

This God is just. God stands in judgment and executes it, in life and death. This God is faithful and is to be remembered for liberating a people who are claimed as his own and consecrated to life and to imitating this God in the world. But the story is not over. Pharaoh regrets letting the people go and sends his army after them. They catch up to them at the Red Sea, with the Israelites trapped between the water and the oncoming Egyptians. Exodus notes that pharaoh is hardened in heart and mind and blind to the workings of glory and the will of God. In their terror, the people turn to Moses, who reassures them that God will fight for them. They just need to "keep still." God then spoke to Moses:

> Yahweh said to Moses, "Why do you cry to me? Tell the people
> of Israel to go forward. You will raise your staff and stretch out

your hand over the sea and divide it to let the Israelites go dry-foot through the sea. I will so harden the minds of the Egyptians that they will follow you. And I will have glory at the expense of Pharaoh, his army, his chariots and horsemen. The Egyptians will know that I am Yahweh when I gain glory for myself at the cost of Pharaoh and his army!"

The Angel of God who had gone ahead of the Israelites now placed himself behind them. The pillar of cloud changed its position from the front to the rear, between the camps of the Israelites and the Egyptians. (Exod. 14:15–20a)

In later lines we are told that Yahweh is in the pillar of cloud and fire that looks toward the camp of the Egyptians and throws it into confusion. The Egyptians want to return to Egypt because they see that God is fighting on behalf of the fleeing slaves, but they are paralyzed. The sea closes back, "returns to its place." "On that day Yahweh delivered Israel from the power of the Egyptians. . . . They believed in Yahweh and in Moses, his servant" (Exod. 14:30–31). In response, Miriam, Moses, and the people all sing the glory and praise of God as they head into the desert to worship Yahweh.

A Jewish legend called "When the Angels Stopped Singing," which tells about this singing, reveals much about Yahweh:

Realizing that they were free at last the Israelites were jubilant and broke into a song of triumph and thanksgiving. But while they were the only ones who sang, they were not the only ones who wanted to sing. The angels also wanted to sing. Before the Egyptians were drowned there was a heavenly debate on how God should deal with them. The guardian angel of Egypt wanted God to deal with them in His attribute of divine compassion. Other angels, led by Michael and Gabriel, urged God to act with His attribute of strict justice. When God agreed to this latter view, and the Egyptians drowned, His ministering angels wanted to break out into song. But they were silenced by God Himself. "This is no time to sing when My creatures, human beings whom I made, are drowning!" This rebuke from God brought the angels to a halt before they could get very far with their singing.[2]

This universal God cares about all human beings and never rejoices in the death of anyone! Later, in the book of Proverbs, it is written:

"Do not rejoice if your enemy falls or let your heart be glad if he stumbles, lest Yahweh see and be displeased and his anger be turned on you. Do not be incensed by the wicked or envious of the ungodly, since there is no future in evil and the lamp of the wicked will be extinguished" (Prov. 24:18–19). The punishment of a people who, through evil and sin, have oppressed another people is not cause for human celebration. God alone is the final arbitrator of justice. All rejoicing must be tempered with the memory of those who are judged and suffer for their actions. We are all the children of the one true God, and we are not allowed to forget that, ever.

Even after the people witness the mighty deeds of God at the Red Sea, Moses seems constantly to need an added dose of patience to deal with them. They continually murmur against Moses (and indirectly against God) about water, about food, about meat in particular, and about whether or not God is really with them. Then they reach Mount Sinai. Moses climbs the mountain, leaving the people encamped at its base. God tells Moses precisely what to say to them:

> This is what you are to say and to explain to the Israelites: You have seen what I did to the Egyptians and how I carried you on eagle's wings and brought you to myself. Now if you listen to me and keep my covenant, you shall be my very own possession among all the nations. For all the earth is mine, but you will be for me a kingdom of priests and a holy nation. (Exod. 19:3a–6a)

Moses relays the message, and the people respond: "All that Yahweh has said, we will do." Moses returns to God with their response. Then God promises to appear to Moses in a dense cloud so that the people can hear God speaking to Moses and learn to trust him always. God then speaks to Moses using the first person, "I am Yahweh your God who brought you out of the land of Egypt," and gives Moses the Ten Commandments for the people. After the decalogue come the meat and bones of the covenant law: chapters 20 to 24 of Exodus. Moses repeats the details of the law to the people and writes it all down and reads it to them. Moses is summoned once again to the mountain where God gives him the tablets of the law that God has written out for the instruction of the people (Exod. 24:12).

When Moses is gone for a long period of time, the people, grown restless and insecure, revert to their old ways and worship their old idols. Yahweh knows immediately and tells Moses to go back down to "your people, whom you brought up from the land of Egypt, because they have corrupted themselves" (Exod. 32:7). Moses resorts to arguing and bargaining with God for the "stiff-necked" people. Moses helps to change the mind of Yahweh (Exod. 32:14), but when he returns to the camp and sees the Israelites singing and dancing while they worship idols, he destroys the slabs with God's own writing on them. A day of reckoning ensues, with each person called to make a choice for or against Yahweh. Again, it is Moses who seeks forgiveness for their sins, and, again, they are granted mercy. The people who have chosen Yahweh gather at the Tent of Meeting to worship. When Moses enters the tent to worship, God comes:

> Now, as soon as Moses entered the tent, the pillar of cloud would come down and remain at the entrance to the tent, while Yahweh spoke with Moses.
> When all the people saw the pillar of cloud at the entrance to the tent, they would arise and worship, each one at the entrance to his own tent.
> Then Yahweh would speak to Moses face-to-face, as a man speaks with his neighbor, and then Moses would return to the camp, but his servant Joshua, son of Nun, would not leave the tent. (Exod. 33:9–11)

Moses is the go-between, a relay runner of messages back and forth between the people and God, yet there are hints and stories of a singular relationship between Yahweh and Moses. Perhaps the most human and revelatory of these stories concerns Moses' desire to see God. It seems that even though God speaks face-to-face with Moses, one on one, somehow Moses does not see him face-to-face. Moses wants to see God, and God, it seems, wants to let him:

> Moses said, "Then let me see your Glory." And He said, "I will make all my goodness pass before you and proclaim the name of Yahweh before you. For I am gracious to whom I want to be gracious and I am merciful to whom I want to be merciful."
> Then Yahweh said, "You cannot see my face because man cannot see me and live." And he added, "See this place near me; you shall stand on the rock and when my Glory passes I will put you in a hollow of the rock and cover you with my hand until

I have passed by. Then I will take away my hand and you shall see my back, but my face shall not be seen." (Exod. 33:18–23)

The story is full of pathos, of tenderness, with God trying to accommodate Moses' wish, trying to do the impossible — to let Moses see him, yet not die. There is an element of playfulness in it, with Moses rock-climbing and God fitting him in a crevice and covering him with his hand and, at the last moment, removing it so that Moses gets a flash of the back side of Glory! It's as though God is playing a game — albeit a serious game — with Moses, letting Moses draw nearer and nearer to God, contradicting the earlier rules when Moses was told to go no closer, because he was on holy ground.

The slabs with the written law are given once more, and God cries out to Moses more about who God is, as he passes in front of Moses. The statement bears remembering for it explains much of what will become a reality for the people of Israel in the centuries that follow:

Yahweh, Yahweh is a God full of pity and mercy, slow to anger and abounding in truth and loving-kindness. He shows loving-kindness to the thousandth generation and forgives wickedness, rebellion and sin; yet he does not leave the guilty without punishment, even punishing the children and their children for the sin of the fathers to the third and fourth generation. (Exod. 34:6b–7)

Moses, the first of the prophets, has the difficult task of first teaching what God expects and asks of his people and that while God is both justice and mercy, the mercy far outstrips the justice. A thousand generations will experience Yahweh's justice while only three or four generations will experience God's judgment. The covenant is again put forth, and Moses lingers with God for forty days and forty nights. When he returns, his face is radiant, so bright that the people cannot bear to look on him. So Moses dons a veil whenever he is in the camp. When he goes to see God, he removes it and leaves it off until he has passed on the words of Yahweh to the people. He does this so they can see reflected in his face a bit of God's shining glory.

The book of Leviticus contains the words of Yahweh — the laws, customs, and rituals that will bind the people together, give them a sense of identity, and call them to obedience before God. They concern diseases like leprosy, the handling of food, ritual sacrifices, the priesthood, what is clean and unclean, and how to atone for sin. In the second portion of the book, called the Holiness Code, God exhorts the people not to ever act like the Egyptians or the Canaanites but to imitate only God. This section includes the call to celebrate the Jubilee Year and the Sabbatical Year, regarding forgiveness and remission of debts; resting the land; establishing cities of refuge and sanctuary; setting free prisoners, aliens, and immigrants; and welcoming all into a relationship of equality by redistributing the land among all the people. These laws are meant to ensure that what developed in Egypt — injustice, inequality, the gap between rich and poor, hatred and oppression — will never be allowed among God's own people in the land of promise. The law will be their safeguard and security net, their boundary fence and protection so that all nations will be led to acknowledge belief in the true God of life, Yahweh: "I will make my Dwelling among you and I will not reject you. I will walk among you; I will be your God and you will be my people. I am Yahweh your God, who brought you out of Egypt to be their slaves no longer. I have broken the bars of your yoke letting you walk erect" (Lev. 26:11–13).

According to tradition, all of these texts are the work of Moses, who attempts to remind the people of the marvels God has worked for them and exhorts them to remember who they are: a chosen people, a covenanted people, and a people called to holiness and justice. Their memories of the desert and their reliance on God for food and water encouraged them to trust in God's providence, to obey his commands, and to be always mindful that his glory traveled and dwelled with them each day and that God would lead them to a land of their own, a place of rest and freedom. Despite that, rebellions will surface and resistance abound, both by individuals and groups. There will be murmuring against Moses, even by Miriam and Aaron, his sister and brother. There will be discouragement and backsliding.

All these stories announce again and again that the Exodus event is the model of liberation, both spiritual and physical, both communal and individual. God wants our liberation to be wholehearted, complete, and free in every respect. In an article in *Sojourners,* Bruce C. Birch writes:

Exodus reminds us that we must not fall victim to the easy temptation of seeking to save the world's soul while its body is in pain. God's salvation is the promise of deliverance for spirit and body, and God is active to bring us fullness of life as whole persons. We must be reminded that spiritual alienation in our time is wedded to great systems of physical dehumanization that crush the spirit of those who suffer, corrupt the spirit of those who oppress, and dull the spirit of those who refuse to see and hear.[3]

Israel's covenant and relationship with God were to be different than others in the world, especially different than what the Israelites had known in Egypt. Egypt relied on military might, economic imperialism, enslavement, cultural identity, forced labor, and a concentration of power in cities that controlled distinct areas. Israel was to be a radically new reality known for its relationship to God and dependence on Yahweh instead of its armies. It was to be characterized by freedom; the care of the vulnerable and the poor; faithfulness to the law and covenant demands; and the worship of one God defined by compassion, justice, and an obvious preference for those who were easy prey to the powers of the world. This God of freedom called the people to fidelity, to imitation, to an enlarging of their hearts, and to obedience. Because of God's intervention in their history of oppression, they were consciously, communally, publicly, and institutionally never to allow that to become a reality among their own people. The necessities of life — food, shelter, wages, water, human dignity — were built into the demands and rewards of the covenant, into the life of the community itself. The social identity of the leaders and elders was defined by their responsibility to make sure that all were cared for. The leaders held positions like Yahweh. They could intervene and save others in need, and they could hear the sighs and cries of those in misery. The book of Deuteronomy declares:

> However you should have no poor in your midst for Yahweh will give you prosperity in the land that you have conquered. If you listen to the voice of Yahweh, your God, and obey all that he has commended you, which I now remind you of, he will bless you as he promised....
>
> If there is anybody poor among your brothers, who lives in your cities in the land that Yahweh gives you, do not harden your heart or close your hand, but be open-handed and lend him all that he needs....

When you give anything, give it willingly, and Yahweh, your God, will bless you for this in all your work and in all that you undertake.

The poor will not disappear from this land. Therefore I give you this commandment: you must be open-handed to your brother, to the needy and to the poor in your land. (Deut. 15:4–5, 7–8, 10–11)

The covenant was to militate against poverty, to endeavor to keep the reality of poverty always in the minds and hearts of Yahweh's people. No one was to be locked into poverty. The Jubilee and Sabbatical Years were to be taken seriously and practiced with justice. The poor must always find provisions for themselves and their families. They were given the right to pick grapes or pluck grain as they passed by vineyards and fields (Deut. 23:24–25), and they were allowed to glean from what remained. In fact, owners were exhorted to leave some of their first harvest for the poor (Deut. 24:19; Lev. 19:9–10; 23:22), and anything that grew in fallow fields belonged to the hungry and poor (Exod. 23:10–11), who were to be accorded tithes every third year (Deut. 14:28–29; 26:12).

The debts of the poor were to be remitted after seven years (Deut. 15:1–2), and those who had become indentured servants and slaves were to be released after seven years and given a new start (Lev. 25:39–55; Deut. 15:12–15). There were laws about lending to the poor and not collecting interest or security on a debt (Exod. 22:25, 26–27; Deut. 15:7–8; 24:10–13). The community of Israel was structured justly to keep it from disintegrating into a nation like Egypt. The Israelites were not to become hard-hearted like pharaoh but were to listen to those who sighed and cried out. This is the source of liberation and freedom. This is the message of Moses.

Moses, however, was not allowed to enter the promised land with the people, because they had driven him in anger to tempt God. Moses was later chastised by God: "You did not trust me nor treat me as the Holy One in the sight of the Israelites; because of that you shall not lead this community into the land that I am giving you" (Num. 20:12). At least twice Moses was given help in administering justice and in instructing the people in the way of freedom. In one instance, Yahweh instructs Moses to select seventy elders from among the people and bring them to the Tent of Meeting. Yahweh tells Moses: "I shall

come down to speak with you and I shall take some of the Spirit that
is in you and put it in them. From now on they will share with you the
burden of the people so that no longer will you bear it alone" (Num.
11:16–23). Two of the chosen elders do not go to the Tent of Meeting and remain behind in the camp. Yet even these two men are given
the Spirit and begin to prophesy, a sign that they can be of assistance
to Moses. Joshua overhears the men prophesying and wants Moses
to stop them. In a fervent prayer, Moses hopes that all the people
will become prophets and that Yahweh will send his Spirit upon all
of them!

Although Moses constantly reminds the people of all that Yahweh
has done for them, they constantly forget. When they approach the
promised land, they grow fearful of entering it without Moses. And so
Moses tells them that God will give them another leader like himself,
which sets a pattern for the prophets in Israel. Moses repeats to the
people the words God had spoken to him:

> I shall raise up a prophet from their midst, one of their brothers,
> who will be like you. I will put my words into his mouth and he
> will tell them all that I command. If someone does not listen to
> my words when the prophet speaks on my behalf, I myself will
> call him to account for it. But any prophet who says in my name
> anything that I did not command, or speaks in the name of other
> gods, that prophet shall die.
>
> You will perhaps ask: "How are we going to know that a word
> does not come from Yahweh?" If any prophet speaks in the name
> of Yahweh and if that which he says does not happen, you shall
> know that the word does not come from Yahweh. The prophet
> has spoken to boast and you shall not pay any attention to him.
> (Deut. 18:18–22)

And so the people are promised the continuing presence of God
in prophets to come, prophets who will sense their problems and feel
their pain and whose hearts will go out to them, seeking answers for
them before God. God will continue to save the people by using other
human beings to share his spirit, his power, and his presence. Because
of Moses' stature, his writing of the Torah and laws, his intercession
for the people, his accompanying them through the desert, and his
radiant face reflecting the glory of God, Moses becomes the model,

the source, and the reference for all interpretation of the law, Midrash, and future understandings of God.

A story in the Talmud tells of how all decisions and rulings within the Jewish community are seen to be founded on Moses' own authority. This story is called "The Crowns of the Torah":

> When Moses was on Mount Sinai to receive the Torah, he saw God adding crowns on several letters each time they appeared in the Torah. "What is the purpose of these little crowns? Couldn't the Torah be given without them?" he asked.
>
> And God answered, "Sometime in the future there will be a great teacher by the name of Akiba ben Yosef who will expound numerous laws which he will deduce from every one of these little lines."
>
> Moses was intrigued and expressed the wish to see this man Akiba. God agreed to the request and gave Moses the power to glance into the future. "Turn around," God said. Moses did so and found himself in the academy of Rabbi Akiba, fifteen hundred years later.
>
> He sat in the back of the lecture hall as Akiba interpreted the law before rows of disciples. But what he heard was all very strange to him. He didn't understand what Akiba was teaching, as it all seemed very different from his own law. Moses became sad, because he thought that his law would be forgotten and replaced by something new. Then suddenly he heard one of the students question Akiba, "Master, what is the source and authority for this law which you have been teaching us?"
>
> Akiba gave his firm and immediate answer, "The source and authority is that it derives from the Torah of Moses our teacher, which he received on Mount Sinai." When Moses heard Akiba's reply he was content, and he went back to his own world.[4]

Moses is Israel's prophet and teacher, and there has never been another comparable to him. The ending of the book of Deuteronomy reads: "No prophet like Moses has appeared again. Yahweh conversed with him face-to-face. What signs and wonders he worked in Egypt against pharaoh, against his people and all his land! What a powerful hand was his that worked these terrible things in the sight of all Israel!" (Deut. 34:10–12).

Yet it is the beginning of Moses' own song that tells much more about him:

Listen, O heavens, as I speak; hear, earth, the words of my mouth. May my teaching be drenching as the rain, and my words, permeate gently as the dew: like abundant rain upon the grass, like a gentle shower on the tender crops. For I will proclaim the name of the Lord and declare the greatness of our God.

> He is the Rock,
> and perfect are all his works,
> just are all his ways.
> A faithful God he is,
> upright and just and unerring.
> Yet he has been treated perversely
> by his degenerate children —
> a deceitful and crooked generation.
> Is this how you repay the Lord,
> you foolish and senseless people?
> He is your father, your creator
> who formed you and set you up.
> Recall the days of old,
> think of the years gone by;
> your father will teach you about them,
> and your elders will enlighten you. . . .
> But the Lord keeps for himself his portion
> Jacob, his chosen one.
> In the wilderness he found them,
> in a barren, howling wasteland;
> he shielded them and cared for them
> as the apple of his eye.
> Like an eagle watching its nest,
> hovering over its young,
> supporting them on its spread wings
> and carrying them on its pinions,
> the Lord alone led them,
> without the aid of a foreign god. (Deut. 32:1–12)

The song continues for many more lines, but the pattern is the same. Moses recounts the wondrous love of God for a people who are stub-

born and stiff-necked, who abandon God at every turn, while God is
faithful, attentive, and just, reduced to threatening them and entreat-
ing them to return wholeheartedly to him. This is Moses' experience
of the people, one that he shares with God in an intimate way. He
pleads with his people to listen, to remember, to obey the covenant,
and to know wisdom in their new land.

Then Moses leaves them, to go off to Mount Nebo, where he will
die, after being given a glimpse of the promised land he will never
enter. Although he gives the people the vision, at the end, he only sees
the reality from afar. The last chapter of Deuteronomy tells of God
showing him the land in detail, pointing out its richness and beauty,
sharing the vision with him in a way that the people who enter it will
never know. Tradition holds that Moses dies alone, according to the
will of Yahweh, and that no one to this day knows where he is buried.

But numerous legends tell of how Moses dies. All of them begin
with a fierce resistance to death and a fierce resistance to obeying the
law of mortals, along with a fierce argument with God on the nature of
his will. Moses longs to walk in the land promised, but the culmination
of his life, the realization of his dream and vision, is denied to him. He
resists, he cries, he prays, he pleads and begs, he screams, and he even
physically fights off the Angel of Death that is sent for him. After that,
he argues with other angels and bests them all in logic, reasoning,
and prayers for life — since God himself is the God of life! Moses is
alone in the wilderness, facing God in an entirely different way than he
was used to. Moses is not arguing on behalf of his people or relaying
messages but having his own life and soul demanded of him. Here is
one story about the death of Moses:

> When Moses realized that his death had been decreed, he fasted,
> put on sackcloth, and drew a small circle on the ground. Then
> he stood inside the circle and proclaimed before God: "I will
> not stir from this spot until You reverse Your decree." Moses
> continued to lament and pray before God, until the heavens and
> earth — the entire order of nature — trembled.
>
> God decreed that Moses' prayer go unanswered; his fate had
> been decided. But so powerful did Moses' prayers become, like
> a sword which rends everything it touches, that all the gates
> of heaven had to be sealed to prevent the supplication from
> penetrating to the throne of the Almighty.

Still, Moses prayed, pleading with God: "Master of the universe, You know how hard I strived to teach the people of Your words and will. I journeyed with them, contended with them, and now that they are to enter the land, will You exclude me from their joy? Is this the recompense for all my struggle?"

God answered only, "The time of your death has come."

Moses would not cease praying, reminding God of their time together: "Master of the universe, remember that day when You revealed Yourself to me, speaking to me from the burning bush? Recall the forty days and nights we were together on Mount Sinai, where I learned Your law to teach to the people. I beg of You — do not now hand me over to the angel of death."

God calmed Moses' fears with a heavenly voice that said, "Do not be afraid. The time comes to all mortals to die. I Myself will attend to your burial."

Upon hearing those words, Moses stood up and sanctified himself like the angels. God Himself came down from the very heights of heaven to take away the soul of Moses. And God took the soul of His servant Moses with a kiss. And God wept.[5]

God himself comes for Moses' soul, as intimate with him in death as he was in life. Moses is taken with a kiss, and God weeps. There is a softness, a kindness, a strange tenderness to the ending of the story, as though the razor edge of death is softened for Moses, God's servant and beloved, obedient friend. There never has been another like him. Other stories tell of God mourning the death of Moses, burying him himself, digging the grave in a cave and carrying his body to its rest, knowing that there would not be another for ages to come who would know him as well as Moses knew him, face-to-face, catching sight of his glory. It is said that God longs for prophets, servants, and friends like Moses and that God's prayer is: "Would that all my people were like Moses, obedient to my spirit, hungry for a glimpse of my face. Would that all my people were so."

✺ THREE ✺

Elijah and Elisha
The Prophet and His Disciples

Judges and seers appeared in Israel before Elijah, but the reality of
what a prophet is begins to develop with Elijah. The image of the
prophet Elijah is decisive and strong, overwhelming and compelling.
He is an uncompromising prophet of zeal for the honor of God. He is
a champion of true worship and justice, and, at the same time, he is a
beloved folk hero whose special gift is working miracles as the protector and defender of the poor, the bringer of peace and reconciliation,
and the teacher of wisdom. Until the Messiah appears, Elijah saves the
faith of worthy and suffering individuals, especially those who practice hospitality, those who are generous to the poor, and those who
love justice. He is the prophet who never died, and so he continues to
bring hope to all those who are desperate and longing for the coming
of the Messiah into the world.

A story in the Zen tradition presents an almost mirror image of
what Elijah has come to portray in our tradition. Richard McLean's
version of this story appears in his collection of stories *Zen Fables for
Today*. It sets the stage for the enormous influence that Elijah exerts in
Israel and in Christianity:

> Once upon a time there was rumor of trouble in one of the
> most famous and prosperous of the Zen monasteries. It had once
> been a luxurious palace, with gardens and pavilions, guest quar-
> ters, slaughterhouses, and kitchens. But the ruler had generously
> given it over to the Zen community for its use. It was located in
> the scenic seaport city of Yokosuka. The head monk heard the
> rumors and worried about what was going on there, about the

45

scandal it was causing, and, if the rumors were true, the state of the monks that lived there. Something had to be done.

And so he called one of his old monks, a trusted disciple, and summoned him into his presence. The man was brilliant and dedicated, enlightened and decisive in his ways, and he trusted him completely. For years he had lived secluded in a cave, meditating and sitting. When the monk arrived he told him of the rumors and commanded him to go to the monastery and investigate the situation. He knew how hard it was to be a monk and to practice one's vows and remain faithful in such a place of beauty and excess with its history and many of its former inhabitants still living nearby or even in the palace. It was understandable if they had fallen and no longer practiced their disciplines. It was his responsibility to check on them and correct the situation. Would he go and see if there was improper conduct or misuse of funds and even worse, debauchery and lavish spending and parties? Of course, he was ready to obey his master.

But the old monk wanted the master to be specific. "Just what do you want me to do?" he asked. The answer: fix it and return the monastery to its practice and schedule so that people can once again go there for enlightenment.

He asked another question: "What kind of authority do I have in this situation with the monks?"

"You have my ultimate authority, to act as I would and do whatever you need to do, if the rumors are true."

"I understand," he answered. "And how long do you want me to take to fix it if there is a problem?"

"However long it takes," was the answer. "I have complete faith in you and your understanding of the gravity of the situation." He asked for the master's blessing and set off.

A number of weeks passed and the master waited for a report to come in, but he was surprised when the old monk appeared on his doorstep instead. "Do you have a report for me?" he asked.

"Yes," the monk replied. "It was as the rumors said; in fact it was a lot worse. I won't go into detail."

"What did you do?"

"I fixed it, of course, as you commanded."

"It's fixed already?" the master asked, with raised eyebrows.

"Yep! Fixed already."

"What did you do that converted them all so quickly and turned it around?"

The monk replied, "It was easy. One night after seeing what was going on, I took a torch and burned the place to the ground!"[1]

The story startles and shocks us! That is the effect that the story of Elijah often has on people as well. The historical background of the story of Elijah is important to understanding *why* he acts as he does and why he acts with such ferocity and passion. As the first of those we come to view as prophets, he is an image of what is to come as Israel matures in its belief in Yahweh, along with its failure and infidelity, and its destiny as the people of God.

First Samuel tells the story of how Samuel is sent to anoint Saul as king in response to the people's pleas for someone to lead them. We read·

> As they went up the hill to the city, they met young girls coming to draw water and asked them, "Is the seer here?" (Formerly, people in Israel who went to consult God would say, "Come, let us go to the seer," for they did not speak of prophets, but of seers.) The maidens answered, "The seer is straight ahead. He has just arrived because they have a sacrifice today on the high place." (1 Sam. 9:11–12)

Samuel, the high priest, will single out Saul as God's anointed, pouring oil over him and assuring him that God is now with him as long as he remains true to the covenant. The seers are consulted in Israel on everything from economic and political issues to the personal divining of information not known to ordinary people. It is interesting that as kingship developed in Israel the prophet's vocation also developed as a system of checks and balances, calling the monarchy and its leaders, along with the people, to conversion and to a return to Yahweh's word. In due course, God will reject Saul for his disobedience and lack of faith and then send Samuel to anoint David in his stead.

When Samuel anointed David, "Yahweh's Spirit took hold of David" (1 Sam. 16:13). This Spirit is given to the king as the one who holds the people of Yahweh together, bringing them security under God and a sense of Yahweh's abiding presence with them, as long as they are faithful to the covenant. When the prophet Nathan speaks

to David after he has had Bathsheba's husband, Uriah, killed in battle so he may marry her, Nathan seems to function more as a private
counselor, who personally calls David to account for his personal life,
rather than as the voice of God on behalf of the people. Nathan reveals
God's glory to David in light of David's sin, teaching David self-
knowledge. David's son Solomon is later born as a sign of Yahweh's
love and forgiveness.

David has many triumphs as king and eventually captures the city
of Jerusalem around 1000 B.C.E. After David's death in 932 B.C.E., the
kingdom is divided. The northern part, known as Israel, exists as a
kingdom for about two hundred years. The southern part, Judah, lasts
until 587 B.C.E., when the temple and the city of Jerusalem are destroyed and the people are forced into exile. These four hundred years
of the kings of Israel are the period when the prophets thrived. It is a
time marked by power, affluence, military allegiances, and decadence.
At the same time it is marked by the development of faith and an
awareness of God's fidelity and the people's response in obedience.

The division of the tribes is caused by Solomon's infidelity and
worship of the idols of his wives. The king who is known in lore for
his wisdom turns from the worship of God through the influence of
his wives. We are told that "Solomon, however, imitated these peoples
because of his love. He had seven hundred wives of royal birth, and
three hundred concubines, and they won his heart" (1 Kings 11:2–3).
Marrying women from other countries was a violation of the law of
Yahweh, and the kingdom was dismembered as punishment for Solomon's sins. His kingdom had grown decadent and obscenely wealthy,
as Solomon attempted to rival the courts of other greater nations. This
was seen as a failure to honor God in the way that Solomon's father,
David, had.

Ahijah of Shiloh, a local prophet, finds Jeroboam, a high official
of Solomon, on a road and tells him of God's plan to dismember the
kingdom of Solomon after Solomon dies. The manner in which Ahijah
announces this to Jeroboam indicates how the prophetic tradition has
begun to develop under Solomon's rule of disorder, greed, selfishness,
and sin:

> Once, when Jeroboam went out of Jerusalem, the prophet Ahijah
> of Shiloh found him on the road. The two of them were alone
> in the open country when Ahijah, who had a new garment on,

clutched and tore it into twelve pieces. He then said to Jeroboam, "Take ten pieces for yourself for this is the word of Yahweh, the God of Israel:

"I am about to tear the kingdom from Solomon's hands to give you ten tribes. Only one tribe shall be left to him for the sake of my servant David and Jerusalem, the city which I have chosen out of all the tribes of Israel. For Solomon has forsaken me and worshiped Astarte, the goddess of the Sidonians, Chemosh the god of Moab, and Milcom the god of the Ammonites. Unlike his father David, he has not walked in my ways to do what is right before me and to keep my commandments and decisions." (1 Kings 11:29–33)

When Solomon died, his son Rehoboam reigned in his place. When Rehoboam went to Shechem to be made king, the people pleaded with him to ease the burden his father had laid on them: "So now lighten the heavy yoke and the hard labor your father imposed upon us and we will serve you" (1 Kings 12:4). But Rehoboam was a true son of Solomon. First, he consulted with the elderly advisers of his father, who told him to go easier with the people; then he consulted with his own cronies, who were cold-hearted and vicious. It was the latter's advice that he followed: "My little finger is thicker than my father's waist. My father laid a heavy yoke on you, but I will make it heavier yet. My father chastised you with whips, but I will fix iron points to the lashes" (1 Kings 12:11). Israel becomes another Egypt. The covenant is as torn and shredded as are the people of the land. The situation is an abomination in the eyes of God, as God's people and the land itself collapse. Jeroboam fortifies Shechem and becomes king there, while Rehoboam is left with only the remnant of Judah. The division follows tribal as well as religious and political lines.

Jeroboam is no better than Solomon, and the kings that arise in Jerusalem follow the same line. They worship other gods, set up shrines to Asherah and Baal, and sacrifice their own children when they build cities. Finally, we come to King Ahab, who marries Jezebel. She controls the kingdom and has Israel serve her gods and goddesses. It is in the time of Ahab that Elijah appears. Elijah is remembered because he battles passionately to save the faith of Israel. The power of the Spirit of God in his mouth resists, corrects, and fights the kings for the hearts and minds of the people of the covenant.

The Christian Community Bible describes how desperate and violent the situation has become:

> The Baals were gods, masters of life, sex, rain and the seasons. Believing that these gods had control over fecundity, people made vows to them about meeting prostitutes consecrated to them. Because of this the word prostitution in the Bible refers both to licentiousness and to abandoning Yahweh by prostituting oneself for other gods. Not everything was bad in this very permissive religion; it did not err in celebrating life. Nevertheless, it kept the people on the level of their instincts....
>
> Jezebel uses her power to bring about a bloody persecution. First to be assassinated are Yahweh's prophets. These are the fellow prophets whom we presented in 1 Samuel 19:18 and 2 Kings 2:15. They are opposed by rival communities of the prophets of Baal.... With the influence of pagan cults, the practice of sacrificing children increases.[2]

This is an internal war: Ahab, Jezebel, their court, and their professional prophets of Baal stand against the communities of prophets dedicated to the covenant of Yahweh and the faithfulness of the people. It is also a battle between the wealthy and powerful people and the poor of the land, who have no resources and are bent under the yoke of their own leaders. The leader of the prophets of Yahweh is Elijah, whose very name means "Yahweh is my God!" He is from a poor, remote region that has remained faithful to Yahweh.

Elijah acts alone. He is driven to take on the monarchy single-handedly. He begins with the rain, which is absolutely crucial in the land of Israel and supposedly controlled by the gods of Baal. Elijah announces: "As Yahweh, the God of Israel whom I serve lives, neither dew shall drop nor rain fall except at my command" (1 Kings 17:1).

And it does not rain for three and a half years. Severe drought and famine cover the land. All the people suffer for the sins of the leaders — believers and apostates alike — but especially the poor, who have so little control over their fate. Elijah's prayer closes the heavens, and its power extends even to morning and night dew so that every stream and *wadi* eventually dries up. Elijah controls the weather!

Rain is considered the blessing of God in many cultures. If it rains on a birthday, a wedding, a funeral, or a feast day, it's a sign of divine favor. When people live close to the earth, rain is part of their faith life. Thus, Elijah uses the rain — or lack of it — to teach people to be a community again and to interpret the rain and all weather as subject to the Lord of creation. The people are forced to examine their lives and to look at their sin, which is destroying their souls as the lack of water is destroying the crops, the land, and their very lives. Water has always had an intimate connection to God in the realm of faith, and water is often used to initiate a new relationship with God (as in baptism).

In the New Testament, the apostle James uses a prayer of Elijah to illustrate the power of prayer for his own community:

> The prayer of the upright man has great power, provided he perseveres. Elijah was a human being like ourselves and when he prayed earnestly for it not to rain, no rain fell for three and a half years. Then he prayed again: the sky yielded rain and the earth produced its fruit. (James 5:17–18)

James is concerned with praying for the forgiveness of sins and the healing of sickness and with helping those who have strayed from the truth to repent and return. Forgiveness is for those who have sinned and for those who seek to save the sinners. This is exactly what Elijah the prophet seeks: calling forth forgiveness for an entire nation.

Elijah acts precipitously and must live with the consequences. However, he relies entirely on Yahweh, who cares for him. Elijah drinks from the waters of a stream, and a raven brings him bread in the morning and meat in the evening. The prophet becomes a hermit, an ascetic, hiding out from the authority that he has confronted head-on. The land waits for rain, and the prophet waits for the people of the land to remember that Yahweh is the Lord of creation as well as their Lord. Creation itself obeys and serves the word of the Lord, even if the people of the land do not obey.

When the *wadi* dries up, Elijah is sent to Zarephath of the Sidonites to be fed by a righteous woman who is not a believer in Yahweh. This poor widow will comfort Elijah. She is an image of the poor who act with hospitality and generosity in the face of drought and impending death, even of their children. These are the *anawim,* God's own chosen and beloved people. The prophet has been sent to remind the king that the king exists to serve these others, in the name of Yahweh.

The widow is remarkable. She obeys! Recognizing that Elijah is an outcast, a fugitive, she still shares her last bit of oil and flour with

him. This woman who lives outside Israel obeys the word of the Lord
through her hospitality. Even in her desperation she obeys the basic
laws that undergird society — she obeys God's covenant with us. It
seems that conversion begins with the least likely people.

After the prophet is fed, his word changes her reality. She becomes
the raven of God for Elijah: "The jar of meal shall not be emptied
nor shall the jug of oil fail, until the day when Yahweh sends rain to
the earth" (1 Kings 17:14). The widow, her son, and Elijah are fed
together on the word of God. No wonder Elijah always has a tender
spot in his heart for all those who once helped him on earth. The poor
widow gave away the last of what little she had, with no knowledge
that there would be more, with no knowledge that there would be life.
A small community of believers has sprung into being that is faithful
to the word of the Lord.

When the widow's child stops breathing, she is once again reduced
to terror. Turning to Elijah, knowing that he is dangerous, she cries
out to him: "What did you do, O man of God? Have you come to
uncover past sins and cause my son's death?" (1 Kings 17:18). She
knows that Elijah's God has power, for it has kept them alive. Even as
one outside the covenant, she knows that prophets do battle with sin
and unrighteousness and so with life and death. Perhaps she knows
that his presence is forcing a revelation of her faults and that the death
of her child is intimately connected to her past sins. Elijah's presence
demands that she examine her conscience, just as it demands that the
rulers and people of Israel examine their sins and lives. From the very
beginning sin and death are linked, as are life, justice, and faithfulness.

Elijah takes her child up to his room, where he prays and calls
on Yahweh, pleading for the child's life because of the kindness the
widow showed him. Elijah knows that God is afflicting the land and
the people, even this widow with whom he sojourns. Three times he
prays and stretches himself out on the body of the child, with the
words: "O Yahweh, my God, let this child's breath return to him"
(1 Kings 17:21). God answers by giving breath back to the child.

When the woman is given back her child she proclaims what she
now knows about Elijah: "Now I am certain that you are a man of
God, and that your words really come from Yahweh" (1 Kings 17:24).
Elijah is, first and foremost, a man of words, and all his words are
God's. God's words can stop the rain and dew, bring the land and
the people — even the king — to their knees with a curse that de-

stroys and kills. But God's words can also bring back life and bring us back to life. And the Spirit of God in one's mouth breathes life. The prophet pleads on behalf of the people, carrying the whole burden of the people's sin, until they hear the word of the Lord.

At last Yahweh commands Elijah to show himself to Ahab the king. It is time now for more than words: it is time for a public presence and public action. During Elijah's absence, Ahab has been looking for anyone who can help him find water and grass for his horses and mules — to keep his kingdom operating and his military and economic structures intact. He has sought out a prophet of Yahweh, Obadiah, who protected one hundred prophets faithful to Yahweh by hiding them in caves and feeding them bread and water during the years of famine and drought.

Ahab and Obadiah divide up the land to search for water, but as soon as Obadiah sets out, he meets Elijah. He calls out: "Is that you, my master Elijah?" Elijah tells him to go to his master to let him know that Elijah wants to see him (1 Kings 18:1–9). Obadiah is terrified that in his rage Ahab will kill him. Ahab, who has been hunting Elijah everywhere, doesn't yet know that Obadiah has been hiding prophets faithful to Yahweh and disciples of Elijah all this time. But Obadiah obeys Elijah, the master prophet.

Elijah goes to meet Ahab, who refers to him as the plague of Israel. Elijah retorts: "Who is troubling Israel? Isn't it you and your family who have disobeyed the commands of Yahweh and followed instead the Baals? Now, therefore, give an order for the Israelites to gather before me at Mount Carmel, together with the four hundred and fifty prophets of Baal who are sustained by Jezebel" (1 Kings 18:17–19). The gauntlet has been thrown down. Jezebel's gods of Baal and her 450 prophets will face off against Elijah and his God, Yahweh.

The contest is simple. The prophets of Baal and Elijah will each build an altar and choose a bull for the sacrifice. They will then cut up the bull, lay it on the wood, and call upon their God to answer with fire and consume the sacrifice. It is very specific: "Then you shall call on the name of your god while I shall call on the name of Yahweh. The God who answers with fire is the true one" (1 Kings 18:24). The issue is which God is the true God and which God the people will serve. One side has one prophet, and the other has 450. The story is gruesome, as the prophets of Baal yell, gash their skin with knives, dance, shout, and rave until evening, exhausted by their failure. Nothing happens. There is no answer from Baal. Elijah has mocked them, egged them on, insulted them and their hollow idols, who seem useless and without power.

Then Elijah calls the people closer. He builds his altar with twelve stones, for Israel's twelve tribes, reminding them how Yahweh named them: "Israel shall be your name." Elijah digs a trench around the altar that will hold thirty liters of water (remember there is a drought). He arranges the firewood, cuts up the bull, and lays it on the altar. Three times he orders the people to soak the bull and the wood with water, filling the trench.

At the time of the evening offering Elijah prays alone. His prayer is the word, the message he has been about for the last three years:

> O Yahweh, God of Abraham, Isaac, and Israel, let it be known today that you are God in Israel and that I am your servant, doing all these things at your command. Answer me, O Yahweh, answer me so that this people may know that you, O Yahweh, are God and that you are turning back their hearts to you. (1 Kings 18:36–37)

Yahweh answers with fire that consumes the offering, the wood, the stones, the dust, and the water in the trench! The people witness God's power, and they fall on their faces, praying: "Yahweh is God! Yahweh is God!" Elijah has made his point! His word is God's word! The people are turned again to the worship of the true God, Yahweh.

At this point Elijah does something that God never told him to do. He orders the people to seize the prophets of Baal and has them slaughtered. Then Elijah goes to the top of Mount Carmel and looks for rain. It comes in the form of a small fist of a cloud that forms over the sea. As it moves toward Carmel it grows into clouds, wind, and strong rain. We know that Elijah has done wrong because suddenly, for the first time, he is afraid of Jezebel. He flees for his life into the desert. Stopping under a broom tree, he prays to die, but God will have nothing to do with his prayer. He is fed again and then travels for forty days and forty nights to Mount Horeb, the mount of God, where he hides in a cave.

The word of the Lord comes to him again, questioning him about what he is doing there. Elijah claims to be jealous for the honor of God because the Israelites have forsaken the worship of Yahweh and slain the true prophets and because there is no faithful person left except him. He no longer says the truth, for the people have turned once again to Yahweh. Elijah acted on his own. He killed in anger and rage and provoked Jezebel to go after him. The bases of power have shifted somewhat. The struggle that began between Yahweh and the gods of Baal and their prophets is now between Elijah and Jezebel.

Because of Elijah's personal actions, he now has trouble perceiving the Spirit of God. He is ordered to stand on the mount and wait outside a cave for Yahweh. We are told that "Yahweh passed by" (1 Kings 19:11a). But it seems that Elijah has trouble discerning or recognizing the presence of Yahweh. First comes a windstorm, rending the mountains and breaking rocks. An earthquake follows and then a fire, but Yahweh is not to be found in any of these things. This is where Elijah the prophet is used to finding God — in power, might, destruction, and death — but at this time God is not to be found there. Elijah needs to learn another aspect of God.

What comes at last is the "murmur of a gentle breeze." Elijah perceives it, covers his face with his cloak, and then goes out to the entrance to the cave. Again, the voice of Yahweh questions him with the same words: "What are you doing here, Elijah?" Unfortunately, Elijah's answer is the same as before, claiming that he is the only true prophet who remains. Elijah seems to have lost some sense of the Spirit of God that he once possessed because of his own sin of violence and murder. By acting like Jezebel in killing the opposing group of prophets, Elijah had not acted with justice, as Yahweh acts. Thus, the time draws close for Elijah to be replaced as the messenger of God.

Elijah is told to return to Damascus to anoint new kings in Syria and Israel and to anoint Elisha, son of Shaphat from Abelmehrah, as a prophet in his place. Elijah obeys. Elijah is remembered as a prophet who was violent, dealing in hellfire and brimstone, acting arrogantly and defiantly. Caught up in his own anger, he sinned by murdering the false prophets. That was not his decision or judgment to make: it was Yahweh's judgment and Yahweh's alone. Nonetheless, Elijah remains great in Israel's history, for he saved the faith of the people in a time of infidelity, human sacrifice, and the oppression of the poor.

It is time now for him to anoint another in his place, on the command of Yahweh. His calling of Elisha, though a model for discipleship among prophets, is unique to this particular relationship and time:

So Elijah left. He found Elisha, son of Shaphat, who was plowing a field of twelve acres and was at the end of the twelfth acre. Elijah passed by him and cast his cloak over him. Elisha left the oxen, ran after Elijah and said, "Let me say goodbye to my father and mother; then I will follow you." Elijah said to him, "Return if you want, don't worry about what I did." However, Elisha turned back, took the yoke of oxen and slew them. He roasted their meat on the pieces of the yoke and gave it to his people who ate of it. After this, he followed Elijah and began ministering to him. (1 Kings 19:19–21)

Elisha is summoned by Elijah's passing near him and casting his own cloak over him. This is the cloak that Elijah pulled over his face when he encountered Yahweh on Mount Carmel in the gentle murmur of a breeze, a whisper (some translations say "a kiss of reconciliation"). This was the breath of God that brought life, that formed the call to repentance. Some Carmelites say that God was trying to breathe on Elijah and open him once again to the force of the Spirit, but that Elijah pulled his mantle over his face and the Spirit passed him by.

This throwing of a cloak over another person to engender a relationship and to transfer power is found in many cultures. In some areas throwing one's cloak over another is the essence of kidnapping. Among some Native Americans, when a man throws his cloak over a woman and she remains under it, they are married. The gesture radically alters both their identities as they become one. In this manner, Elijah throws his cloak over Elisha, thus choosing him as his disciple, his servant, the one who will take his place in Israel. Elisha disappears into the mantle of justice. Yoked with the word of the Lord, Elisha will follow behind Elijah, planting the word of the Lord in the community. (Also in the Native American community, if someone wants to pray or be alone in the midst of community, he or she pulls their cloak around them, hiding their face, and everyone gives them space apart. "Going behind your blanket" is echoed in the Christian tradition of a baptismal garment that covers us so that now "We live no longer for ourselves alone, but live hidden with Christ in God.")

The story of the passing on of prophecy is laced with symbols: a field of twelve acres, with Elisha at the end of the twelfth acre, "the land of Israel, God's portion of the earth." Elisha, who knows what is being asked of him, runs after Elijah. But he needs a moment before radically shifting his life and leaving everything behind. He wants to ritually let go, saying goodbye to his parents. But Elijah's response is forceful. None of that is allowed. The only thing that functions in a prophet's life is total obedience to the word of the Lord. The translation of Elijah's response is better rendered in the New American Bible: "Go back! Have I done anything to you?" He throws the words in his face. Elijah has acted on the word of God, and Elisha knows what is demanded in response. He turns from Elijah and responds ritually. He sacrifices the oxen he was plowing with and gives the meat to the people to eat. He severs all his connections to his old life to follow in Elijah's footsteps and be apprenticed to the word of God. One throw of a cloak cuts to his heart, and he is wrenched away from his life. Now, for the sake of the people, he lives in the realm of Yahweh. He will spend the rest of his life feeding them and teaching them the true nature of sacrifice. He has been drawn into the memory of Israel and all that Yahweh has done for Israel.

Now comes the disappearance, the passing of Elijah from this world to the world of the Spirit. Elijah and Elisha have become close friends, bound to each other in the work of God. Elisha, along with all the prophets of Bethel, Jericho, and the Jordan, know that Yahweh is calling Elijah to him. In response to Elijah's request, Elisha stays with him. The story of Elijah's passing is the basis for all the stories about Elijah in the Jewish tradition.

Yahweh took Elijah up to heaven in a whirlwind. It happened this way:...

When Elijah and Elisha stood by the Jordan Elijah took his mantle, rolled it, and struck the water with it. The water parted to both sides and they crossed over on dry ground.

After they had crossed, Elijah said to Elisha, "What shall I do for you before I am taken away from you? Ask me." Elisha said, "Grant that I may have the best of your spirit." Elijah answered, "Your request is most difficult. Yet if you see me while I am being taken from you, then you shall have it. But if not, you shall not have it."

As they were talking on the way, a chariot of fire with horses of fire stood between them, and Elijah was taken up to heaven in a whirlwind. Elisha saw him and cried out, "Father, my father, chariots of Israel and its horsemen!"

When Elisha lost sight of him, he took hold of his own clothes and tore them. He then picked up the mantle which had fallen from Elijah and returned to the banks of the Jordan. There he struck the water with the mantle, but it did not part. So he asked, "Where is Yahweh, the God of Elijah?" And as he struck the water again it parted. Elisha crossed over. (2 Kings 2:1a, 7b–14)

The spirit of Elijah now rests on Elisha. All the other prophets know that the mantle has been passed. Elijah has crossed into God's time, and Elisha crosses back into Israel. He has witnessed Elijah's passing and has requested the best of Elijah's spirit to be given to him. (In the words of the New American Bible, "Grant me a double portion of your spirit.") And Elisha's request is granted. He will need it: following Elijah is no easy trick. And neither is dealing with the Israelites and their kings. They are still as hard of heart and backsliding as they were in Elijah's time.

The relationship between Elijah and Elisha is the classic one of master and disciple. Elijah's cloak drops from the chariot of fire as he leaves. It is left on earth to be picked up and used, continuing and developing the tradition. Elisha will continue the work of Elijah. Another widow, this one the wife of a prophet, will go to Elisha for help in paying her husband's debts to prevent her sons from being sold into slavery. She explains she has only a little oil to her name. Elisha will give her and her sons a chance at life. He gives her instructions, and she obeys. She borrows as many vessels as she can from her neighbors, and those she then miraculously fills with oil, one after another (remember the unlimited oil of Elijah's encounter with a widow?). There is enough oil to pay off the debts and then to live on. Elisha creates a community around the widow in need; her debts are paid; and there is more than enough to live on.

Later, during his travels, Elisha is befriended by a wealthy barren woman who builds an addition to her house so he can rest on his way. Elisha prophesies that a son will be born to her in a year and leaves a good gift for her, and his prayer gives her a son. When the son becomes ill and dies, she leaves him on Elisha's bed and rides to find Elisha to plea for his life. Elisha sends his servant to lay Elisha's staff on the boy's face, but to no avail. Elisha goes himself and lays upon the child, prays, stretches himself out on the child, breathing life into him, and the boy comes back to life. Elisha also multiplies loaves so that there is food with an abundance of leftovers. He purifies water and destroys what is harmful in communal pots of food. Many of the stories about him have to do with the scarcity of food or with healing.

And there is the singular story of the healing of Naaman, a Syrian general, an enemy of Israel. Stricken with leprosy, Naaman seeks out Elisha based on the word of a servant girl. Again, it is an outsider who obeys the word of the prophet of Israel and is cured. When Elisha refuses his grateful gifts, Naaman departs, taking with him soil from Israel to build an altar in his own country to worship the God of Israel.

The stories of Elisha spread throughout the land, as is shown in one peculiar story from 2 Kings. Elisha returns to the woman whose son he brought back to life and warns her of the beginning of a famine that will last for seven years. She obeys Elisha's order to uproot her family for the seven years. Then we read:

> At the end of the seven years, the woman came back to her land and went to ask the king for her house and field. The king was talking with Gehazi, the servant of the man of God [Elisha], saying, "Tell me all the marvelous things Elisha has done." As Gehazi was narrating how Elisha had restored the dead to life, the woman showed up, she whose very son Elisha had raised from the dead. She was claiming back from the king her house and field. Gehazi said, "This, my lord, is the woman, and this is her son whom Elisha raised from the dead." (2 Kings 7:3–5)

These stories, started during the lifetime of the prophet, were passed from mouth to mouth, from generation to generation, as part of the tradition of the word of God, part of the memory of Israel. They became the basis for the stories of Elijah that began to arise after his death. The image of the chariot and horses of fire connected to Elijah's passing is also associated with Elisha. When it comes time for Elisha to die, Joash, the king, goes to him and cries out: "My father! My father! Chariot and horses of Israel!" And Elisha, like his master Elijah, tries to pass on a gift with his death.

Elisha commands Joash to take a bow and arrows and shoot an arrow out the window to the east. Thus Joash is given victory over his enemies to the east. Then Elisha commands him to strike the arrows on the ground. The king does, but stops after three strikes. Elisha is angry and tells him he should have done it five or six times, that because he stopped at three, he will defeat his enemy only three times.

Again, Joash's lack of trust and reluctance to obey thwart the will of
the prophet and change history.

The story does not end when Elisha dies and is buried. Elisha's
power is still potent:

> Elisha died and they buried him. A little later, a detachment of
> Moabites conducted a raid as they used to do at the beginning of
> every year. It happened that at that time some people were bury-
> ing a dead man, when they saw the Moabites. So they quickly
> threw the body into the grave of Elisha, and then fled to safety.
> But as soon as the man's body touched the bones of Elisha, the
> man revived and stood on his feet. (2 Kings 13:20–21)

Even his bones can bring the dead to life! The stories are told with
wonder and awe because it is the power of Yahweh that remains in the
prophet's bones!

It is Elijah, however, who becomes the prophet who captures the
imagination, the memory, and the hearts of Israel in all generations.
After all, Elijah doesn't die — he disappears, ascending to heaven in a
whirlwind, in a chariot of fire pulled by horses of fire. And so he can
return time and again to help the Jewish people, just as he did when
he was on earth, as champion of the poor, of God's honor and justice.

In a collection of stories about Elijah, Louis Ginzberg tells us some
important traditions about Elijah the prophet:

> Elijah's miraculous deeds will be better understood if we re-
> member that he had been an angel from the very first, even
> before the end of his earthly career. When God was about to
> create man, Elijah said to Him: "Master of the world! If it be
> pleasing in Thine eyes, I will descend to earth, and make myself
> serviceable to the sons of men." Then God changed his angel
> name, and later, under Ahab, He permitted him to abide among
> the sons of men on earth, that he might convert the world to the
> belief that "the Lord is God." His mission fulfilled, God took
> him again into heaven, and said to him: "Be thou the guardian
> spirit of My children forever, and spread the belief in Me abroad
> in the whole world."
>
> His angel name is Sandalphon, one of the greatest and
> mightiest of the fiery angel host.

Elijah [has] special vigilance as protector of the innocent, as a friend in need, who hovers over the just and the pious, ever present to guard them against evil or snatch them out of danger. With four strokes of his wings Elijah can traverse the world. Hence no spot on earth is too removed for his help. As an angel he enjoys the power of assuming the most varied appearances to accomplish his purposes. Sometimes he looks like an ordinary man, sometimes he takes the appearance of an Arab, sometimes of a horseman, now he is Roman court-official, now he is a harlot.[3]

Peninnah Schram, the author of a marvelous collection of stories called *Tales of Elijah the Prophet,* describes why Elijah holds such a fascination for the Jewish people:

Elijah is central in Jewish folklore because he is a figure we Jews have needed throughout the ages to help us and to heal us. After all, there are more Elijah stories than stories about any other Jewish hero in all of Jewish folklore. Why? Whenever Jews were in trouble (which was often), or lived in poverty conditions, or were caught in a web of injustice or a blood libel, who else could we call upon to help? Well, of course, God. But Elijah came to us, often in an earthly form or in a dream, as God's messenger and brought with him the most important ingredient that helped us to survive, namely hope. As the one who would announce the arrival of the Messiah, Elijah helped the Jews maintain the hope and optimism of a better world soon to come, a world filled with peace and justice and harmony. He is our compassionate angel.[4]

The prophet Elijah continues to be the watchdog of Israel, the one who looks out for those we overlook, especially the poor and those who are hungry for wisdom and the word of the Lord. Elijah intervenes in the lives of the powerless facing evil, injustice, and dominating violence. He is a matchmaker and especially watchful for the women of valor who will be the force behind the children of Israel as they wait for the coming of justice and peace. A friend, he visits regularly with those who seek to serve God by studying the word of God, giving alms, tending to the poor, and defending the honor of God by standing for justice. He prefers those who care for others' needs be-

fore taking care of their own, and he is a consultant to those who study
the law and expound its meaning to the people. But Elijah's primary
work is to prepare for the coming of the Messiah and to make sure that
Israel and the whole world are ready for his coming. For this reason,
a place is left for Elijah at every Passover celebration and a cup of
wine is consumed in his honor, remembering the faith he kept alive in
Israel. At Passover, a door is always left open so that if Elijah passes
by, he will know that he is welcome.

We end with a story of the prophet Elijah, a very famous story that
hits home today. Its closing line has been passed on to us in our tradition using the words of Jesus. This version is from *A Jewish Reader:
In Time and Eternity:*

> Rabbi Joshua came upon the prophet Elijah as he was standing at
> the entrance of Rabbi Simeon ben Yohai's cave. He asked him:
> "When is the Messiah coming?"
>
> The other replied: "Go and ask him yourself."
>
> "Where shall I find him?"
>
> "Before the gates of Rome."
>
> "By what sign shall I know him?"
>
> "He is sitting among poor people covered with wounds. The
> others unbind all their wounds at once, and then bind them up
> again. But he unbinds one wound at a time, and binds it up again
> straightaway. He tells himself: "Perhaps I shall be needed — and
> I must not take time and be late!"
>
> So he went and found him and said: "Peace be with you, my
> master and teacher!"
>
> He answered him: "Peace be with you, son of Levi!"
>
> Then he asked him: "When are you coming, master?"
>
> He answered him: "Today!"
>
> Thereupon he returned to Elijah and said to him: "He has
> deceived me, he has indeed deceived me! He told me, 'Today I
> am coming!' and he has not come."
>
> But the other said to him: "This is what he told you:
> 'Today — if ye would but hearken to His voice.' "[5]

Jesus turns to his community in the synagogue and says: "Today
these prophetic words come true even as you listen!" (Luke 4:21). If,
today, we listen; if, today, we hear; if, today, we let the word soften our
hearts and transform our lives; if, today, we turn again and obey the

word of the Lord — then that word will come true. The message has been transmitted down through the generations. The message endures though the prophet dies. The story unfolds, and hope and faithfulness are like rain and dew on the earth, bringing life and resurrection wherever the word is taken to heart.

In every generation the cloak is dropped, passed on, or thrown over another to pick up. Who wears the cloak and carries the mantle of justice today? Where are the disciples of the word of the Lord? Are they still hiding out in a remote *wadi,* sojourning with a poor widow and her child, traveling the roads and resting in borrowed upper rooms, climbing into caves at the top of mountains and living attentive to the whisper of God's murmuring Spirit? Do even their bones bring life? What stories of hope and memory are they telling today? Who comes to us in disguise — prophet, angel, or the very presence of the word of the Lord? Who disturbs by their very presence among us? Who keeps the faith alive and remembers the poor? Who will pick up the cloak and grasp a double portion of Spirit for the earth today?

FOUR

Amos and Hosea

The Northern Prophets

Amos

Amos is one of the first "minor" prophets, but in his case "minor" has nothing to do with the extent of his influence, the vitality of his message, or his stature as a prophet. It merely refers to the length of the book of Amos. Amos is also one of the first of the "writing" prophets. This doesn't mean that these prophets wrote down their words — rather, it signifies that a scribe or someone after them used their words to restore the memory of their announcement of what Yahweh had demanded of the people. What had transpired in the past would happen again in the history of Israel.

Amos is often referred to as the prophet of social justice, the one who revealed that God was the champion of the poor and the needy. He was also the prophet who pronounced judgment and annihilation on those with no pity for the numberless masses of people reduced to servitude in their own land.

An old Jewish folktale sets up the issues facing the land of Israel in the middle of the eighth century, when the nation was prosperous and rich, trading with its neighbors commodities produced by the labor of peasants who were generally destitute because they were forced to raise cash and export crops rather than food for themselves. Small farms and properties that had been in families for generations were being bought by the wealthy, and, as the saying goes, the rich were getting richer and the poor were getting poorer. The rich were a small minority, and the poor formed the majority in the land. The battleground was the land, and the victims tended the fields and vineyards, harvested and prepared the crops, but did not eat of the fruit of their labors. This is the folktale:

Once upon a time there was a pious man who had inherited a vast amount of landholdings and wealth in oil, wine, and wood products. He blessed God daily for his good fortune and began preparations for the Sabbath hours before sundown, taking time off from his business affairs to make sure that the finest of wines, candles, meats, and delicacies were bought for the celebration.

One day before the stars rose in the sky that heralded the beginning of the Sabbath he was called out on business. He attended to it quickly and was rushing back to be inside before his wife would light the candles and welcome the Spirit of God in exile to spend Sabbath with the Jewish people. Just blocks before his own house he ran into a poor man who aggressively begged alms from him, pleading for any amount of money so that he too could celebrate Sabbath with his family and have something to eat with them.

But the pious man was enraged and he brutally counter-acted his begging saying: "Who do you think I am? Do you think me stupid? Why have you waited until this last minute to beg? Everything is closing. Everyone is hurrying home to their own families. Nobody waits this long to prepare for the Sabbath! Do you think your trick will get me to give you more money? Has this worked for you before? Well, it won't work with me. Get away from me!" And he left the man empty-handed in the street.

Once he got to his own door, his wife was waiting, with the door open so that he could quickly enter. He was still livid at being accosted on the street and almost made late to his celebra tion. He sputtered out in anger what had just happened to him — and the gall of these people nowadays.

But his wife stared at him hard and told him to his face that he was wrong. In a stern voice she told him: "You have no idea what it's like to be poor. You've never tasted the humiliation and weariness of being poor. I grew up in a poor family. You don't know how many times we waited in the dark when it was nearly the Sabbath and we all were crying, hoping against hope that father would bring something home to us — even a piece of dry bread, a stub of a candle thrown out, leftover food from a rich man's garbage. You have sinned against that man and his family! You cannot sit down to the Sabbath meal tonight!"

Immediately the man turned and ran out the door again, running around the neighborhood looking for the poor man who was still seeking Sabbath food as the stars came out. Some say the story ends with him finding the man and giving him bread and meat, salt and wine for the Sabbath, begging him for his forgiveness. Others say the story ends with him not being able to find him and returning to his wife downcast, intent on making amends when the Sabbath was over. But that Sabbath, at least, the memory of the man's desperate face and outstretched hand remained in the flicker of the Sabbath candles and tainted the taste of all that was eaten.

On an individual basis the story is heartrending and sad. And the plight of the poor has been an issue that is central to the ethics and spirituality of the entire Jewish people. One of the many commentaries states:

> There is nothing in the world worse than poverty — it is the most terrible of all sufferings. A person who is crushed by poverty is like one to whom all the troubles of the world cling and upon whom all the curses mentioned in the Bible come.
>
> Our rabbis said: If all the sufferings and pain in the world were gathered on one side of the scale, and poverty was on the other side, poverty would outweigh them all. (*Exodus Rabbah* 31.14)

This situation of poverty is seen in the relationship of one human being to another and one family to another. From Israel's very beginning in the Sinai desert, the people were to be aware of one another and to have pity on the destitute. This was laced throughout the code of ethics and behavior demanded of the people by Yahweh's covenant:

> If there is anybody poor among your brothers, who lives in your cities in the land that Yahweh gives you, do not harden your heart or close your hand, but be open-handed and lend him all that he needs. . . .
>
> When you give anything, give it willingly, and Yahweh, your God, will bless you for this in all your work and in all that you undertake.

The poor will not disappear from this land. Therefore I give you this commandment: you must be open-handed to your brother, to the needy and to the poor in your land. (Deut. 15:7–8, 10–11)

From the beginning the poor were to trigger the memory of being slaves in Egypt, and their very presence was to move the heart of the community to relieve their suffering. Because this was the land that Yahweh had given to his chosen people, it was never to even begin to look like Egypt. The books of the laws contained codes to rectify the imbalance of poor and rich, to militate against it developing, and to lessen the consequences of its harshness among Yahweh's own people. The presence and plight of the poor are meant to be communal pricks of conscience announcing that all is not well in the land or among the people who worship Yahweh. All of life — agriculture, economics, farming, trade, and so on — was to be carried out in such a way that the poor had a place in society and a chance to survive with dignity. This is written again and again, as in the book of Deuteronomy:

When you harvest the wheat in your fields, if you drop a sheaf, do not return to pick it up, but let it be there for the foreigner, the orphan and the widow. Yahweh will bless you for this in all your work.

When you harvest your olives, do not go back to beat the trees another time, what is left shall be for the foreigner, the orphan and the widow. When you gather the grapes in your vineyard, do not return to look for what has been left. This will be the share of the foreigner, the orphan and the widow. Remember that you were a slave in Egypt. This is why, I command you to do this. (Deut. 24:19–22)

In later days, Rabbi Israel Salanter wrote: "A person should be more concerned with spiritual than with material matters, but another person's material welfare is your own spiritual concern." There has always been a connection between the gestures of individual persons and the code of the law. It has always been core to the covenant and the very existence of the people of God that when the poor become the majority in the land it is because of injustice, callousness, greed, and disobedience to God's word. This is essential to our tradition even today, as found in these words of Thomas Merton: "You for your part can draw up a new code of just laws; I for my part will give my coat to a beggar. And until you have given your coat to the poor and shared your own bread with those who starve, you will not know much about just laws and your code will be a joke, say the prophets and the saints."[1]

This is the backdrop of Amos's call as a prophet. The situation in Israel has deteriorated to the point that a wealthy few are utterly without pity, intent on greedily producing more cash crops and insensitive to the desperate situation that is cracking the very foundation of their lives and, more importantly, their relationship with Yahweh. A Jewish saying sets up the scene: "If you pervert justice, you shake the world." In Israel there is almost a symbiotic relationship between the wealthy and the poor; each profoundly needs the other and reveals the other's character and soul, mirroring the world through each other's eyes. But the connection is rooted in the obligation of the people to not "deal deceitfully or falsely with one another" in regards to farming, labor, trade, consumption, the marketplace, or any other form of business and finance. And this reality is subtly connected to the practice of worship. Ethical behavior and commitment to the welfare of others determine the faithfulness and sincerity of one's rituals and devotions, especially in regard to the Sabbath. The Sabbath exists to connect the memory of what God has done for Israel with what the people of Israel, in turn, must do among themselves, as light to other nations.

> Take care to keep holy the sabbath day, as Yahweh, your God, commanded you. You have six days to work and do your tasks. But the seventh day is the Day of Rest in honor of Yahweh, your God. Do not do any work, you or your child, or your servant, or your ox, or your donkey, or any of your animals. Neither will the foreigner who lives in your land work. Your servant will rest just like you. Remember that you were once enslaved in the land of Egypt from where Yahweh, your God, brought you out with his powerful hand and outstretched arm. For that reason, Yahweh, your God, commands you to observe the sabbath. (Deut. 5:12–15)

The people were reminded over and over again to be consistent in all their dealings — business, interpersonal, and religious — from their weights and measures to their purity of heart:

You shall not keep in your bag two weights, one heavier and the other lighter, nor shall you have in your house a large measure and a small one. You shall have a full and exact weight, and an equally just and exact measure, that you may lengthen your days in the land which Yahweh, your God, gives you. Because Yahweh hates him who does such things and any kind of injustice. (Deut. 25:13–16)

In that last line lies the crux of the matter. This is why Amos is commanded to go to the people of the Northern Kingdom to declare God's wrath and hatred. Injustice rules the land, and the poor are being swallowed up in the greed of those who conveniently forget that their relationship with Yahweh is founded on justice and faithfulness.

Amos is not the kind of prophet we are used to, those who preach "Repent or else!" No, Amos's oracles were preached to the wealthy ruling classes of Samaria in the north, and they call for their complete destruction and annihilation. The oracles, by themselves, taken and strung together, are utterly distinctive from the rest of the book of Amos. In fact, many scholars believe that Amos's words are primarily contained in just these oracles.

The material in the book of Amos can be separated into three sections. The first includes the original oracles, found primarily in Amos 2:6b–8; 2:13–3:8; 4:1–3; 5:1–2, 7–20; 6:1–8; 8:4–7, 9–10; and 9:1–4. Scholars feel that after the Samarians in the north were conquered in 722 B.C.E., a scribe took some of Amos's oracles and wove his own words around them, calling on the people of the Northern Kingdom to look at their immediate history after the death of Jeroboam, when four kings died by the sword between 745 and 732. Then again, later in history, another scribe sought to interpret Amos's words for the people of Judah, when once again the ruling elite and wealthy were punished by exile in Babylon in 587 B.C.E. and a remnant hoped to return to live in the land of promise and justice.

The first scribe's text covers most of the descriptions of Amos's call and his five visions, whose tone is one of repent, change, and listen to the word of the Lord. The second scribe weaves in the pieces of hope, adding primarily the beginning and the end to instill a sense of a future into the exiles.

Amos's original oracles can easily be lifted out of the text. They are written in a poetic style, and many translations of the Bible present

them as poetry. They were delivered orally and are direct and ac-
cusatory. Each delivers an accurate sword thrust. These characteristics
single them out from the rest of the book.[2]

Nine oracles scattered in chapters 2 through 9 are directed toward
the wealthy urban landowners and traders of Samaria. Amos has a
habit of being very specific about descriptions of people, of what they
have done, and of what will happen to them because of their actions.
Themes are repeated over and over again. The brutality of the rich
will be rewarded with the wrathful justice of God, as God leaves them
to their own devices and to the viciousness of politics in the world.
These are the issues:

> The powerful have oppressed the powerless; the ruling elite, the
> poor. In the midst of this oppression, in fact on the very foun-
> dation of it, the powerful enjoy a luxury whose most offensive
> manifestation is an extravagant festivity. God rejects this state
> of affairs and will reverse it. In a typical measure-for-measure
> response of justice, God will answer the violence done to the
> powerless by the elite with his own violence against the elite.
> He will wage war on them, killing many and leading others into
> exile, where they too will be killed. God will answer their festive
> revelry by turning it, through war, into lamentation and wailing.
> For oppression, war. For revelry, wailing. These four terms sum
> up the whole basic message of the prophet Amos.[3]

Amos is fond of pronouncing judgments and oaths and announcing
war and dirges. All are devastating. What is prophesied is inevitable
and catastrophic. The judgment, which Amos has already rendered,
will be carried out. Amos's duty is to moan, weep, cry out, lament, and
condemn. There is no turning back the wrath of God. It is the direct
consequence of the injustice that has caused the death and humiliation
of so many of the people. Amos's very name means "burden," or, in
some translations, "oracle delivered."

And now to the prophet Amos. We know little or nothing about
him, although his words echo and resound throughout the ages. In
Amos 7, he describes his call to prophesy to Amaziah, the priest of
Bethel. (Remember that references to Bethel, high places, and rituals
or worship are usually attributed to the first scribe.) Amos is told to go
back to the south, where he came from, and earn his bread by prophesying there rather than in the king's sanctuary and national shrine

(7:12–13). Amos's description of why he is in the Northern Kingdom is brief but powerful: "Amos replied to Amaziah. 'I am not a prophet or one of the fellow-prophets. I am a breeder of sheep and dresser of sycamore trees. But Yahweh took me from shepherding the flock and said to me: Go, prophesy to my people Israel' " (7:14–15).

That's it! Amos was minding his own business, literally. He says, "Yahweh took me" and said "Go, prophesy!" Amos was summoned. Earlier, in chapter 3, Amos describes that summons. Its bite is hidden in the form of the text as well in its word:

> Do two walk together unless they have agreed?
>
> Does a lion roar in the forest when it has no prey? Does a young lion growl in its den unless it has seized something?
>
> Does a bird get caught in a snare if the snare has not been baited?
>
> Does a tiger spring up from the ground unless it has caught something?
>
> If a trumpet sounds in a city, will the people not be frightened?
>
> If disaster strikes a city, has not Yahweh caused it? Yet Yahweh does nothing without revealing his plan to his servants, the prophets. If the lion roars, who will not be afraid? If Yahweh speaks, who will not prophesy? (Amos 3:3–8)

Nothing will silence him, except the command of God. Although his call was a complete surprise, Amos is compelled to obey. God is described as a lion who has already seized his prey, has it in his den, and is roaring before consuming what he has caught! All are deaf to the roar, to the word of God, except Amos, and he must speak. He must roar out the judgment of God. Amos stands before God and the people. It is agreed: God has opened his mouth, his mind, his heart, and his intent to the prophet, and the prophet is only his servant. Amos carries the burden of judgment, but he also carries the burden of a people who have long been destroyed by their own neighbors and leaders. His sympathies and compassion are with the poor and the needy, as our God's own sympathies. This is the secret God gives to Amos to share with Israel and with all of us.

Amos's words and oracles condemn as though in a court of law. They list grievances, spell out injustices in detail, point fingers, deliver vivid, sharp-edged observations of injustice. Amos, with his keen sense of outrage, is the conscience of God using a human voice, revealing the limit of God's patience with those who disdain the cries of the poor or ignore the desperation created by greed and selfishness. The poor — and God — can bear only so much pain. Amos roars out:

> They sell the just for money and the needy for a pair of sandals; they tread on the head of the poor and trample them upon the dust of the earth, while they silence the right of the afflicted; a man and his father go to the same woman to profane my holy name; they stretch out upon garments taken in pledge, beside every altar; they take the wine of those they swindle and are drunk in the house of their God. (Amos 2:6b–8)

Their punishment will be swift and without recourse or mercy because they have shown none:

> "Behold, I will crush you to the ground, as a cart does when it is full of sheaves. The swift shall be unable to flee and the strong man shall lose his strength. The warrior shall not save himself nor the bowman stand his ground. The swift of foot shall not escape nor the horseman save himself. Even the most stouthearted among the warriors shall flee away naked on that day," says Yahweh. (Amos 2:13–16)

Judgment is rendered and the punishment announced, usually with images that are meant to instill fear — just as the sound of a lion roaring close by would terrify you and render you incapable of escaping. Amos, who is intent on reminding the people that nothing is hidden from God, tries to convey the reality of God's horror over people who are steeped in self-importance, greed, hedonism, and violent practices that reduce the majority of the population to a living death of squalor. The images of what the unjust will experience should instill fear within us! This is what will happen: "Yahweh says this: As the shepherd rescues from the mouth of the lion a pair of legs or the tip of an ear, so shall some of you be saved, O Israelites of Samaria who loll on comfortable couches and rest on pillows of Damascus" (Amos 3:12).

With each oracle Amos builds his case against the wealthy. He singles out groups within the wealthy, naming them in such a way that we can recognize them readily:

Listen to this word, you cows of Bashan, you women who live on the hills of Samaria; who oppress the weak and abuse the needy, who order your husbands, "Bring us something to drink quickly!"

The Lord Yahweh has sworn by his holiness, "The time is coming upon you when you will be dragged away with hooks, even the last of you with fishhooks. Through the breaks in the wall you will go out, straight ahead, driven all the way to Hermon." It is Yahweh who has spoken. (Amos 4:1–3)

Death and exile face them when they are driven out from the land they have abused and misused. The land of promise is God's and only given to them to care for and live upon as the light of justice for all nations. Because they have betrayed that trust and no longer walk in agreement with God, Amos's words become a lament, a dirge, a curse upon those who have done such evil. They are words that have come down through the ages to describe injustice and the rising up of one class against another. Never for a moment have the rich thought that they would have to pay for their crimes and be punished for how they fabricated their lifestyles at the expense of so many others:

Woe to you who turn judgment into bitterness and do no justice in the land!

You hate him who reproves in court; you despise him who speaks the truth.

Because you have trampled on the poor man and extorted levies on his grain, though you have built mansions of hewn stones you will not dwell in them; though you have planted choice grapevines, you shall not drink of their wine.

For I know the number of your crimes and how grievous are your sins: persecuting the just, taking bribes, turning away the needy at the gates. (Amos 5:7–12)

Again, retribution is thorough and deadly:

Woe to you who long for Yahweh's day!
Why should you long for that day?
It is a day of darkness, not of dawn,
as if a man fled from a lion
only to run into a bear;
or as if he entered his home,

> rested his hand against the wall,
> only to be bitten by a viper. (Amos 5:18–19)

In chapter 6, Amos describes those who are "overconfident," secure in their dwellings built in the hills to get away from the heat of the summer. They spend their days and nights lounging and gorging themselves, "on beds inlaid with ivory." They "sprawl on couches; eat lamb from the flock and veal from calves fattened in the stall" (6:4). They pass time making music on harps and new instruments and drink wine by the bowlful. Amos condemns them for anointing themselves "with the finest oils, but you do not grieve over the ruins of Joseph" (6:6). Amos says that they will be the first to go into exile. Their revelry will be over and done with, forever.

Finally, he returns to his opening words:

> Hear this, you who trample on the needy to do away with the weak of the land. You who say, "When will the new moon or the sabbath feast be over that we may open the store and sell our grain? Let us lower the measure and raise the price; let us cheat and tamper with the scales, and even sell the refuse with the whole grain. We will buy up the poor for money and the needy for a pair of sandals." (Amos 8:4–6)

And God's response to all this is: "Yahweh, the pride of Jacob, has sworn by himself: 'I shall never forget their deeds' " (Amos 8:4–7). The injustices inflicted on God's own people have been cold-blooded and calculated. This hasn't been done by just one individual or a few — rather, the power-brokers have institutionalized a whole pattern of stealing from the land and those who work it, the poor. This theft has been done for gain, for greed, for profit, for export, for international esteem. The words of God in Amos's mouth cut through all the lies and distortions, leaving not a shred of excuse for their behavior. Not only will the unjust system they have constructed be dismantled — it will be utterly destroyed as a consequence of their evil. There will be no ground to stand on when the justice of God turns toward them.

Amos's actual words end in the middle of chapter 9. They offer no hope for his immediate hearers. He is not there to encourage repentance or change. What has been done is beyond salvage. Their savagery is too extensive. Their injustice runs too deep. Their hearts are too hardened by excess, greed, decadence, and their long history of ignoring the sufferings of their neighbors and fellow human beings. They are approaching the end and there is no recourse. This is the sentence of death:

> The Lord Yahweh says, "On that day I will make the sun go down at noon and darken the day in broad daylight.
>
> "I will turn your festivals into mourning and all your singing into wailing. Everyone will mourn, covered with sackcloth and every head will be shaved. I will make them mourn as for an only son and bring their day to a bitter end." . . .
>
> "Strike the top of the columns, so that the beams shake and the roof falls down on the heads of them all. Those who are left I will slay with the sword; not one shall flee, not one shall escape.
>
> "Though they dig down to the netherworld, my hand will take them from there; though they climb up to heaven, I will bring them down from there.
>
> "Though they hide on the top of Carmel, I will search them out there and take them; though they hide from me in the depths of the sea, I will bid the sea-serpent bite them.
>
> "When they are led into captivity by their enemies, there I will command the sword to slay them." (Amos 8:7–10; 9:1b–4)

These were not threats; they were a sentence pronounced and, in due course, carried out in history. Amos's God is a God of justice who acts in the world, who is witness to injustice and the cries of the poor, and who will not allow such a horror to continue unabated. The balance of power will tilt. Those who built their kingdoms on injustice and greed will know the harsh taste of justice meted out to them. The scales will balance. This is primitive justice, a justice that reverses fortunes and mirrors the horrors inflicted upon others. They have brought this sentence upon themselves. They have reached a point of no return.

Amos has been ordered to prophesy. He must. His prophecy is an outcry against injustice, against destroying the lives of those who are precious to God. He can't call for "reform" because the oppressors don't even see what the outcry is about. The outcry of the poor and the desperate is as poignant as the cry of the prophet roaring out a sentence of exile and death. In the end, the fulfillment of Amos's prophecies confirms the truth of his words and the truth of the horrors we inflict upon one another.

Later, when scribes returned to the oracles of Amos, they added information appropriate to their time in history, including a condemnation of worship and festivities in "high places" and an emphasis that Jerusalem was the only place to celebrate the feasts. These texts differ from those of Amos. The scribes do not condemn univocally as Amos did, but instead encourage the people to repent. While Amos's lion tears and devours his prey caught in his claws, the scribes' lion bellows and roars that if they heed his warning, the whole catastrophe can be averted. Amos understands that God has already made a choice for justice. The scribes seemingly feel that the people can choose. If only these hearers will "turn," they can still be saved. It all hinges on the present.

We are told nothing of the fate of Amos. We know he was not listened to; his pronouncements were ignored; and the people suffered the consequences. Did he just go home to the south and take up his businesses where he left off? Did he ever make it home? Was he caught up in the destruction and exile? Amos obeyed God. He had no other existence besides this, no other memory. His words served to teach the people of Israel about injustice, about the poor, and about God's intolerance of our evil.

Though Amos's words reveal a harshness perhaps unparalleled in the prophets, they also reveal the tenderness with which God holds the poor and needy of the earth, for these are the people that move God to roar out in indignation. The Indian poet and mystic Rabindranath Tagore writes of the poor and their God in his poem "Gitanjali 10":

> Here is your footstool
> and there rest your feet
> where live the poorest,
> and lowliest, and lost.
> When I try to bow to you,
> my obeisance cannot reach
> down to the depth
> where your feet rest
> among the poorest
> and the lowliest, and the lost.
>
> Pride can never approach
> to where you walk
> in the clothes of the humble

among the poorest
and the lowliest, and the lost.
My heart can never find its way
to where you keep company
with the companionless
among the poorest
and the lowliest, and the lost.

Amos's God is a lion intent not only on eating its prey but also on feeding its young so that they might live as lions of Judah, lions of God. Amazingly, the situation that arose in northern Israel in the eighth century is the same today worldwide. Julius Nyerere, the president of Tanzania who died in 1999, wrote:

It is the minority which is well fed, and the minority which has secured control over the world's wealth and over their fellowmen. Further, in general that minority is distinguished by the color of their skins and by their race. And the nations in which most of that minority of the world's people live have a further distinguishing characteristic, their adoption of the Christian religion.

Amos's indictment is repeated in our times, and it is directed at us. The focus of God's justice is squarely on those who claim to be in covenant with God and who are commissioned to be the light to the nations.

In the writings of the prophets, wealth is not necessarily a blessing from God. It is more often than not a lure, an easy slide into oppression, and a threat to the social order that God demands among people. In a nutshell, God condemns the use of commerce and business, especially anything related to food production, to oppress the poor and then cast them into slavery to pay their debts. Lenders, who often are regular, hypocritical attendants at rituals of worship, usually charge the poor exorbitant interest on their debts. Such lucrative business practices drive a wedge between rich and poor people or rich and poor nations. They speak louder than any liturgical prayer or ritual sacrifice made or sanctioned by those who reap the benefits from the dominant system.

The scribes who followed in Amos's footsteps sought a transformation of society by institutionalizing the oracles of Amos. But the corruption of power, which penetrates equally religion, commerce, and politics, was too strong. And so, once again, the elite of the generations that came after the destruction and exile of 722 fell into the same trap. Their fate was sealed by the destruction of the temple in Jerusalem. Similarly, the last of the scribes to use Amos's material sought to give heart back to those returning from exile. He exhorted them to remember and to not fall under the same sentence of death.

Even today Amos's roar comes to every nation, to every people in every generation. To borrow a phrase from journalist Arthur Jones, Amos is the prophet who announces that the only economics allowed among the people of God are "economics as if people mattered."[4] Yet the spirit of our age is a quest for wealth and power that is itself a form of idolatry. The largest endangered species on this planet today is the poor. How are these continuing issues of power evaluated in light of God's will, the dignity of earth and those who dwell upon it, and especially its poor? In the article referred to above, Arthur Jones quotes Old Testament scholar Norman Gottwald: "The Bible also provides a 'communitarian' yardstick: Do the mode of production and the power relations governing it build up the whole community, providing its basic services and creating opportunities to realize the life possibilities of the greatest number of people?"[5]

Jones continues his critique:

Is modern capitalism doing that? No. Not worldwide. Not now. The standard of living and per capita income from Latin America to the Philippines has dropped back to 1970s and, in some places, 1950s levels. The evidence is in the debtor nations and the West's declining industrial regions. Globally, quickly said, and allowing that local Third World cupidity had a role, the capitalists made easy loans at cheap interest rates.

Indebted countries around the world have since paid — where they knuckled under to capitalism's debt collector, the International Monetary Fund — a billion in interest on every billion borrowed and still owe more than the original loan.[6]

What underlies these questions is the refrain shouted loudly — often on deaf ears — by the prophets: God's will is a passionate concern for the poor. It is expressed in laws that reveal God's commandments rooted in the Sabbath, in the Jubilee Year, and in the Codes of Holiness enjoined upon the Israelite community. Economic redistribution that draws in those on the margins of society and that is based on just distribution, not greed or hoarding or amassing capital, is the rule that undergirds any truly Judeo-Christian society.

This idea goes back to the early months of the Exodus, in the desert, when the people of Israel were taught how to be God's people. The command was simple: "Each day the people are to gather what is needed for that day. In this way I will test them to see if they will follow my teaching or not" (Exod. 16:4). Yahweh has declared a new social order based on an economic system in which everyone's need for sustenance was provided for and any excess accumulation was prohibited (Exod. 16:16–21).

Later, according to the proclamation of the Jubilee Year, originally called the Sabbath Year and practiced every seven years, the land was not tilled, no seed was sown, and no harvest was reaped so that the land could know a time of rest and restoration. Both economic and ecological equilibrium would be reestablished (Exod. 23:10–11). Core to this Jubilee celebration was the idea of debt remission and relief and the liberation of slaves (Deut. 15:1, 12). Every seven years, the cycle of poverty, of slavery, of debt, of slow death by starvation, and the division of society into rich and poor, powerful and powerless, was broken on a regular ritual basis in memory of the people's liberation from Egypt.

At the end of the twentieth century, this issue of debt reduction and relief was picked up in Latin America and in Europe as a way to celebrate the Jubilee Year decreed for the year 2000. As early as 1991, two bishops, Carlos Maria Ariz and Romulo Emilliani, and many missionaries wrote a manifesto addressed "To the World Bank, International Financial Institutions, Governments of the Industrialized Countries, Governments of Latin America, and the Christian Churches." It reads in part:

> In union with God and our peoples, we invite you to pray, "Pardon, O God, our debts as we pardon our debtors. Amen." As we share in this life of Indian, Afro, and peasant peoples here, we cannot fail to recognize that the stripping of resources and the consequent impoverishment which began 500 years ago is expressed in a very concrete form by the inhuman, immoral, and unpayable external debt; this debt continues to permit the technological growth of the North at the cost of the impoverishment and death of the South.

In the name of Jesus Christ and the peoples of Latin America, we demand:

- of the World Bank and International Financial Institutions, the cancellation of this unpayable foreign debt;

- of the governments of Latin America, that they cease payment of this debt, which is causing the slow death of our peoples;

- of the Christian Churches, that 1992 be proclaimed the Year of Grace for debtors and creditors, canceling the debt, so the authentic New Evangelization can begin today.

Amos would have recognized true followers in these bishops and missionaries who, like the scribes of the eighth century B.C.E., knew that periodically "the earth must be allowed to rest, and slaves freed, and all debts must be forgiven." Without this practice that seeks to restore balance nationally and internationally, cities and nations will continue to concentrate wealth and power among the few, which will result in starvation and deprivation for the majority and lead inevitably to violence.

In an address to Canadian Catholics, John Paul II used the language of the prophets:

Poor people, and poor nations — poor in different ways, not lacking food but also deprived of freedom and other human rights — will sit in judgment on those people who take these goods away from them, amassing to themselves the imperialistic monopoly of economic and political supremacy at the expense of others.

The institutionalization of injustice and the widespread acceptance of capitalism, greed, and inequality, combined with the complexities of the market, the regulations of economies and of loans and payment policies, do not excuse us in any way. As Christians, "We should have a great love for our age, but make no concessions to the spirit of the age, so that in us the Christian mystery may never lose its sap."[7] We have to be reminded by "prophets" that there is an unbroken relationship between, on the one hand, injustice and the evil we perpetuate and, on the other hand, what the prophets would call a divinely inspired catastrophe. Curses follow upon our refusal to fulfill our obligations to the poor. God has never seemed to favor the rich, though the rich often claim their wealth as a blessing of God. Instead, in both testaments God's favorites are the poor, the oppressed, and the marginalized.

Amos gave greater responsibility for the care of the poor to the guardians and makers of the law. He railed against the absence of justice and righteousness and especially against those in society who perverted justice for their own ends. He cried out: "But you have turned justice into poison and the fruit of righteousness into worm-wood" (Amos 6:12). Such a perversion of justice is a bitter and poisonous herb. Instead of the sweetness of justice (often compared by the prophets to the grape and wine of the vineyard), the bitter-ness of injustice is the only taste of life afforded to the poor. Only when "righteousness" — civil justice — is the experience of all will "justice roll down like waters, and righteousness like an everflowing stream" (5:24).

Amos castigates all the nations for their injustice but reserves the depth and extent of the wrath of God for his own people who have been taught the wisdom of God to practice among themselves. To reject these laws; to be aware of the gravity of the situations of in-equality; to use religion to validate their choices and shore up the dominant culture through liturgy and an individualized spirituality that allow the rich to ignore justice and blame the victim — this calls down condemnation against ourselves, just as it did with our ances-tors in faith. Those who are chosen bear greater guilt: "You only have I known of all the families of the earth; therefore I will punish you for all your iniquities" (Amos 3:2). Amos then singles out the cities as well as specific social groups within the culture: men, women, even the wealthy elite will know agony worse than those they oppressed. Israel will be overwhelmed by the power of other nations. Injustice invokes imperatives. Present injustices demand immediate remedies. Guilt is definite. In the end, men and women will meet God, whom they have conveniently forgotten in their quest for wealth and secu-rity. Amos's words do not give hope, although the book itself ends with a promise:

> I shall bring back the exiles of my people Israel; they will rebuild the desolate cities and dwell in them. They will plant vineyards and drink their wine; they will have orchards and eat their fruit.

I shall plant them in their own country and they shall never
again be rooted up from the land which I have given them, says
Yahweh your God. (Amos 9:14)

As the recipients of this tradition, we are called to repentance, to
"justice or else," to live in such a way that the poor know justice in the
land and that the world knows that we stand with Amos. By standing
with Amos, we also stand with the poor and the indigenous of the
world, with God, and against oppression, the exploitation of resources,
and the persecution of those who seek justice. What can that look like?

David Fernández, a Jesuit priest who is director of the Jesuits'
Miguel Agustín Pro Human Rights Center in Mexico City, reflected
on the intimidation and threats to which Mexican Jesuits have recently
been subjected:

The Mexican Jesuits have identified themselves with the indigenous peoples of the country. This has earned them the enmity
of the wealthy landowners who link themselves to the ruling Institutional Revolutionary Party (PRI) to maintain political
control. The landowners are accused of abusing the indigenous
peoples. Since the Chiapas uprising in 1994, attacks against the
Jesuits, especially those working with poor communities, have
increased.[8]

Persecution of Jesuits, and others, active in places where social injustice is most severe is the price they pay in the struggle for the rights
of the poor. As Father Fernández says, being the victims of malicious
stories and aggression is part of their mission. This is the practice of
solidarity and speaking out on behalf of the poor, both giving voice
to their concerns and standing with them as they rise up to take possession of the land that is theirs. This practice of prophetic justice is
central to religious community life and to the life of all Christians.
Whom do we defend? Where do we stand, and whom do we stand
with? Whose voices do we support? Do we raise our voices economically, politically, culturally, and even religiously against the prevailing
culture of excess? Do we speak out against the dominant modes of
finance, prerequisites for loans, and resistance to debt relief? Do we
speak together and employ our rich tradition of social justice statements from the last one hundred years and incorporate that clout into
our electoral process? Do we seek alternatives to the unjust treatment

of immigrants, farmworkers, the undocumented, the poor, the indigent, and the underemployed? Do we work with others for a just wage for all? These hard questions are just the beginning of the examination of conscience that Amos would detail for us today.

On a personal and corporate level, do we succumb to the marketing practices and advertising of companies and institutions that engage in unjust labor practices? NIKE's ads are short and demanding: "Just do it!" Do we "Just NOT do it"? As Global Exchange, an organization that seeks to bring information to the public, states:

> NIKE factories in China, Indonesia and Vietnam pay their workers 20–30 cents an hour. The employees work long hours with minimal breaks. Emotional and physical abuse is common. Meanwhile NIKE executives and athletes make millions. They can afford to treat and pay their workers better. Show your outrage for NIKE's greed and hypocrisy by buying a JUST DON'T DO IT T-shirt. The proceeds from the sales enable us to keep the heat on NIKE through media work, education, and protests.[9]

The prophet Amos roars at us that we are not allowed to enhance our lifestyles at the cost of the poor, the workers, and the farmers of the world. We are enjoined to investigate where our money goes when we buy shoes, uniforms, electronics, and clothing. Ignorance does not necessarily let us off the hook. Information is available and it is crucial to changing our lives and spending practices. We are supposed to be appalled at injustice. But how do we in fact react to it?

> Compare what NIKE pays its workers with the pay of NIKE's executives and celebrity promoters. CEO Philip Knight is one of the richest people on the planet. To match Mr. Knight's $5.2 billion dollar worth, a young Chinese woman would have to work 9 hours a day, six days a week — for 100 centuries! Michael Jordan gets $20 million a year to promote NIKE sneakers, more than the annual income of 30,000 Asian women who make NIKE shoes.[10]

This brutality would make Amos wince, and then he would turn and roar out the word of the Lord at us, the elite of the Western world and of the kingdoms of the north. Many of us reap the harvest of injustice from these massive issues. But the prophet Amos allows us no excuse. There is only immediate radical change or imminent annihilation. We must respond together now. It is imperative.

How can we persuade others to do what is right? Generally, there are three ways that we can use: encourage them, demand and threaten, or trick them into doing right. A story told about a mayor from the Northern Sung dynasty (970 to 1127 C.E.) illustrates a mixture of all these methods. (Note that this story, used to illustrate the teaching of a prophet from northern Israel, comes from a northern Chinese kingdom and addresses the present-day nations of the North!)

Once upon a time the newly appointed mayor Fan Chwen-Zan wanted to promote the silk industry in his region, but the majority of his constituents were farmers. He thought about ordering them all to change their methods and plant mulberry trees instead of their usual crops and then punish those who disobeyed, but he knew how they'd react. They'd grumble, do it only reluctantly, and both farm production and his reputation would take a beating. He didn't know how to trick the farmers into planting the trees, but he did know that tricking people often led to mistrust and a climate of deceit that encouraged cheating and lies.

What was he to do? He studied all the records of the previous mayors, the prison and work systems, penalties and retribution, and decided upon an idea. He decreed that anyone who was convicted of a misdemeanor could plant mulberry trees in their backyards and on their land instead of the usual hard labor. It was their choice. The number of trees that were to be planted depended on the severity of the violation or the crime. He even decided that sentences could be reduced or penalties made more lenient according to the quality of the cultivation of their allotted trees.

It worked! Practically no one chose the hard labor sentence and instead planted mulberry trees. After all, who would choose jail over the task of planting a few (or many) trees? In just a few years, there were thousands of mulberry trees in yards, on streets, in once-empty lots, on roadways in and out of town, on every available piece of unused land, and they were carefully cultivated and tended. And people began to breed silk worms since the trees were already there — and the profits were substantial. Of course, the mayor was praised for his ingenuity and the people shared in the wealth that the scheme brought to the region.[11]

A saying usually accompanies the story: "Redirect idle human resources to other useful fields. You will be surprised by the result." Pragmatism, imagination, and human craftiness, mixed with a bit of incentive and mercy, can alter society quickly, if we only learn to think of what might enhance life together rather than just for ourselves.

Hosea

Hosea began to preach in the north sometime between 745 and 723 B.C.E., before the Northern Kingdom fell to Assyrian troops and toward the end of the prosperous and idolatrous reign of King Jeroboam II. Jeroboam was notorious for his lavish spending, his persecution of the prophets (see 1 Kings 13), and for doing evil in the land, setting an example for the people.

First Kings 14 tells the story how, when his son Abijah fell ill, he sent his wife to an ancient blind prophet in disguise to find out what would become of the child. But Yahweh warned the prophet Ahijah that she was coming. He prophesied to her thus:

> I have been told to give you unpleasant news. Go, therefore; bring Jeroboam this message of Yahweh, the God of Israel: I made you rise from the midst of the people and established you as the leader of Israel. I took the kingdom from David's family to give it to you. Yet you have not been like my servant David, who kept my commands and followed me with his whole heart, doing only what was pleasing to me. You have done worse than anyone before you. You have made me angry with your strange gods and the images you have made; and you have forsaken me. (1 Kings 14:6b–9)

Jeroboam's wife was then told news that would be horrifying for any mother, for anyone in a family. God's punishment would "cut off every male in Jeroboam's line, whether slave or freeman in Israel, and . . . wipe out the descendants of Jeroboam just as they wipe out the dung until it is gone" (1 Kings 14:10). And there was more: none of these males would be given burial, and as soon as she stepped through the city gates at the entrance to her own house, her child would die. However, this one child would be buried and mourned because God found something good in him alone.

As with Amos, this is a time of great gulfs between the poor and the rich, aided and abetted by corrupt courts of law and a general break-down in public morality. Although Yahweh was loosely acknowledged as the God of Israel, there was little practice that expressed that belief. The emphasis was instead on rites of prostitution, sacrifice (even fire sacrifice of the Israelites' own sons and daughters), and divination of the fertility gods of Baal (see 2 Kings 17:9–24). In many places, with its share of exhortations, angry declarations, and images, the book of Hosea sounds like the ferocity of Amos. But what distinguishes Hosea from Amos is the beginning of the book, which situates this rage within the context of Hosea's relationship to Gomer, a temple prostitute of the cult of Baal, the woman chosen by Yahweh to be Hosea's wife.

Amos never mentions the covenant between Yahweh and the people, but Hosea's entire structure of symbols is built on this rela-tionship of intimacy, created when God adopted Israel as his beloved son: "I loved Israel when he was a child; out of Egypt I called my son. But the more I called, the further from me have they gone — sacrificing to the Baals, burning incense to the idols" (Hos. 11:1–2). God is also the devoted, attentive husband of Israel who courted her as she wandered in the desert: "So I am going to allure her, lead her once more into the desert where I can speak to her tenderly" (2:16). Yahweh has provided for his beloved's and his children's needs with tender devotion and yet was spurned and ignored. "Yet it was I who taught Ephraim to walk, taking them by the arms; yet little did they realize that it was I who cared for them. I led them with cords of human kindness, with leading strings of love, and I became for them as one who eases the yoke upon their neck and stoops down to feed them" (11:3). The images are those of family, between husband and wife and between parents and children.

There is a sense of agony, of internal wrestling and terrible struggle within God between justice and mercy, between righteous indignation, jealousy, and compassion:

They insist on turning away from me, they cry out because the yoke is upon them and no one lifts it. How can I give you up,

Ephraim? Can I abandon you like Admah or make you like Ze-
boiim? My heart is troubled within me and I am moved with
compassion. I will not give vent to my great anger; I will not
return to destroy Ephraim for I am God and not human. I am
the Holy One in your midst and I do not want to come to you in
anger. (Hos. 11:7–9)

But the relationship is, more often than not, one-sided. There is little
or no mutuality. God reaches out, chooses, draws near, envelopes, and
embraces Israel, but Israel is fickle and childish, and any expressions
of love are short-lived. When God begs, cajoles, pours out his heart,
his people, his children, and his beloved shun him for other stupid
lifeless gods:

O Ephraim, what shall I do with you?
O Judah, how shall I deal with you?
This love of yours is like morning mist,
like morning dew that quickly disappears.
This is why I smote you through the prophets,
and have slain you by the words of my mouth.

For it is love that I desire, not sacrifice;
it is knowledge of God,
not burnt offerings. (Hos. 6:4–6)

Here is the crux, the heart of the matter — knowledge of God. This
is knowledge of God that is intimate and born of long faithfulness,
knowledge that is mutual and expressive, strong and consistent in private devotion and public worship. This kind of knowledge of God
has become unknown and unpracticed in the land. Thus, it is in reference to this intimate relationship that Hosea hears Yahweh's call
and the message is intertwined and interlaced with Hosea's disastrous
marriage to Gomer, a temple prostitute.

The details of the relationship between Hosea and Gomer and exactly how it aligned with the relation between God and Hosea is not
of great concern. In a sense the details and the historicity of Hosea
and Gomer's relationship are not important because this is prophecy.
The life of a prophet is the word of God received and taken into one's
flesh and blood and then translated into words and actions for others
to respond to. The personal life of the prophet exists only in the context of God's call and demand for truthfulness. At the beginning of the

twenty-first century, we should not seek to avoid the message because we are appalled by the medium. We should not reduce the prophetic agony, which distills God's own agony, because we are adverse to a relationship between a man (the prophet) who is faithful to the covenant (and so to his wife and children) and a woman, a prostitute, who is unfaithful. We are the prostitute, whether male or female, and we are the selfish and destructive children. Yet God is pursuing us, intent on sharing his unbounded love and faithfulness with us. It is our salvation that makes us human.

It is not surprising, then, that the book of Hosea begins with Yahweh's command to Hosea to initiate a relationship like that which God has long since entered into with Israel:

> When Yahweh began to speak through Hosea, the Lord said to him, "Go, take for your wife a woman involved in sacred prostitution and have children born of prostitution, for the land is wholeheartedly lapsing into prostitution and turning away from Yahweh."
>
> So he married Gomer, daughter of Diblaim. And she was with child and bore a son. Yahweh told him, "Name him *Jezreel,* for I will soon punish the family of Jehu for the massacre at Jezreel. I will put an end to the kingdom of Israel. The days are coming when Israel will be defeated in the Valley of Jezreel."
>
> Gomer was again with child and gave birth to a daughter. Yahweh said to Hosea, "Name her *Unloved,* for I will have no more love for the nation of Israel, nor will I forgive them."
>
> After weaning Unloved, Gomer was with child again and had another son. Yahweh said, "Name him *Not-my-people,* for you are not my people, nor am I *I-AM* for you." (Hos. 1:2–9)

Hosea and Gomer and their children are a microsymbol of God's universal covenant with the people of Israel. Yahweh commands Hosea to act toward Gomer as God acts toward Israel: "Welcome once more this woman who makes love to others. Love her just as Yahweh loves his people who turn to other gods" (Hos. 3:1). Just as Hosea hopes against hope that Gomer will be satisfied with his love enough to leave behind her way of life, so Yahweh God hopes — with patience, frustration, and ultimate promise — that his people Israel and we, his people today, will turn from our worship of other gods and the destruction of the peoples of the earth to the justice and faithfulness that God lavishes upon us. With the words of God in the prophet's mouth, this image of marriage broken and sundered is used to describe what will be — what is — the ultimate will and design of God. God's will is for a new covenant, more intimate and complete than the original. It is for a deeper and truer relationship that encompasses not only God and humankind but all of creation.

God breaks out in a love song, a paean of promise, a hymn to holiness and peace, to justice and integrity for the whole of the universe and all its peoples. God sorrows that we settle for so little, that we grovel before empty idols and seek after wealth and violence instead of the joy, delight, and freedom that are offered to us by the One who loves us so passionately. As a people we are called to be the beloved of God, healing the earth, binding the wounds of violence and distrust, and making of earth a dwelling place of enduring justice and peace:

> On that day, Yahweh says,
> you will call me *my husband,*
> and never again: *my Baal.*
> I will take the names of Baals from her lips
> and no longer will they be invoked.
> That day on her behalf I will make a covenant
> with beasts of the field and birds of the air,
> with creatures creeping upon the ground.
> I will wipe out the sword and war in the land;
> I will make people rest safe and secure.
>
> You will be my spouse forever,
> betrothed in justice and integrity;
> we will be united in love and tenderness.
> I will espouse you in faithfulness
> and you will come to know Yahweh.
>
> This is what Yahweh says of those days, . . .
> "I will show my love to *Unloved;*
> I will say to *Not-my-people,* 'You are my people';
> and they will answer, 'You are my God.'"
>   (Hos. 2:18–23, 25b, c)

Ah! The wild promises begin. The future is laid out in unbelievable terms. The word of God is already creating a new thing in the mind, the memory, and the soul of God's people. This is what it was meant to be: a marriage between heaven and earth, between God and all peoples in a world of integrity, justice, and peace. This is the knowledge that God wants to share with his own beloved children and those he has called to be his beloved. This is knowledge more powerful, more expansive and life-giving, than even the knowledge of a man and woman united by marriage and family. This is faithful, freely shared love with God.

But God is torn in pieces by his people, by his children's rejection and blatant disregard for honesty or justice in the land, by the hollow and disgusting worship of fertility gods and war gods, and by the machinations of political alliances, greed, and the suppression of the poor. His beloved, those he has called by name, have forgotten all they learned from God in the desert: the knowledge of justice, the knowledge and memory that they belong to God and that God is their only support, defense, and power. God's *hesed,* God's tender-hearted intimate love, cannot find a crack through which to enter their lives or their relations with one another.

And so Yahweh is torn. The tenderness of love is rooted deep in God, but so is the knowledge of justice that surges in anger against the people who destroy one another and turn their backs on him. Hosea cries out: "I will be like a leopard for Ephraim and like a lion for Judah. I will tear them to pieces and leave them. When I carry them off, no one will rescue them. Then I will go away and return to my place until they admit their guilt and come back to me, for in their anguish they will earnestly seek me" (Hos. 5:14–15). The nation of Israel is in league with other nations. Worship of the true God is a mockery. Monstrous injustice is tolerated in the land.

Judgment will come from across the borders, from Assyria, the very nation that God's people turned to for help, instead of to God. This learning of the knowledge of God is not easy or immediate. It will be a long struggle, generation to generation, since we so rarely learn from those who have gone before us in faith. Only when times are filled with terror and insecurity, with violence at home and abroad, when we sense we are losing control, do we turn once again to the word of God and say to one another:

> Come, let us return to Yahweh.
> He who shattered us to pieces, will heal us as well;
> he has struck us down, but he will bind up our wounds. . . .

Let us strive to know Yahweh.
His coming is as certain as the dawn;
his judgment will burst forth like the light;
he will come to us as showers come,
like spring rain that waters the earth. (Hos. 6:1, 3–5)

Sadly though, Israel's turning to Yahweh will be short-lived, without sincerity, based on empty offerings of sacrifice and prayers. Israel will turn again to Assyria and back into the old ways of crushing the poor so that a few can amass fortunes. The people will build idolatrous high places and forget the honor of God. And so they will set in motion the terms of judgment, and they will be destroyed. Hosea cries out: "You must return to your God, practice love and justice and trust in your God. Canaan has dishonest scales and likes to cheat. Ephraim boasts, 'I have become rich and possess a fortune.' Yet he will be left with nothing of what he has treasured for he was doing wrong" (Hos. 12:7–9).

Hosea again uses the image of a child, but this time it will be stillborn. "The wickedness of Ephraim is deep-set; his sin is stored up. The pangs of woman in labor come upon him. But the child is capricious. When it is time he does not leave the womb" (13:12–13). Samaria will be captured in 721, and the deportation of its inhabitants will begin.

But the book of Hosea ends with encouragement. Hosea exhorts the people to pray, to use these words:

Return to Yahweh with humble words. Say to him,
"Oh you who show compassion to the fatherless
forgive our debt, be appeased.
Instead of bulls and sacrifices,
accept the praise from our lips.

"Assyria will not save us:
no longer shall we look for horses
nor ever again shall we say 'Our gods'
to the works of our hands." (Hos. 14:3–4)

And God will answer:

I will heal their wavering
and love them with all my heart

for my anger has turned from them.
I shall be like dew to Israel
like the lily will he blossom.
Like a cedar he will send down his roots;
his young shoots will grow and spread. . . .

I am like an ever-green cypress tree;
all your fruitfulness comes from me.

> (Who is wise enough to grasp all this?
> Who is discerning and will understand?
> Straight are the ways of Yahweh;
> the just walk in them, but the sinners stumble.)
> (Hos. 14:5–7a, 9b–10)

Even though Israel will be broken up, the temple destroyed, and the people driven into exile, Yahweh, the faithful one, will return again and again to the people. One day all of humankind will be reconciled with God in a marriage founded on integrity and justice, and all of the earth will reap the fruits of such justice and mercy.

Abraham Joshua Heschel sums up the basic similarities and differences between Amos and Hosea. They both rail against Yahweh's people, and the substance of their argument, God's case against the people, is basically the same. But "Amos knows God as the selfless and exalted Being Whose sensibilities and concern for justice are pained by the sinful transgressions of Israel." The emotions of Amos are primarily "resistance and abhorrence leading to rejection." On the other hand, it is Hosea who "flashes a glimpse into the inner life of God as he ponders His relationship to Israel. In parables and in lyrical outbursts the decisive motive behind God's strategy in history is declared. The decisive motive is love."[12]

Stronger than any other motive, emotion, or action on God's behalf is the drive for communion, union, and reconciliation. God, more than anything else, desires to "know" the people he has created, chosen, and loves. Hosea's primary complaint against the people of God is that they do not "know" him. Hosea fashions the phrase *daath elohim*, usually translated as "knowledge of God." In Middle Eastern languages this knowing signifies sexual union but much more. It has a strong history in Israel's beginnings. In the book of Exodus we first meet the God who hears the groaning and cries of his people in bondage, and

God "remembers his covenant, sees the people of Israel, and knows their condition" (Exod. 2:24, RSV). But the real meaning of the word "know" is that God has "pity" on them.

The next chapter tells of how God has seen the affliction of his people in Egypt, hears their cry, and "knows their sufferings" (Exod. 3:7, RSV). Again, the text means that God has pity, is affected by what he sees, and knows it deep within. It also carries the meaning of sexual union, of marriage that is physical, emotional, and life-altering, as in Genesis 4:1, when "Adam knew [or attached himself] to Eve his wife." It is a mutual, reciprocal, totally engaging relationship. Abraham Heschel points out that "Hosea seems to have seized upon the idea of sympathy as the essential religious requirement. The words *daath elohim* mean *sympathy for God,* attachment of the whole person, his love as well as his knowledge; an act of involvement, attachment or commitment to God."[13] Those words summarize the word of God spoken by Amos and Hosea.

The contrast between Amos and Hosea is seen both in what they condemn and in what they stress. To Amos, the principal sin is *injustice;* to Hosea, it is *idolatry.* Amos inveighs against evil *deeds;* Hosea attacks the absence of *inwardness.* In the words of Amos:

> I hate, I despise your feasts . . .
> I will not accept your sacrifices; . . .
> But let justice roll down like waters,
> And righteousness like a mighty stream.
> (Amos 5:21, 24)

In the words of Hosea:

> For I desire love [*hesed*] and not sacrifice,
> attachment to God rather than burnt offerings.
> (Hos. 6:6)[14]

There is one image that binds together both these prophets and the inner core and the outer expressions of their messages and God's intent and will. It is a brutal image that is first experienced within one's own body and then corporately within the body politic or the community. A dear friend of mine has suffered for years from a debilitating and deadly disease called scleroderma. It is basically the development and growth of fibrous tissue in the skin and internal organs that hardens them. The skin and organs lose their elasticity, stiffen, and harden into what could be called a stone shroud. In essence, one's own body becomes a tomb, as every movement, every breath becomes unbearably painful. There is no position that is comfortable. Contact with anything or anyone can be excruciating.

This word *sclerokardia* is used in the Bible. Many translations of the psalms say: "If today you hear his voice, harden not your hearts." This phrase is found in the opening prayer of Matins. The prophets are told that the hearts of the people are stubborn, hardened against God and against their neighbor. The connection between hard hearts and deaf ears also runs through the stories of the gospel. This also is a deteriorating disease — a disease of the soul and spirit characterized by constant turning away from the word and the knowledge of God, resisting the hand outstretched in forgiveness, reconciliation, and love. It develops quickly with one's refusal to do justice and live in obedience to the covenant. As it progresses, one can easily and without remorse break the hearts of others and break the heart of God. It shatters the holiness of creation and the wholeness of relationships. According to the prophets Amos and Hosea, this disease of the soul leads to destruction and can be healed only by the mercy of God. The word of the Lord shatters that hardness while it speaks tenderly to us, leading us with strings of love and never abandoning us. All we must do is turn — turn and love one another with the love God lavishes on us. This is the cry of Amos and Hosea: Turn!

FIVE

Jeremiah and Zephaniah

*The Long March to Jerusalem —
the Temple Destruction and Exile*

We begin with an old Hindu story that I call "Whose Name Is on the Stone?"

Once upon a time a great king came to power. He was part of a long line of kings intent on being warriors, on extending the borders of their lands and wealth. They were all arrogant before the nations, but this king was the worst of all. He wondered how he himself, among all his ancestors, could be remembered. And he hit upon a unique plan. He would build a temple to the gods, a temple unlike any seen in the history of the last thousand years. It would be his temple, his gift to the gods, and his hand would be in every aspect of its design, construction, artifice, and ornament. So a decree went forth throughout the land that no one, absolutely no one, was to do anything in regard to the temple unless ordered to do so by the king himself. This was his project, his grand monument.

Over the next twenty-six years the temple was built. From the blueprint stage to the construction of the foundation, from artistic touches and gold detail to statuary and color, the king was the last word and decision maker. Every resource in the kingdom and all of the people were involved in building this temple to the gods. And it was magnificent, unlike anything anyone had ever seen before, in size, magnitude, and detail. No expense was spared. It was to have the best of everything: wood beams intricately carved and brought from afar, stone and gleaming marble, inlaid jewels and gold borders. Each statue, though it was one among hundreds, was executed with careful design, and only the best artisans were allowed to work on the final touches.

Each day the king rose and went to the outskirts of his city to inspect the temple and urge on the builders. Nothing escaped him. He would examine a new piece of work and exclaim, "Who is the one who did this shoddy work?" And the hapless soul would be jailed, sent into slavery, or killed on the spot. However, when the work was exquisite the artisan was rewarded and given even more important work to do. And so the temple rose in glory.

Soon the day of dedication drew near, which all the country had been planning for months. The dedication stone would be at eye level at the only entrance to the temple, and it would bear only the king's name and the year of its completion. There were just four days until the ceremony when the king had a dream. It was a terrible dream. He was standing in front of the temple, in front of the dedication stone, and a towering angel in an immense shaft of fiery light blocked out his view. The angel appeared to be carving a name into the stone. The king peered around the angel's shimmering wing and caught but a glimpse, but he was sure it was not his name! He awoke, furious. But as the day wore on, he put it out of his mind. That night, with three days until the festival of dedication, the angel came again. The king strained to see the letters that the angel was chiseling into the stone, but could only make out the first few letters. Then the king awoke again. The letters did not help him at all. They were the beginning letters of the names of practically all the masses of the poor in his country. The following night the dream came for the third time and the king was steeling himself to read the name. As the angel carved, he committed it to memory and then awoke. He had the specific name!

Immediately, soldiers were massed and sent out in every direction to find the person and bring him or her before the king. Late in the day, they arrived back, dragging with them a ragged and shaking woman, an old widow. She was terrified, groveling in fear before the king. He bellowed at her, "What have you done? There have been strict orders that no one was to have anything to do with my temple! What have you done?"

In tears of terror she stuttered out: "Forgive me, master. I love God so much. I only wanted to honor him, to do something, but I had nothing to offer. But one day I watched the horses bringing the great cedar beams that would form the doorway of the temple. And they were straining so in the heat, weary and exhausted, and no one was paying any attention to them. All I did was take the straw from my pallet that I sleep on and feed the horses. It was all I had and I just wanted to do something, to have a part in building the temple."

The king was livid and had her thrown into jail to rot. That night, the night before the dedication, the angel appeared again, towering over the stone and the king. The angel chiseled away at the stone and when he finished he turned his wrathful gaze directly on the king. He pointed his finger at him: "Tomorrow you are to carve that woman's name into this dedication stone. If you do not, then your name and memory will be forever erased from history and it will be as though you never existed. Carve her name there!" And the king awoke, shaking.

Whose name did the king carve on the dedication stone? This story has two possible endings. In the first, the king carved the name of the woman. After all, what real choice did he have? In the second ending, he carved his own name, and he let the old woman rot in prison until she died. Of course, most people want it to end with her name on the stone. But no one knows his name, and there is no memory of him except in a story. And the story is about her!

This story is also about religion — religion and politics, religion and the building of temples that are about the temporal and dominant power of the ruling class. These temples are monuments to monarchy as opposed to temples for the true worship of God by people trapped in economic misery. And their misery is usually caused by the decisions and rule of their leaders.

Zephaniah and Hulda

The towering prophet Jeremiah and his close contemporary Zephaniah arrived on the scene in Israel during a time of absolute disarray. The towns of Judah had been destroyed, and the kings were attempting to gather their forces around the city of Jerusalem. By the end of the eighth century, the prosperity of Judah had already collapsed. Jerusalem was the administrative center for taxation, tribute, and excessive military spending. It was a time of massive migration, with perhaps 2 percent of the population controlling half or more of the national income. The country was surrounded by warring armies, and the elite of the country exploited the populace through economic institutions that were tightly controlled by the king, his administration, and the military. Any profits were reserved for luxury consumption. The prophet Zephaniah appeared out of nowhere after a silence of seventy years. The last prophet heard from was Isaiah, who concluded his mission around 690. Zephaniah's opening salvo was one long threat:

> When Josiah, son of Ammon, reigned in Judah, the word of Yahweh was addressed to Zephaniah, the son of Cushi, son of Gedaliah, son of Amariah, son of Hezekiah. [Yahweh] said:
> "I will wipe out everything from the face of the earth. I will put an end to humans and animals, to the birds of heaven and the fish of the sea. I will wipe humankind from the face of the earth. I will raise my hand to punish Judah and all the inhabitants of Jerusalem; and I will bring out of that place all the remnants of Baal with their priests. . . . "
> Silence before Yahweh! For his day is near: Yahweh has prepared his sacrifice and consecrated his invited guests. Yahweh says: "On the day that sacrifice is made, I will call to account the officials, the king's sons and all who clothe themselves in foreign fashion. I will also give the corresponding punishment to everyone who jumps over the threshold without stepping on it and fills the House of their Lord with the fruits of their crimes and thefts.
> "On that day, a great cry will be heard from the Fish Gate, a wail from the new city and frightful noise from the nearby hills. Wail, inhabitants of the lower district, for all the traders have disappeared, all who counted the silver have perished.
> "On that day I will explore Jerusalem with torches, and call to account those who have sunk in their vices and think in their hearts: Well, Yahweh does not do good or evil! Their riches will be pillaged, their houses demolished." (Zeph. 1:1–13a)

As befits the prophetic tradition, the description is thorough and detailed. Jerusalem will incur punishment because of the evil perpetuated by the people who dwell there. Zephaniah sums it up succinctly: "The land of Judah will be burned in the fire of his zeal when he destroys even the traces of all who dwell in that land" (1:18b). His short book of only three chapters is one long, seamless barrage of destruction except for one line: "Seek Yahweh, all you poor of the land who fulfill his commands, do justice and are meek, and perhaps you will find refuge on the day Yahweh comes to judge" (2:3). The very end of the book picks up long after the destruction of the city when there is a "poor and meek people who seek refuge in God. The remnant of Israel... On that day I will face your oppressors; I will be good to you and gather you to make you famous and honorable among all the peoples of the earth, when I bring back the captives before your eyes — this is Yahweh's word" (3:12, 20).

The backdrop for Zephaniah's prophecy is the story of Josiah the king and Hulda the prophetess that is told in 2 Kings 22–23 and again in 2 Chronicles 34–35. Many people have never heard of either of these people, yet their story presents issues that must be dealt with in relation to the prophets, specifically the tension between the monarchy and the prophets and who truly speaks for God.

Josiah was only eight years old when he became king, and he reigned in Jerusalem for thirty-one years. When he was sixteen years old, he began to "seek the God of his father David" (2 Chron. 34:3). When he was twenty he began a purge in Jerusalem and all of Judah of the high places where other gods were worshiped. He had the altars and symbols of other religions destroyed. He participated in this himself, "burning the bones of their priests on their altars" (34:5), and he traveled throughout the land, purifying it. Then he imposed tribute on all the towns to repair the house of God in Jerusalem. The money was collected so that it could be used to repair and restore the temple.

This was a well-organized endeavor, involving the governor, Maaseiah; Josiah's secretary, Shaphan; his herald, Joah; the high priest, Hilkiah; the Levite gatekeepers; and the masters of work in the temple. And while Hilkiah was in the process of repairing the temple and melting down the silver in Yahweh's house, he found a book of the law, which he asked Shaphan to take to King Josiah. When it was read to Josiah, he tore his garments and told his minister, his secretary, and the high priest to consult Yahweh about what was written there (2 Chron.

34:8–21). They immediately consulted Hulda the prophetess. We are given a great deal of information about her and her prophecy.

> Hilkiah and the king's men went to Hulda the prophetess, wife of Shallum, son of Tokhath, son of Hasrah, the keeper of the Temple robes; she lived in Jerusalem in the new town. They spoke to her about this, and she answered, "This is the word of Yahweh for the man who sent you to me: I am going to punish Jerusalem and all its people, carrying out all the curses written in the book that has been read in the presence of the king of Judah, because they have abandoned me and have burned incense to other gods, stirring up my anger by everything they have done. Because of this my anger is aroused against Jerusalem, and it will not die down.
>
> "And you will tell the king of Judah who sent you to consult Yahweh, that thus answers Yahweh, the God of Israel, regarding the words you have heard: Since your heart has been touched and you have humbled yourself before God on hearing what he has threatened against Jerusalem and those who live in it, since you have humbled yourself before me and torn your garments and wept before me, I for my part have heard — this is Yahweh's word. The punishment which I am going to bring on Jerusalem will not come until after your death. I will let you die in peace." They took this answer to the king. (2 Chron. 34:22–28)

What book did Hilkiah discover in the temple? Traditionally, exegetes and historians say that it was probably the scrolls of chapters 12 to 22 of the book of Deuteronomy. These scrolls would have contained laws regarding the destruction of all sanctuaries to other gods that the people would find when they entered Canaan, a description of the Passover ritual, laws concerning tithes and the celebration of the Sabbath Year every seven years, and pragmatic laws regarding war, cities of refuge, and treatment of the poor and enslaved. Josiah seems to have decided to concentrate on laws governing the celebration of Passover, believing that the city described in Deuteronomy 16 is Jerusalem. "You may not offer the Passover sacrifice in any city which Yahweh gives you, but only in the place chosen by Yahweh as the dwelling place for his name" (Deut. 16:5). He concentrated on the specifics of the sacrifice itself: how the lambs, oxen, bullocks, and goats were to be prepared and offered.

And so Josiah committed everyone in Jerusalem to this practice. He made no mention, however, of the requirements for the Sabbath Year in regard to slaves, the poor, forgiveness of debts, foreigners, and so on. The focus was on ruthless enforcement of the cult directives: "For the rest of his life he made sure that every member of Israel served their God" (2 Chron. 34:33). The following chapter (35) describes how the Passover was celebrated in Jerusalem, with Josiah providing thirty thousand lambs and kids and three thousand bulls from his own herds. The officials of his court and the priests also provided animals from their obviously huge flocks. After the sacrifices, pots and pans were provided with the roasted lambs so that the people could take the meat home. The Passover is described in glowing terms:

> No Passover like this one had ever been celebrated in Israel since the days of the prophet Samuel; no king of Israel had ever celebrated a Passover like the one celebrated by Josiah with the priests, the Levites, all of Judah and of Israel who were present, and the people of Jerusalem. (2 Chron. 35:18)

This is Josiah's claim to fame and reputation in Israel. Then, later, he became embroiled in a dispute with Neco, the king of Egypt, who was jockeying for position against the Assyrian king. Josiah marched out to stop him. And then we learn of Josiah's untimely end:

> Josiah marched out to stop him. Neco sent him messengers to say, "There is no quarrel between me and you, king of Judah. I have not come today to attack you, but to fight my enemies, and God has told me to hurry. Do not oppose God who is with me, lest he destroy you." (2 Chron. 35:20b–21)

But Josiah continued to challenge him, for he was determined to fight him and would not listen to what God was saying through Neco. When Josiah went out to fight on the plain of Megiddo, Egyptian arrows struck him. He said to his followers, "Take me away; I am badly wounded." His servants "took him back to Jerusalem, where he died" (2 Chron. 35:23b–24a).

Recall Hulda's early prophecy that Josiah would die in peace because of his humility before God. Some distortions and contradictions in the prophecy seem apparent. While it is true that the calamity that befell Jerusalem happened after his death, Josiah was guilty of not listening to God, who can speak outside his own kingdom. In addition,

according to the prophet Zephaniah, Josiah did not always obey God
within his own kingdom:

> Woe to the rebellious, the defiled, the city that oppresses. She did
> not pay attention to the call nor accept the correction; she did not
> trust Yahweh nor did she approach her God. Her kings are like
> roaring lions, her rulers like evening wolves that do not leave
> even a bone for the next day. Her prophets are blabbermouths
> and treacherous people; her priests defile whatever is sacred with
> no respect for the Law. (Zeph. 3:1–4)

It seems that the history written in both 2 Kings and 2 Chronicles is directly contradicted by Zephaniah's words. The indictment is
specifically against the city, the rulers, the judges, the prophets, and
the priests — *not* against the people. Those individuals mentioned in
the historical accounts — Josiah, the high priest Hilkiah, the secretary Shaphan, the king's minister Asaiah, Josiah's friends, the elders,
Levites, those refurbishing the temple, and Hulda, the in-house court
prophetess — fall into the category of those rebellious against Yahweh. There is no praise in the mouths of Zephaniah or Jeremiah, the
prophets of Josiah's time, for anyone in power in Jerusalem. With all
the political conflicts raging around Judah during this time, it seems
likely that Josiah's motivation was purely political, part of a military
maneuver to claim independence from Assyria. (It should be remembered, however, that the leaders of Jerusalem oppressed their own
people even more than the Assyrians.)

Major questions remain. Why was the book found just then? Why
was it read only by the king and his advisers? Why was Hulda, the
court prophetess, consulted rather than Zephaniah or Jeremiah? Hulda
had no "call" from Yahweh, and her lineage was described through her
husband, who was in the employ of the king. Her words were vague,
more of an analysis of why the king would be spared and how good
he was than a call to repentance and return to Yahweh's justice. Hulda
lived in the "new city," which was singled out for destruction because
it was where the wealthy dwelled in their extravagant homes. Hulda's
words were partial truths and distortions that left out crucial pieces
of Deuteronomy. She neglected anything that would call the ruling
powers to radical conversion and concern for their own people. She
was in Josiah's employ, and her message served his plans.

Josiah must have realized that removing religious celebrations from the domain of the people would break down any sense of community or of connection to their own towns and further his own plan to centralize all offices in Jerusalem: political, economic, cultural, and, now, religious. The Passover ritual was central to providing the people with a sense of the power of Yahweh raised in their defense, seeking liberation and freedom. Before, each family took a lamb from its own flock and celebrated together or with their neighbors. By moving the feast and its celebration to Jerusalem, Josiah generated propaganda for himself and his rule; he was even written about as being greater than David, because "no king had ever celebrated a Passover like this one!" (2 Chron. 35:18).

The propitious "finding" of the book in the temple legitimized everything Josiah sought to do. His reforms were carefully designed and executed by the ruling elite to further their own economic, political, and military ends. It was no longer Yahweh's or the people's Passover but Josiah's Passover, which further demoralized the people. In the end, Jerusalem's rulers and rich leaders appropriated even the central symbol of Yahweh's choice of Israel as his people, his nation, for themselves. Zephaniah rails against them, and Jeremiah will be equally torn in mind and soul over what is happening to the cherished inheritance of the people of Yahweh.[1]

Jeremiah

The prophets continually protested any use of cult or ritual to validate the ruling elite's power or to beggar the populace. With the exception of Amos, they all focused on the abuses of religious practice while the real issue of justice for the poor was ignored or neglected or, worse still, while injustice was practiced with a vengeance. The Jewish community has long taught the connection between justice and truth:

> Do not make a mockery of justice, for it is one of the three pillars of the world. Why? Because our sages taught: "On three things the world stands: on justice, on truth, and on peace." Know, then, that if you pervert justice, you shake the world, for justice is one of its pillars. (Rabban Simeon ben Gamaliel, in *Deuteronomy Rabbah* 5.1)

As Amos sought to uphold the pillar of justice, Jeremiah sought to uphold the pillar of truth and later Isaiah would uphold the pillar of peace. "The call to be a prophet came to Jeremiah in the year 635 B.C.E., and he was active during the reigns of the last kings of Judah — Josiah (640–609), Jehoiakim (609–598), Jehoiachim (598–597), Zedekiah (597–587) — and continued for some time after the fall of Jerusalem in 587 B.C.E."[2] All of this history is conveyed in the paragraph that opens the book of Jeremiah.

From the first words of Yahweh's call to Jeremiah, we know we are in the presence of a passionate man, torn and broken by what he must say and what he will witness among his beloved people. His relationship with his God is braided together with his relationship with his people, and both are sources of grief, agony, tears, and, on rare occasions, joy and delight. The words of his summons are some of the best-loved words of Yahweh:

> Now the word of the Lord came to me saying,
> "Before I formed you in the womb I knew you,
> And before you were born I consecrated you;
> I appointed you a prophet to the nations."
> Then I said, "Ah, Lord God! Behold, I do not know how
>   to speak, for I am only a youth." But the Lord said
>   to me,
> "Do not say, 'I am only a youth';
> For to all to whom I send you, you shall go,
> And whatever I command you, you shall speak.
> Be not afraid of them,
> For I am with you to deliver you, says the Lord."
>
> Then the Lord put forth His hand and touched my mouth;
>   and the Lord said to me,
> "Behold, I have put My words in your mouth,
> See, I have set you this day over nations and over
>   kingdoms,
>
> > To pluck up and to break down,
> > To destroy and to overthrow,
> > To build and to plant.
> "... Arise, and say to them everything that I command you. Do
> not be dismayed by them, lest I dismay you before them. And

I, behold, I make you this day a fortified city, an iron pillar, and
bronze walls, against the whole land, against the kings of Judah,
its princes, its priests, and the people of the land. They will fight
against you; but they will not prevail against you, for I am with
you, says the Lord, to deliver you." (Jer. 1:4–10, 17–19; RSV)

Jeremiah has been chosen, from before birth, in his mother's
womb. This is Jeremiah's guts, his meaning, his destiny, his glory,
and his grief. His life begins and ends with the words, "The word of
the Lord came to me" (Jer. 1:11; RSV). More than any other prophet,
Jeremiah is reluctant to be so designated, singled out, and sent. The
life of a prophet is hard, hard as nails, hard as iron, hard as bronze.
It is a life of resistance, of being set over against others, of being a
cry that is not heard or a cry that is opposed. It is a dangerous life.
This was especially true for Jeremiah because his message, from its
very beginning, is frightening: it is a message of impending doom, of
destruction, of exile, and of a God in opposition to his own people.
Jeremiah wants to bow out, but God moves in on him, counteracting
his words, and then touching his mouth, putting the words inside him.
Yahweh's message can be reduced to six verbs: pluck up and break
down, destroy and overthrow, and build and plant (Jer. 1:10). The battle lines are drawn. Jeremiah is to dig in and hold his ground no matter
what — and his only defense and shield are the words: "I am with
you,... to deliver you" (1:19; RSV).

Basically, we know Jeremiah from his words, which are very revealing. His message is hard for him to deliver, and he hopes against
hope that the people and his beloved city will turn again toward God.
He is wedded to God and to God's word, and he knows he stands in
opposition to the entire land. The word "against" is repeated over and
over again. This is an exhausting, frustrating, dangerous position to
take. Any resistance to the word of God, to the judgment and destruction that are aimed at Jerusalem and its inhabitants, will be directed
toward Jeremiah. This will pervade his whole life — just as resistance to the will and law of Yahweh has pervaded the whole life of
Israel. The king, the rich, the temple, the priests, and even the people
stand resolutely against Yahweh and against Jeremiah. Yahweh and
the people have faced off.

Jeremiah is supposed to be as hard as any metal known at the
time. Yet we are given strong evidence that Jeremiah's heart is, in-

deed, crushed by his message, by the necessity of what he is saying, by the people who refuse to believe, and by even his own friends who are intent on killing him and silencing him. We are given access to Jeremiah's heart in his confessions and prayers to Yahweh, his ravings, his moans, his questions, his cries, his screams, and his tears. When he is scorned by the people, he turns to God, and his relationship to God is stunning in scope and depth.

Perhaps the two sides of Jeremiah's message and heart can be described as wrath and anger or heartbreak and anguish. As we read the book of Jeremiah, we come to realize that these emotions and conflict actually reside in God, but they are expressed through Jeremiah's conflicted soul. Jeremiah's God is passionately in love with his cherished people, who are described as beloved children and beloved spouse. "For I am a father to Israel, and Ephraim is my first-born" (31:9). Or, as the Jews translate, Yahweh calls Israel "my darling child." Yahweh cries out softly, "I thought how I would set you among my sons, and give you a pleasant land, . . . and I thought you would call me, My Father, and would not turn from following me" (Jer. 3:19; cf. 3:4; RSV).

At this point, Israel is a nation without honor, without justice, without any tenderness in its soul for its poor and needy, for the fatherless, the widow, and the orphan. Yahweh's children are dangerous, engaged in deceit, in planning murder, in lies, and in greed and lust (Jer. 5). Jeremiah's God, who loves deeply, cannot believe that Israel, his love, is abandoning him. Yet he knows just as deeply that the people are vicious and have betrayed every gesture and gift that have been given to them. Over and over again, when Yahweh speaks to Jeremiah about the people, he calls them "my people, my dear people." God grieves over his people, his lost children, his lost love. He has loved them since the beginning, when he created them as a people and brought them out of bondage and settled them in their land. And yet he knows that "they know me not; they are stupid children; they have no understanding" (Jer 4:22).

Jeremiah must try to convey God's love and anguish, God's justice and judgment, and God's agony over what will happen to his people. They are always his people, even when they sin grievously against him, even when they destroy the poor, even when they themselves will be caught by foreign powers, slaughtered, with their temple and city burned to the ground and those who do not die led into exile. They are always his beloved people, his children. God pleads with his people through Jeremiah, and it is painful to read the words that are torn out of God and out of Jeremiah.

> "You shall say to them this word:
> 'Let my eyes run down with tears night and day,
>   and let them not cease,
> for the virgin daughter of my people is smitten
>   with a great wound,
>   with a very grievous blow.' " (Jer. 14:17; RSV)

God is just! God is the Holy One of Israel, the only king. God is the Lord of heaven and earth. Sovereignty is his alone. But God is also now the abandoned bridegroom (Jer. 2:2); he is a father who has been hurt and betrayed (Jer. 3:19), whose heart is deeply troubled (Jer. 8:18); and he is a potter who formed and holds Israel in his hands (Jer. 18:1ff.). He sends Jeremiah on a quest, like Abraham, to roam through the city to see if he can find even one person who acts justly and seeks the truth so that he can forgive the entire city (5:1–4). But Jeremiah's words are scorned, as are God's, and the reaction of the prophet and God is one of anger: "I am full of the wrath of the Lord; I am weary of holding it in" (6:11a). This is God who is speaking. His people have forgotten. They take him for granted, ignore him, and refuse to worship. What God wants is as clear as the people's refusal:

> It is Yahweh who speaks:
> "Let not the wise boast of his wisdom,
> nor the valiant of his valor
> nor the wealthy of his wealth!
> But if someone wants to boast,
> let him boast of this:
> of understanding and knowing me.
> I am Yahweh, the merciful;
> I implement justice
> and rule the world with righteousness.
> For in these things I delight"
> — this is Yahweh's word. (Jer. 9:23)

God is both just and merciful, two forces that are not really in opposition in God. It is God who did the planting and God who will do the plucking. God did the building up, and God will do the tearing down. As once God led the people out of bondage into freedom, so it will be God who overthrows them and takes them down. But love, faithfulness, and compassion are always there, and so God will still be there among his people after the destruction. When he has mourned them and their deaths, he promises newness: "But after I have done this, I will have compassion on them and bring them back to their possession, each one to his own land.... But if then any nation does not obey me, I will uproot and destroy it — it is Yahweh who speaks" (Jer. 12:15, 17). God bears and suffers the pain of Israel in himself. The people are his intimately. He has freely attached himself to them and will not let go, no matter what happens to them.

This is expressed most deeply and poignantly in the symbol of the linen belt, or waist or loin cloth. The telling is layered with pathos and intimacy as well as destruction and loss:

> Thus said the Lord to me, "Go and buy a linen waistcloth, and put it on your loins, and do not dip it in water." So I bought a waistcloth according to the word of the Lord, and put it on my loins. And the word of the Lord came to me a second time. "Take the waistcloth which you have bought, which is upon your loins, and arise, go to the Euphrates, and hide it there in a cleft of the rock." So I went, and hid it by the Euphrates, as the Lord commanded me. And after many days the Lord said to me, "Arise, go to the Euphrates, and take from there the waistcloth which I commanded you to hide there." Then I went to the Euphrates, and dug, and I took the waistcloth from the place where I had hidden it. And behold, the waistcloth was spoiled; it was good for nothing.
>
> Then the word of the Lord came to me: "Thus says the Lord: Even so will I spoil the pride of Judah and the great pride of Jerusalem. This evil people, who refuse to hear my words, who stubbornly follow their own heart and have gone after other gods to serve them and worship them, shall be like this waistcloth, which is good for nothing. For as the waistcloth clings to the loins of a man, so I made the whole house of Israel and the whole house of Judah cling to me, says the Lord, that they might be for me a people, a name, a praise, and a glory, but they would not listen." (Jer. 13:1–11; RSV)

The story wrenches. It has intimations of the past, when God took Moses, his beloved prophet, and hid him in a cleft in the rock and passed by him, so that Moses could see him and not die. It has intimations of closeness, daily intimacies, even familiarity between God and his people. But, at the same time, it is clear that because of the actions and refusal of Israel, and especially the people of Jerusalem, the bond is broken. God who had taken them out of Egypt and dwelled with them in the desert, who had kept his tent with them, is now abandoning his place with them. Israel must be purified and made worthy of living with God again before God will remake his dwelling place among them. He is pulling back, becoming as a stranger to them, a foreigner, because in reality they have already made him that. Jeremiah senses this and cries out:

> O Yahweh! Hope of Israel,
> you who save in time of distress,
> why are you as a stranger in this land,
> or like a traveler who stays only a night?
> Why should you be as if bewildered,
> like a warrior unable to save?
> But you are in our midst Yahweh,
> and on us your Name has been invoked.
> Do not abandon us! (Jer. 14:8–9)

The images God gives to Jeremiah are all about brokenness, things that cannot be repaired or saved. God is the potter at the wheel whose pot has been spoiled in his hands, so he tries reworking it into another pot. Yahweh's message is that the people are clay in his hands and he can do with them as he wishes (Jer. 18:1–11). Yahweh then tells Jeremiah to buy a jar and take it out of the city, bringing with him some elders and priests. After declaring that God is going to destroy them, Jeremiah throws down the pot and shatters it before the elders of the people as a sign of what God will do to them, their city, the temple, and their lives (Jer. 19).

In all of this, Jeremiah struggles with God and struggles with the people who laugh at him and scorn him. He continues to speak of destruction while his own heart is breaking. Caught in the maelstrom of God's own torn heart at what will happen to his people because of their evil and injustice, he lashes out against God in his own prayers and confessions. His message is one of violence and devastation, and he is caught in that violence and devastation. He prays — or cries — in agony:

> Yahweh, you have seduced me
> and I let myself be seduced.
> You have taken me by force and prevailed.
>
> (Jer. 20:7)

Jeremiah's words are even stronger in the Hebrew translation. Abraham Heschel translates these lines more forcibly:

> O Lord, Thou has seduced me,
> And I am seduced;
> Thou hast raped me
> And I am overcome.[3]

Heschel notes that "the words used by Jeremiah to describe the impact of God upon his life are identical with the terms for seduction and rape in the legal terminology of the Bible."[4] The relationship between the Divine and the prophet is overpowering, all-invasive, violent. It also suggests being lured and invited into an all-encompassing intimacy. Heschel's description of the relationship between God and the prophet clearly delineates the separation between the two and yet shows the power that bleeds from one into the other:

> The call to be a prophet is more than an invitation. It is first of all a feeling of being enticed, of acquiescence or willing surrender. But this winsome feeling is only one aspect of the experience. The other aspect is a sense of being ravished or carried away by violence, of yielding to overpowering force against one's own will. The prophet feels both the attraction and the coercion of God, the appeal and the pressure, the charm and the stress. He is conscious of both voluntary identification and forced capitulation.
>
> This dialectic of what takes place in the prophetic consciousness points [to], . . . on the one hand, the divine pathos which stirs and entices the prophet, and, on the other hand, unconditioned power which exercises sheer compulsion over the prophet.[5]

Jeremiah knows God in a way no one has known him before. His intimacy with and his freedom before God are revealed in lines such as, "Cursed be the day I was born!" (Jer. 10:14). Jeremiah is caught between justice and mercy, between humanity and divinity, between truth and his inability to express this knowledge of God. He willingly submits to God and speaks his word, but, at the same time, he resists what is happening all around him, and he resists what is happening to him. What he must prophesy is horrible, but it is the truth and must be told. Because he has such closeness to God, such access to the aching heart of God, he is at a loss. He knows sorrow along with wrath and anger. It is too much for him to bear. Yet he has known God! And that knowledge has been a source of unbridled joy. He tells of this joy while he also pleads for protection from his enemies.

> Remember! For you I have suffered great humiliations.
> I devoured your words when they came.
> They were my happiness
> and I felt full of joy
> when you made your Name rest on me. (Jer. 15:15b–16)

Jeremiah is shunted back and forth between extremes. He knows in his flesh and mind and heart that God's words are "like fire, like the hammer that shatters a rock" (Jer. 23:29). Because Yahweh's continual call to repentance has been ignored, it becomes a judgment handed down: "All the land will be a ruin and a desolation and for seventy years these nations will serve the king of Babylon" (Jer. 25:11). Jeremiah knows that this word of Yahweh is directed not only to Judah and Jerusalem but also to all the nations of the earth:

> You will communicate all this to them and say, "Yahweh roars on high and from his holy dwelling threatens all the inhabitants of the world. His mighty roar echoes to the farthest ends of the earth. For Yahweh judges all the nations and passes sentence against all humankind, and the wicked he abandons to the sword — word of Yahweh." (Jer. 25:30–31)

Because of the fierceness and surety of Jeremiah's words and the strength with which he proclaims them, he suffers what will become the earmark of the true prophet: persecution, humiliation, plots against him, and attempts to murder him. Jehoiakim, the son of King Josiah, arrests him and has him sentenced to death. It is only when Jeremiah is befriended by Ahikam, son of Shaphan, that the plot to put him to death is foiled (Jer. 26). Jeremiah continues to do battle with the kings of Judah and the court prophets as Nebuchadnezzar's army draws closer. When one of Jeremiah's opponents, the false prophet Hananiah, deceives the people, Jeremiah foretells his death within the year.

Jeremiah deals harshly with any false prophets, as those who have gone before him have done.

The first twenty-eight chapters of Jeremiah tell of the time before the destruction of the city, the razing of the temple, and the departure of the people into exile. Then Jeremiah's prophecies shift to the exiles, instilling hope in them once again, based on a call to repentance and a heartfelt and radical altering of their lives. They must worship and trust only in God. In a letter to the exiles, he writes:

> This is what Yahweh says, "When the seventy years in Babylon have been completed I will come to you and fulfill my gracious promise to you and bring you back to this place. For I know what my plans for you are, plans to save you and not to harm you, plans to give you a future and to give you hope."
>
> And Yahweh says, "When you call on me I will listen. You will seek me and find me when you search for me with all your heart." For Yahweh says, "I will let myself be found by you and I will gather you from among all the nations and from all the places where I have driven you and bring you back to the place from which I sent you into exile." (Jer. 29:10–14)

Jeremiah has brought the message of tearing down and dismantling, of routing and destroying. Now begins the harder work of rebuilding and planting again and instilling fresh heart into those who have lost everything. Their army has known the wrath of God that slaughtered them and reduced their temple and city to ashes and ruins. Jeremiah turns his energies and words to those who have survived the sword but have been driven into exile as slaves. His words of hope sing with possibilities not yet experienced:

> Thus says Yahweh: The people who survived the sword have found grace in the desert. As Israel marched to his rest Yahweh appeared from afar saying, I have loved you everlastingly, so I have kept for you my mercy. I will restore you again, and you shall be rebuilt, O virgin Israel!
>
> You will take up your tambourines and go out to dance joyfully. You will plant vineyards again on the hills of Samaria, and the farmers who plant them will enjoy their fruit.
>
> A day will come when watchmen will call out on the hills of Ephraim, "Come, let us go to Zion, to our God Yahweh!" . . .

Proclaim your praise and say:
"Yahweh has saved his people, the remnant of Israel!"
Look, I will bring them back from the land of the north,
gather them from the ends of the earth.
All of them — the lame and the blind, mothers and women in
labor — a great throng will return.
They went weeping, they will return in joy.
I will lead them to streams of water, on a level path so that
no one will stumble, for I am Israel's father and Ephraim is my
firstborn. (Jer. 31:2–9)

Jeremiah's heart was broken within him, as was God's, by the people's arrogance and pride. The prophet and the people have borne a terrible burden of punishment, deserved and justly meted out, but God will not abandon them. All have known anguish and lamented over so many deaths. They have all suffered: men, women, women in labor, children, and those who were their leaders, rulers, and priests. God and Jeremiah, who has been drawn into God's designs and heart, alone have known the extent of what has happened to the people, the land, and the temple. Jeremiah writes:

But if you will not listen,
    my soul will weep in secret for your pride;
my eyes will weep bitterly and run down with tears,
because the Lord's flock has been taken captive.
(Jer. 13:17; RSV)

Jeremiah lived both extremes and in-between as well. As intercessor for the people, he sought to save them, even though they considered him a traitor, an enemy, an interloper. People whom he loved and trusted and regarded as friends turned on him and sought to kill him. He become a man alone with God. Jeremiah knew that God was the Lord of Hosts and that he was but a human servant through whom God sang and shouted. There were times when Jeremiah himself had to learn conversion and repentance and to turn to God once again. God did not allow him to turn against the people, even his own accusers. God chastises him:

Therefore thus says the Lord:
"If you return, I will restore you,
    and you shall stand before me.

> If you utter what is precious, and not what is worthless,
>   you shall be as my mouth." (Jer. 15:19; RSV)

Though he is a prophet, Jeremiah is still one of the people, and God can and does rebuke him. He too knows God's compassion and true loving nature: "I the Lord search the mind and try the heart, to give to every man according to his ways, according to the fruit of his doings" (Jer. 17:10; cf. 11:20; 20:12). Jeremiah's own heart can be as cold, stubborn, and rebellious as those of the people. Now their stubborn hearts have been broken and rent asunder, and they need new hearts. Jeremiah is given a vision: of two baskets of figs, one basket ripe and ready for eating and the other rotten. These are the two kinds of people, and Jeremiah must make this people believe that God intends something absolutely unheard-of for them:

> This is what Yahweh God of Israel says: "Just as I see these figs are good, so do I consider good those who have been deported from Judah to the country of the Chaldeans. I will look kindly on them and bring them back to this land. I will build them up and not destroy them, plant them and not uproot them. I will dispose their heart to know me as Yahweh. They will be my people and I will be their God for with all their heart they will come back to me." (Jer. 24:5–7)

This is the final intent of God, the plan God has for his people. It is a new thing, never before seen, even among his own people. The new covenant that God will make with the people is described in the most famous lines of the book of Jeremiah:

> This is the covenant I shall make with Israel after that time: I will put my Law within them and write it on their hearts; I will be their God and they will be my people.
>   And they will not have to teach each other, neighbor or brother, saying: "Know the Lord," because they will all know me, from the greatest to the lowliest, for I will forgive their wrongdoing and no longer remember their sin. (Jer. 31:33–34)

This new covenant is linked to a person and brings a promise for the future: "In those days and at that time I will make him who is the shoot of righteousness sprout from David's line; he will practice justice and righteousness in the land. In those days Judah will be saved and Jerusalem will live in safety. He will be called Yahweh-Our-Righteousness" (Jer. 33:15–16).

The city is gone. The temple is gone. The land is ravaged. Many of the people are dead. Those who survived are slaves in a foreign country. Yet Jeremiah preaches hope and unbounded, unbelievable possibilities once again. The God of Jeremiah and of Israel can create something new, fresher and more true than the original covenant. The people's weeping will be turned into tears of joy and gladness, their dirges and mourning into gladness and wild exaltation at the goodness and mercy of God.

When Nebuchadnezzar, the king of Babylon, takes the city of Jerusalem, Jeremiah goes into exile with everyone else. He continues to warn and to encourage, and his servant-secretary writes down his words. They sum up the tension he always carries with him: the knowledge and the belief, the burden of grief and hope for a future for the people, the anger and the compassion. The prophet Baruch penned these words:

> "Alas for me! I am weary of sighing and I find no rest!" Yahweh says: "When I am knocking down what I have built and pulling up what I planted, why do you want great things for yourself? Don't look for them! Yet, though I am about to send disaster on everyone — word of Yahweh — you will be safe wherever you go." (Jer. 45:3–5)

Jeremiah has been given to see the world as God sees it, rather than through the lens of history or politics or economics, or as religious leaders of Jerusalem and Judah want to see it. He sees it through a relationship, through a covenant, through the love of God reaching out for his beloved children whom he wants to cherish, to lavish affection and life upon, even when they turn their backs on his face. But God's love and faithfulness are never-ending and everlasting. They are ever-creative and ever-imaginative, full of grace and based on both justice and mercy. God wants his people to know him, to understand him, to respond to him freely, to become more human. They are to become his dwelling place where righteousness and truth are honored and the poor know his presence as justice. There is no escaping this God who is called "The Healer of Shattered Hearts" by a young rabbi, David Wolpe.[6] The name is taken from one of the psalms that sums up the story of Jeremiah:

> The Lord rebuilds Jerusalem;
> He gathers the exiles of Israel;
> He heals their broken hearts
> And binds up their wounds.
> (Ps. 147:2–3)

During the exile, Jeremiah disappears into the people. But his words sing, echo, and reverberate throughout the centuries in the hearts of those who wait for the coming of "Yahweh-Our-Righteousness." There will come one who, like Jeremiah, will weep over his people, his city, and his nation, over all creation that rejects and refuses to believe in love, justice, truth, and peace. This period of exile is filled with mourning and weeping. It reminds us of the mournful song we hear after Christmas of Rachel weeping for her children who are no more:

> Thus speaks Yahweh:
> "In Ramah, a voice
> of mourning and great weeping is heard,
> Rachel wailing for her children
> and refusing to be consoled,
> for her children are no more."
>
> Yahweh says this to her:
> "Weep no more and dry your eyes;
> your sorrow will have redress.
> They will come back from the enemy's land.
> There is hope for your descendants;
> your sons will return to their own borders."
> (Jer. 31:15–17)

There will be another man who weeps, whose name — one of many — is Yahweh-Our-Righteousness. He and Jeremiah and God are of one heart. Later, he cries and prays over his beloved city and people who have outright rejected him and are already planning his murder. Unlike Jeremiah, who escapes, he will not. He will be caught in the snare and crucified outside the city:

> O Jerusalem, Jerusalem, you slay the prophets and stone your apostles! How often have I tried to bring together your children, as a bird gathers her young under her wings, but you refused! From now on *your Temple will be left empty for you* and you

will no longer see me until the time when you will say: *Blessed is he who comes in the name of the Lord.* (Luke 13:34–35)

The image is vintage Jeremiah, complete with tenderness, pathos, and hurt born of rejection and violence. In its face there is only love and sorrow for what will befall the people and the city once again. And Jesus will weep, as did Jeremiah and Yahweh, for in his person God and human meet and the grief is still unbearable:

When Jesus had come in sight of the city, he wept over it and said, "If only today you knew the ways of peace! But now your eyes are held from seeing. Yet days will come upon you when your enemies will surround you with barricades and shut you in and press on you from every side. And they will dash you to the ground and your children with you, and leave not a stone within you, for you did not recognize the time and the visitation of your God."

Then Jesus entered the Temple area and began to drive out the merchants. And he said to them, "God says in the Scriptures: *My house shall be a house of prayer:* but you have turned it into a *den of robbers.*" (Luke 19:41–45)

Jesus is quoting Jeremiah on the nature of true worship, the only thing that God wants of his people. Worship is not a matter of sacrifices, burnt offerings, or empty rituals. From the beginning God has only wanted one thing: the hearts of his people, for his people to walk in the ways that he commands, and to listen to his voice and be his people (Jer. 7:21–24). Jeremiah is very specific about what "walking in the ways of God" entails and what being his people means:

Amend your ways and deeds and I will stay with you in this place. Rely not on empty words such as: "Look, the Temple of Yahweh! The Temple of Yahweh! This is the Temple of Yahweh!"

It is far better for you to amend your ways and act justly with all. Do not abuse the stranger, orphan or widow or shed innocent blood in this place or follow false gods to your own ruin. Then I will stay with you in this place, in the land I gave to your forefathers in times past and forever.

But you trust in deceptive and useless words. You steal, kill, take the wife of your neighbor; you swear falsely, worship Baal

and follow foreign gods who are not yours. Then, after doing
all these horrible things, you come and stand before me in this
temple that bears my Name and say, "Now we are safe."
   Is this house on which rests my Name a den of thieves? I have
seen this myself — it is Yahweh who speaks. (Jer. 7:3–11)

It has always been this way. God sees and cares. God will not tolerate empty, insulting worship while his people tread on their neighbors
and crush the poor and the powerless. Those who bear his name must
act with justice and integrity outside the temple before daring to enter
it. This is what the justice of God demands. But God's mercy means
that he will send the one who is called "Our Righteousness" and "Our
Justice" to weep over us, to live with us, to die with us, to even be
killed by us so that once again we may know the unbearable tenderness of God's compassion for us. We should cry with Jeremiah: "How
long, O Lord, how long? Will we ever learn? Have we learned this
truth yet?"
   Jeremiah is a poet, a theologian, and someone intent on altering the
history of the people. Jeremiah's theology is dense and evocative, reminding all religious people in the Jewish and Christian traditions that
religion is all of a piece. Old Testament scholar Walter Brueggemann
described five characteristics of Jeremiah's brand of history-making
that should be the church's curriculum of study:

> One, the capacity for anguish, pathos, and incongruity, which we
> take into our very own persons. Two, a confidence in the moral
> coherence of the world that is not negotiable. Three, assertion of
> the raw sovereignty of a God who will not fit into our schemes.
> Four, the capacity for discerning social analysis and criticism.
> And, five, the bold conviction of hope that God will not quit
> until God has done God's thing.[7]

Jeremiah's "messing with history" put him in the center of Israel's
growing sense of nationalism and power-brokering among the nations. Undergirding Jeremiah's words was the command to confront
and speak the truth to power: to the king and his advisers, his military, and the religious leadership that acted hand-in-glove with the
monarchy and wealthy of the nation. Because of Yahweh's specific
directions on where Jeremiah was supposed to do his preaching — the
court of the temple, the gates of the city, within the palace grounds —

he was arrested, jailed, dropped into a cistern, starved, and persecuted. He was accused of "aiding and abetting the enemy" (Jer. 32:2–4), of being a threat to national security, of deserting to the enemies of Israel (37:13–16), and of terrifying the people. He was whipped and put in the stocks (20:2; 26:8–10). And he was condemned to death, though his sentence was later commuted (38:10), with the result being that he was simply kept in custody.

Jeremiah deliberately disobeyed civil and national laws, what we call civil disobedience today, and mired himself in the sticky business of politics and religion. He returned to his basic message again and again: stop the shedding of innocent blood; do not oppress the resident alien; rescue the victims of injustice; protect the weakest members of society. In other words, do what is right and just! Because he insisted on placing himself in the presence of power, he learned intimately how the penal and judicial systems of his day worked   they served the king, the economy, the military, and, unfortunately, the religious leaders, all of whom seemed to be in collusion against the will of Yahweh.

Jeremiah's God is tender in the extreme for those who are in need or turn to him with their whole hearts, but he is altogether different to those who resist doing good and endanger the lives of his people and heritage. There are very disturbing images of this God who is personal but who may be someone we would not want to meet. Yahweh is described as "a fire that cannot be quenched because of your evil deeds" (Jer. 4:4). Still more threatening is:

> Run for your lives, do not tarry,
> for I will bring evil and great destruction from the north.
> The lion has come out of his den; the destroyer of nations has
>   set out
> to devastate your country and make your cities ruins without
>   inhabitants! (Jer. 4:6–7)

Or,

> That is why the lion from the forest will slay them and the wolf from the desert will destroy them, while the leopard lurks around their cities. Anyone who comes out is torn to pieces, for great is their sin and many are their desertions. (Jer. 5:6)

It seems we today could do with a good dose of fear of the Lord. There have been Jeremiahs among us whenever it has come to the shedding of innocent blood, and they often walk the way of the prophet, ending up in jail. The writer Henry David Thoreau, who dwelled in the woods, was vehemently opposed to the Mexican War, seeing it as an attempt to extend the slave-holding territories of the United States. Because the taxes imposed supported the military, he refused to pay them and was jailed. Ralph Waldo Emerson, another philosopher and writer, who was Thoreau's friend and also opposed to the war, visited him in jail. It is said that Emerson asked him: "Thoreau, what are you doing in here?" Thoreau looked him right in the eye and answered: "Waldo, why aren't you in here with me?"

It seems there must be an issue, a place where one refuses to bend, refuses to participate, refuses to allow nationalistic rhetoric, massive sums of money, or saber-rattling to form one's choices. Jeremiah shouts until he is hoarse that a definitive taboo is the shedding of innocent blood and/or collusion with any national program that destroys the poor of the land. A very famous spiritual asks, "Is there no balm in Gilead?"

God's grief is situated at this critical point. The heart of the people is stopped dead. There is only death by injustice, callousness, selfishness, systemic violence, and military excursions. There is a crippling burden on the poor that reduces them to misery and slavery within their own land. God's indictment rests on his nation because they are no longer a people attentive to the marginal, the vulnerable, and the powerless. What about our country? Has it become a brutal society, where large numbers survive without dignity, living with debilitating despair, underemployment, poor housing, inadequate medical care, second- and third-rate educational systems, separated by race and economic level with public policies that could at best be called rapacious? Is our national pride built on military defense, a medieval penal system, and a justice system that is skewered toward the wealthy?

For Jeremiah, for the prophets, and for Yahweh, the first response to this sad state of disrepair is to speak the truth and call for justice *now,* or else. Religious zealotry, patronizing authority, the correctness of answers, the manipulation of religious ritual and teaching to validate one's lifestyle, and the denial of evil are no different today than in Jeremiah's time. When the religious establishment uses rituals and liturgy to reinforce the dominating economic, nationalistic, and racist culture and to concentrate on personal transformation, piety, self-knowledge, and spirituality, the prophet needs to speak out on behalf of God's weakest and most loved members of society. There is no place for religion that is more intent on being "correct" or "saved" or "belonging" or on venerating its believers than on sacrifice, justice, and protecting the honor of God, which means the care of his poor and the oppressed of the earth.

In *The Healer of Shattered Hearts,* David Wolpe writes of a marvelous legend:

> A Jewish legend holds that redemption will come when the tears of the Jewish people have filled a giant vat in heaven. Surely even the authors of that sentiment, centuries ago, must have marveled at the dimensions of a vat so vast as to contain the tears shed by the Jewish people in that oppressive age. Yet what is significant about the legend is not only the redemptive hope. It is the essential symbolism — tears are measured. Barring salvation, the greatest hope is that cries are heard, that human agony is not a tiny, pitiful squeal to an indifferent cosmos, but has the dignity of true outcry — it is listened to.[8]

Jeremiah wept because the people had refused. They would not weep for the honor of God or in response to the sufferings of their fellow Israelites or for the lack of justice and knowledge of God in the land. This ability to weep in sorrow is essential to the practice of religious people.

We end with another story about a temple. It is one of the legends of how the temple was built in Jerusalem and why only the western wall of the temple, the one known as the Wailing Wall, remains:

> Once upon a time when there was peace in the land of Israel, David the King began having dreams, marvelous dreams every time he slept. He would rise up to the heavens and roam through paradise. He was surprised to learn that everything in heaven had a counterpart on earth! And what he saw in heaven was a city, a temple to Yahweh called Jerusalem. From then on he vowed that he would build that city, that temple, here on earth.

All of the people were gathered together and told of the dream and asked to be a part in the building. Everyone from the least to the greatest shouted that they would do their part in building the city. Lots were drawn, and different groups among the people were assigned different portions of the temple to build.

The first group to draw the lot was the priests. They would build the eastern wall and provide the vessels and inner court of the temple. Next the nobles and wealthy chose, and they would build the northern wall and provide oil for the lamps. Third were the business and military people, and they would build the southern wall and provide the steps between the various levels of the temple. Lastly the poor got the western wall, and they would provide the curtains for the sanctuary. Building started immediately. The first three groups built theirs quickly, because they had the money, the investments, and paid others to do the work. It went much more slowly with the western wall.

When the poor, the workers, mothers and fathers, would finish their daily work and chores, they would begin to work on their portion of the wall of the temple. Fathers and sons would painstakingly make bricks and carry them to the wall and insert them, stacking them higher and higher. Mothers and daughters would work together sewing miles and miles of cloth by hand for the great curtains of the sanctuary. Years passed and finally it was time for the dedication of the temple. It was a ceremony and celebration unparalleled in Israel's history. The sacrifices, the music and dancing, the singing and prayers were attended by all of the people. And the poor — mothers and daughters, fathers and sons — stood close to their wall, pointing out what they had made, fashioned, and contributed with their hard labor and the love of their hearts and hands.

They say that is why, when the temple was destroyed, Yahweh would not allow the western wall to be completely ruined. It was the wall he treasured the most because it came from the hands of his poor ones. Even today when Jews gather at the western wall, all that is left of the temple, and put tiny scraps of paper into its cracks between the stones, they weep for the honor of God and for the loss of the temple. And they say that early in the morning, the wall is covered with dew. But those who know say no, it isn't dew — it is the tears of the angels who weep because God weeps still for the destruction not of his temple but of his people, especially the poor, whose innocent blood is still shed and who so often live as slaves in their own lands. One must weep. It is true worship and the beginning of the heart's turning and the people's just acknowledgment that they are God's own possession and Yahweh is their God.

❧ SIX ☙

Micah and Isaiah

The Southern Prophets

At the time of the prophets Micah and Isaiah, the two kingdoms of Israel — Israel in the north and Judah in the south — are prosperous and thriving lands, with a few very rich people and many, many poor. King Uzziah has had an exceptionally long rule (783–742 B.C.E.), though he is afflicted with leprosy and his son Jotham rules in his name. In the year of Uzziah's death, the prophet Isaiah will be summoned to become the prophet of Jerusalem. Micah and Isaiah are contemporaries, but Micah probably preached a bit farther north of Jerusalem. He will be the first to declare the coming destruction of the temple and its city, Jerusalem.

Let us begin with a Jewish story to introduce the prophets Micah and the man who is called "first Isaiah," the poet and singer of the first thirty-nine chapters of Isaiah. The story tells of a Persian emperor, Chosroes, who had many advisers, including one who was a Jew. Many of the Jews in exile, the Jews of the diaspora, were well educated and rose to places of importance even during exile:

> Once upon a time King Chosroes grew fatally ill. He was sick for a long period of time and nearly died a number of times. But he always seemed to rally and come back. Finally he was well again. He had been to the edge himself and he had seen what it meant to be mortal, king or not. So he gathered all his advisers around him, those to whom he had assigned different areas of his kingdom, the military, those who were in charge of weights and measures, those who oversaw roads, immigration, slaves, building projects, and education.

124

He spoke to them: "I want to know the truth. I want you to tell me the truth about what you really think of me as king. I don't care how you phrase it. I'm here to get the truth out of you. In order to help you and encourage you to tell the truth I will give a stone to each one of you: a ruby, a diamond, a gem of great value. I want the truth."

Immediately they began to babble, telling him all the great things he had done in his kingdom and that his army was the most powerful, that the economy was great, and that the people were happy and loved him. They said that they were overjoyed that he hadn't died. Each one bested the one before and went on and on. But Elim, the Jewish adviser, didn't say a word. The king noticed Elim's silence and cut the others off in midsentence. He said: "Elim, what do you think?" And Elim answered: "The truth cannot be bought. I will tell you nothing."

Chosroes looked at him and said, "All right. I won't give you a stone. I will give you nothing. Now, tell me the truth."

Immediately Elim answered: "On occasion you are a very good king and a very good man. But you have weaknesses, inclinations like everyone else. Except when you act on them, everyone suffers for them, and the responsibility you incur is much worse. You spend money terribly. You constantly are throwing parties, giving away gifts like this to others who will flatter you up one side and down the other. Your people are starving to death. But worse than that you spend too much money on your army and you look on your people as fodder and fuel to fight. Your people don't love you. They are in absolute terror of you, wondering which place you are going to invade next. On occasion you are a good man, but as a ruler, you are selfish, you are mean-spirited, you are arrogant, and you are not a good king. That is the truth."

The king responded, "I need to think about this." He quickly ordered his servants to give each of those who had spoken first a stone and to Elim he gave nothing. The next day, everyone was back in the court chambers, and all the ones who had spoken first the day before cried out: "Master, whoever gave you those stones that you then gave to us is dishonest. They're thieves. The stones are worthless."

The king eyed them and said: "Yes, and so is everything you told me." Turning to Elim, he said, "Elim, you are my new adviser. Perhaps some day I will be a good king."

This is a disturbing story because it makes us think about our enemies. Enemies may tell us what we need to hear — the truth. It may be a vision not shared by everyone or the vision that we seek. This vision is our shadow side. Another reaction to the story is — oh, that's a story with a happy ending. It says, yes, goodness does triumph. That is the fervent hope of every prophet who speaks in the presence of unjust authority and power. The story also makes people look at both their lack of courage when confronted with power and how easy it is to be co-opted by power.

The words that strike home are "The truth cannot be bought." Elim is interested in the truth, which is the only thing of interest to a prophet. The prophet's truth is seen from God's vantage point, and, for us, that is looking the truth of death right in the eye. Violence, evil, sin, injustice, hate, and power used wrongly all are forms of death. When confronted with a question such as the king's, truth-tellers have something to lose. Oftentimes, the very life of a prophet is at stake. Death may be their last word, their final witness to the world of the truth of the word of God.

The story is about power, but the history of Israel and the constant interruptions of God into history through the prophets reveal that the only power is truth. The story also shows that truth is best seen by those outside, by those who are closer to the eye of God, closer to the truth. Applying that insight to contemporary America, we see that those who understand what power is and how it operates may be those outside, those underneath, or those on the borders: immigrants from the south, the people and children of Iraq, those who cannot get their voices heard within their own country, those without health insurance, those who do not speak English as their first language, those who are so ground down by poverty that their lives are eclipsed by daily misery.

Micah

Both Micah and Isaiah are called to speak a hard word to power, to the king and the ruling class in Jerusalem. And their call comes when the rulers are at the height of their temporal power, when they have forgotten that Yahweh should be the only king in Israel. Micah prophesied during the reigns of Jotham, Ahaz, and Hezekiah, and his visions concerned both Israel in the north and Jerusalem in the south. Micah was harsher in word and judgment than even Amos and was the first to warn of the complete destruction of the temple and the beloved city of Jerusalem. Balancing this prediction of loss was a prophecy of peace. We often look to Isaiah as the Advent-Christmas prophet and singer of peace, but, indeed, one of those famous lines is found first in Micah:

> In the last days, the mountain of Yahweh's house shall be set over the highest mountains and will tower over the hills. All the nations will stream to it, saying, "Come, let us go to the mountain of Yahweh, to the house of the God of Jacob, so he may teach us his ways and we may walk in his paths. For the Teaching comes from Zion and from Jerusalem the word of Zion."
>
> He will rule over the nations and settle disputes for many peoples. They will beat their swords into plowshares and their spears into pruning hooks. Nation will not raise sword against nation: neither will they train for war any more. But each one will sit in peace and freedom under a fig tree or a vine of his own, for the mouth of Yahweh of hosts has spoken. (Mic. 4:1–4)

Zion, the city of God, the city of peace, the dwelling place of the Most High, had already become the heart of the people. The people believed that Yahweh really was enthroned in their midst. Deep inside the temple was the Holy of Holies, where the Ark of the Covenant was kept. It was a rectangular box with a gold slab on top called "the mercy seat," and on either end was a cherub with outspread wings. Above the cherubim's wings, the Lord was invisibly enthroned (see 1 Sam. 4:4). Micah alternately warns of God's desertion of his people, leaving them bereft, and of peace, of God coming once again to bring his people together and be their king once more.

His target audience is, as always, the wealthy, but he reserves special ire for the rulers and the prophets and the horror of what they do to the people:

Then I said, "You rulers of the house of Israel, is it not your duty to know what is right? Yet you hate good and love evil, you tear the skin from my people and the flesh from their bones.

"Those who eat my people's flesh and break their bones to pieces, who chop them up like meat for the pan and share them like flesh for the pot, when they cry, Yahweh will not answer. He will hide his face from them because of their evil deeds."

This is what Yahweh says of the prophets who lead my people astray:

"You cry: 'Peace' when you have something to eat, but to anyone with nothing for your mouths, it is 'War' that you declare. So night will come to you without vision, and darkness without divination. Then sun will set for the prophets and the day will be dark for them." . . .

Hear this, leaders of the nation of Jacob, rulers of the house of Israel, you who despise justice and pervert what is right, you who build Zion with blood and Jerusalem with crime. Her leaders judge for a bribe, her priests prophesy for money, and yet they rely on Yahweh and say, "Is Yahweh not in our midst? No evil, then, will come upon us." Therefore, because of you, Zion will become a field, Jerusalem will be a heap of ruins and the temple mount a forest with sacred stones. (Mic. 3:1–6, 9–12)

It is not surprising that Micah's warnings were seen as empty threats, for it was unheard-of that Yahweh would desert his people or let his temple be destroyed. Such a judgment was ridiculous. It could not be imagined, and so his words were ignored. His raw and brutal images accused the rulers of cannibalism and of being infected with diseases of greed, corruption. He addressed them as liars who preached — for pay — what the people wanted to hear. They had forgotten the covenant made when they were a people wandering in the desert. They refused to remember that they were connected to each other and responsible for each other before God and the nations. They no longer remembered that they were to be a nation unlike any other so that their very existence would witness to God's presence in the world.

The code to which they were witness demanded that they never become like Egypt. An underclass was never to emerge, but if it did, then ritual celebration of the Sabbath and Jubilee Years would cancel any debts and restore the balance. The yearly celebration of Passover

was a ritual of memory, of the great events that shaped their identity
and liberated them from slavery. It was to be used to interpret their
present reality when they were threatened by other nations. Politically,
they were God's portion, and all royal or military authority and power
were subject to God's word in the Torah.

Old Testament scholar Walter Brueggemann succinctly pulls together the elements that fashion this nation of Israel:

> To be sure, the traditions of Isaiah (royal), Micah (peasant), and
> Deuteronomy (Mosaic-covenantal) give differing nuance to the
> life of Judah. All are agreed, however, that in every sphere of
> its life, Judah must be a community of intentional resistance,
> refusing to let dominant, imperial definitions confiscate the life
> of Judah. The community is enjoined to great vigilance, lets it
> lose its raison d'être, which is as a Yahweistic, alternative mode
> of life in a world of acquisitive, exploitative power (compare
> Deut. 8:1–20).[1]

It is because they have betrayed that reason for existence that the
unthinkable will happen: they will cease to exist as a nation and will
be driven into exile. Micah uses the metaphor of a court of law, with
Yahweh bringing suit against his people, with the very mountains and
earth bearing witness against them. The people retort with a list of
"What do you want from us, you who are God the Most High?" Their
litany is their own indictment. Do you want "burnt offerings, with
sacrifices, with yearly calves, . . . with thousands of rams, with an over-
abundance of oil libations? Should I offer my firstborn for my sins,
the fruit of my body for my wrongdoing?" (Mic. 6:6b–7). The very
answer is an insult to Yahweh, who has always wanted only one thing
from his people: their obedience and worship. Yahweh's answer to
their arrogant mocking is probably one of the most famous lines in
the Bible. Many Jews believe that it sums up the entire ethical and
moral code of Israel: "You have been told, O man, what is good and
what Yahweh requires of you: to do justice, to love mercy, and to walk
humbly with your God" (Mic. 6:8).

According to God, this is life. This is the call of the prophets in a
nutshell, the meat at the heart of their very existence. The words used
are significant. "Do justice" — the Hebrew word *mishpat* means more
than specific acts of justice. It defines God's order in the world; it is
the covenant guide for living in community; and it is the memory of

God's words and deeds past and present and the people's response in gratitude toward one another. In a word it says, Be the Torah; do God's justice; imitate God in your life. In Deuteronomy we read: "Justice, justice shall you pursue" (Deut. 16:20). Its written corollary is "that you may live." This is the fundamental attitude of God that is to be imitated and emulated. This is why the rabbis teach:

> Said Rabbi Chama b. Chanina: As God clothes the naked ("And the Lord God made garments of skins for Adam and his wife, and clothed them" [Gen. 3:21]) so you must clothe the naked; as He visits the sick ("The Lord appeared to him [Abraham, after his operation of circumcision] by the terebinths of Mamre" [Gen. 18:1]) so must you care for the sick; as He comforts the mourners ("After the death of Abraham, God blessed his son Isaac" [Gen. 25:11]) so must you comfort those who mourn; as He buries the dead ("He buried him [Moses] in the valley in the land of Moab" [Deut. 34:6]) so must you attend to the burial of the dead. (*Sotah* 14a)[2]

"Do justice" means to be faithful as God is faithful, holy as God is holy, to set those in bondage free, to hear compassionately the cries of those in slavery, to do for one's neighbor what God has so graciously done for you. It is the teaching of the Torah, the source of abundant life. These two words — Do justice — point to the way of God and simply say: walk in it! Whatever the concept of justice might be, it is only by doing acts of justice, by solidly standing with those in need of justice, and by resisting injustice that justice can become a reality.

The second demand is "Love mercy" (or "Love tenderly"). The Hebrew word *hesed,* compassion, means coming to the rescue of the poor, the outcast, the alien, the slave, the powerless, hearing the cries of those in misery, giving love that is faithful, sustaining, enduring. It is the way God loves his people, and God's people are to return that love by loving one another. This urgent command shoots right to the heart of every individual and to the community. What one does *outside* the temple is worship, and nothing done *inside* the temple can undo or change that attitude or practice.

The third admonition is to "Walk humbly with your God." The Hebrew word *hasene* means lowly, attentively — we are to walk humbly in awe of God's goodness, God's presence, God's power, remembering and knowing God. This is power. This is living. This is the summons to *tikkum olam* — to repair the world. This is worship. This is the way God is to be pursued. This is the way into the heart of God. This is the way to dwell in God's presence and to know that God is in our midst. Again, David Wolpe writes of how God has walked with others in the tradition, such as Abraham and Noah:

> The Rabbis point out an interesting contrast in the biblical descriptions of Abraham and Noah. Of Noah, the Bible writes that he walked with God (Gen. 6:9). When speaking to Abraham, God enjoins him to "walk before Me" (Gen. 17:1). At first glance you might consider Noah to be the greater figure, since he walked *with* God. In fact, the Rabbis contend, the contrast is intended to be a compliment to Abraham. For Noah was like a small child who needed the support of his parent, and so walked with God so that he might not stumble and fall. But Abraham's strength was such that he could walk alone, unaided, with only the reassuring certainty that God was behind him. (*Tanh. B. Lech L'cha* 26)
>
> ... Perhaps one day, having learned to walk with God, we will be able to become a world on the model of Abraham, to take the burden of justice more squarely on our own shoulders, and to show that we have learned peace. Then we shall walk before God, and His presence will gaze from behind, still close, now proud.[3]

Micah's legacy is this understanding of peace based on justice, on mercy, and on walking humbly with our God. In Micah's short book, we read the ancient prophecy of Advent: "But you, Bethlehem Ephrathah, so small that you are hardly named among the clans of Judah, from you shall I raise the one who is to rule over Israel. For he comes forth from of old, from the ancient times" (Mic. 5:1). Micah condemns, and the sentence is one of death, but he also sings of hope. Another will come, sent by God, who will be a king in Israel and who will shepherd the people: "He will stand and shepherd his flock with the strength of Yahweh, in the glorious Name of Yahweh, his God. They will live safely while he wins renown to the ends of the earth. He shall be peace" (Mic. 5:3).

This is Micah's resounding plea, prayer, and hope for his people: that the new king shall be peace. Micah ends with a prayer to God, the God the people have forgotten but also the God one day a remnant will know again:

Who is a god like you, who takes away the guilt and pardons
crime for the remnant of his inheritance?
Who is like you whose anger does not last? For you delight
in merciful forgiveness.
Once again you will show us your loving kindness and
trample on our wrongs, casting all our sins into the depths of
the sea.
Show faithfulness to Jacob, mercy to Abraham, as you have
sworn to our ancestors from the days of old. (Mic. 7:18–20)

This is Micah's faith, Micah's belief, Micah's prayer. He stands between Yahweh and his people, grieving over their immediate future
yet trusting that Yahweh will be faithful as in the past. When Micah
sees his people resisting the word of God that he proclaims, he prays:
"As for me, I will watch expectantly for Yahweh, waiting hopefully
for the God who saves me. My God will hear me" (Mic. 7:7). The
prophet's prayer is enough for the whole nation.

Isaiah

The book of Isaiah, with its sixty-six chapters, has traditionally
been broken up into three segments: chapters 1–39 form First or
Proto-Isaiah; chapters 40–55 comprise Second or Deutero-Isaiah; and
chapters 56–66 are known as Third or Trito-Isaiah. We will focus
on the core of the prophet Isaiah's actual teaching from First Isaiah,
specifically chapters 1–12, 28–32, and 36–39. (The last-named chapters, which describe the history and backdrop for Isaiah's prophecy,
are also found in segments of 2 Kings 16–21.)

During the time Isaiah preaches, the Northern and Southern Kingdoms are on a steady slide toward ruin. The Northern Kingdom is
doomed, and its people will cease to exist (Isa. 7:8). Isaiah's word
goes out to Judah in the south. The city of Jerusalem, the nation, and
the surrounding countries are rife with political intrigues and wars.
It is not surprising, then, that one of the underlying concerns of the
prophet is the need to trust in God, not in political alliances, not in
might or preparation for war. God is in Jerusalem, and this is Judah's
only defense because Yahweh has committed himself to his people
and to David and his dynasty.

God confronts Isaiah in the temple in the year that King Uzziah dies and his son Jotham becomes king (742 B.C.E.). When Jotham dies around 735 and is succeeded by his son Ahaz (735–715), Ahaz finds himself embroiled in plots to overthrow him and replace him with a king who would bring the Kingdom of Judah (all that remains of Israel) into an anti-Assyrian coalition. That would end the dynasty of David. Much of Judah is already devastated; Jerusalem is threatened; portions of the Southern Kingdom have been annexed by the Philistines and the Edomites (see 2 Kings 10:5; 2 Chron. 28:16–18); and King Ahaz and his people are in a state of panic. Ahaz and his advisers can think of only one possible way out: to petition Assyria, their hated enemy, for help to try to save Jerusalem. Ahaz decides to turn to Tiglath-pileser III, the king of Assyria. His petition is an outright betrayal of David's covenant with Yahweh: "I am your servant and your son. Come up, and rescue me from the hand of the king of Syria and from the hand of the king of Israel, who are attacking me" (2 Kings 16:7; RSV). It is at this point that the prophet Isaiah comes forward to accuse Ahaz of unfaithfulness and of having a lack of faith in God.

Isaiah's dramatic call to prophecy includes a revelation of God that will inspire Isaiah's poetry and songs and sustain him throughout his terrible ministry, condemnation, and eventual death. His call comes in the temple, with an image of God who is glory, might, power, and holiness — in contrast to the kings ruling Israel at that time:

> In the year that King Uzziah died I saw the Lord seated on a throne, high and exalted, the train of his robe filling the Temple. Above him were seraphs, each with six wings: two to cover the face, two to cover the feet, and two to fly with. They were calling to one another: "Holy, holy, holy is Yahweh Sabaoth. All the earth is filled with his Glory!"
>
> At the sound of their voices the foundations of the threshold shook and the Temple was filled with smoke. I said, "Poor me! I am doomed! For I am a man of unclean lips living among a people of unclean lips, and yet I have seen the King, Yahweh Sabaoth."
>
> Then one of the seraphs flew to me; in his hands was a live coal which he had taken with tongs from the altar. He touched my mouth with it and said:
>
> "See this has touched your lips; your guilt is taken away and your sin is forgiven." (Isa. 6:1–7)

Isaiah's experience of the living God was essential for grounding his mission to Jerusalem and the temple. The main thrust of his prophecy would be to sustain, encourage, and fortify the king's resolve to rely on Yahweh's promise of faithfulness made to David and his descendants. David's throne, David's dynasty, David's city and temple would last forever. The power of God stands behind the existence of his people and his dwelling place with them. Isaiah's mystical experience and the revelation of the Holy One of Israel color everything he says and sustain him in the face of disbelief all around him. His knowledge of Yahweh is a mystery that evokes fear and guilt, an awareness of sinfulness, and awe. His experience is extraordinary because Israel's tradition is clear: "No one can see God and live" (Exod. 33:20). But Yahweh sends the seraph to Isaiah to purify him with divine fire that comes forth from the altar. Yahweh shares with Isaiah his radiance, his holiness, his word, and his power. The center of this force, the geographical place, is the temple. For the Jewish people, it is the center of the universe. Now purified, Isaiah hears the voice of Yahweh speaking:

> Then I heard the voice of the Lord, "Whom shall I send? And who will go for us?" I answered, "Here I am. Send me!" He said, "Go and tell this people: 'Much as you hear, you will not understand; much as you see, you do not perceive.'
>
> "Let their hearts be hardened, make their ears deaf and their eyes blind; what a misfortune for them, should they hear and see! Yet if they understood and came back to me I would heal them."
>
> Then I said, "For how long, O Lord?" And he answered,
>
> "Until towns have been laid waste and left without inhabitant; until the houses are deserted and the fields ruined and ravaged; until Yahweh has sent away the people and the fields are left deserted.
>
> "Even though a tenth remain in it, it will be burned. Yet there a stump will remain like that of a fallen oak; this stump is a holy seed." (Isa. 6:8–13)

Poor Isaiah! His mission is to a hard-hearted and deaf people who will not hear, will not repent or turn, and who will end as a stump. Yet he must constantly hold them together and instill courage and trust in them while all around them other nations are intent on destroying them. He has the paradoxical task of making the people stand up and face their enemies, of teaching them to trust in God's glory as support, knowing they will refuse to trust God and so bring the end upon themselves.

His task begins. He obeys Yahweh, and with God's encouragement he takes his son who is named "A-remnant-will-return" to meet Ahaz. The message to Ahaz is blunt and short: "Stay calm and fear not; do not lose courage before these two stumps of smoldering firebrands — the fierce anger of Rezin the Aramean and the blazing fury of the son of Remaliah." He is told to stand firm in faith, hang on because in fifty-six years "Ephraim will be shattered and will no longer be a people." But Ahaz is also warned: "But if you do not stand firm in faith, you, too, will not stand at all" (Isa. 7:3–9b).

But this isn't what Ahaz wants to hear. He has already made his plans and decided. His decision is not for God, but for Assyria, which Ahaz sees as a more pragmatic and reasonable alliance. Isaiah will try to make him understand that he must obey the covenant and rely on God. That is really his only option, the only way to save the people from total destruction. So Isaiah approaches him again, knowing that Ahaz is tottering on the brink of a complete collapse of faith. Isaiah tells him to ask for a sign from Yahweh — anything at all — and it will be given to him, to shore him up. Ahaz refuses, not out of humility but out of political choice and desperation. He has already turned from Yahweh and has sent his fealty and obeisance to the king of Assyria. The die is cast. But Isaiah and Yahweh will not be put off so easily. Ahaz will be given a sign, whether he wants it or not. And it is then that the ancient promise of advent, of who and what is to come because of the will of God, is spoken:

> Therefore the Lord himself will give you a sign:
> *The Virgin* is with child and bears a son and calls his name
> *Immanuel.* He will live on curds and honey by the time he learns
> to refuse evil and choose good. For before the child knows how
> to reject evil and cherish virtue, the land of the two kings that
> you abhor will be deserted. (Isa. 7:14–16)

Isaiah's prophecy, God's word, is spit out in anger. God will not be so easily shunned by his own people. And here begins the first of many promises that can be interpreted on a number of levels. First, in the actual time of Isaiah and Ahaz, a child will be born, another king in the Davidic line. God will not desert his chosen people.

On another level, this is not just a promise about the next king in line to the throne, but a promise extended further into history. No matter what happens to the dynasty of David, to the city of Jerusalem and the people of God, Yahweh will be with them. The name of the child to be born is literally "God-is-with-us." Isaiah's prophecy reiterates God's faithfulness in spite of the people's betrayal and turning to others for political and military support. The prophecy is cast into the far future, the unknown, as a promise that one day there would be fullness of justice and that the presence of God would once again reside with his people as it did in the Ark of the Covenant. There would be a Messiah who would be the presence of justice in the land and among the people and who would proclaim by his presence that God was with them. It would be proclaimed for all the nations to see. The glory of God would be revealed again in a king who would be true and faithful — like God. This seed of hope is planted in Israel.

As Isaiah's prophecy continues, it becomes terrifying. It tells of how the seed will eventually be trampled underfoot and razed to the ground. Because the king and the people refuse the power of God, they will fall under the wrath of other nations. Isaiah reports that Yahweh has told him to go in to his own wife, who will conceive a son to be named "Quick-to-plunder–Booty is close." Before the child knows how to say "father," Yahweh pronounces that the kingdom of Samaria will be destroyed by Assyria. The die is cast. Isaiah tells the people: "Only Yahweh Sabaoth must you hold in veneration, only him must you fear, only him must you dread" (Isa. 8:13). The nations are nothing before the face of the Lord. He writes down these words:

> He will be a sanctuary and at the same time a stumbling-stone, the rock that brings down, for both houses of Israel. He will be like trap and snare for the people of Jerusalem. Many of them will stumble, many will fall and be broken, be trapped and captured. . . . Here am I and the children he has given me. We are signs and portents in Israel from Yahweh Sabaoth, who dwells on Mount Zion. (Isa. 8:14–15, 18)

Isaiah and his family are themselves a sign and a portent, an enduring reminder, a goad for the people of the city, a burr in the side of the king. Isaiah is trying to tell Ahaz that not only Jerusalem but all the nations and, indeed, the whole world are subject to Yahweh Sabaoth. Isaiah is advising him not to make alliances with anyone, but to hold fast. No matter the outcome politically or militarily, a remnant will remain that one day will know a reign of everlasting peace with justice. A huge maw is opening between the king and the prophet. In the end, what the king does hastens the end.

In 722 B.C.E. Samaria fell and the Northern Kingdom disappeared forever. The royalty and most of the people were sent in chains to Assyria. In 715 Ahaz died and his son Hezekiah (715–687) came to rule, apparently the king announced in Isaiah's prophecy. A good king, he initially tried to bring about religious reforms in Judah. He was technically a vassal of the Assyrian king and paid out enormous sums of money in taxes and tribute. He knew that fighting or joining with other states against Assyria would be courting death. However, many of the other nations, Egypt among them, sought to lure Jerusalem into an alliance that would try to break Assyria's dominance. Isaiah was appalled that Hezekiah would think of aligning Judah with Egypt and the others against Assyria. Yahweh commanded Isaiah to hang sackcloth around him, to take off his sandals, and to walk naked and barefoot through the city as a sign of what would happen to Egypt and Ethiopia — Assyria would lead them away as captives (Isa. 20).

In the end, Judah did not participate in the revolt against Assyria, but chose to bide its time. The next nation to court Judah in its fight against Assyria was Babylon. Hezekiah thought this might be the time to move against Sennacherib of Assyria, a new king who had not yet solidified his power. He not only signed but was in the forefront of those who tried to break Assyria's power. Jerusalem prepared for all-out war. The city and its people exulted; everything turned to preparation for war: raising an arsenal of forces, fortifying the walls of the city, and feasting as they whipped themselves up to fight.

Isaiah wailed against them in what is called "an oracle concerning the Valley of Vision" (Isa. 22). In this gruesome description of slaughter, Yahweh cries out: "Look away from me. I will weep bitterly. Do not try to comfort me over the ruin of the daughter of my people" (22:4). The people looked to their weapons, horses, and chariots as their security instead of to God. They gave no thought to their Maker. "You had no regard for him who had planned it [the city] long ago" (22:11b). The world of Israel was turned upside down. The rulers were irresponsible, proud, and arrogant. Isaiah cried out: "You turn things upside down, as though the potter were the clay, and of him you could say, 'He did not make me; he knows nothing' " (29:16). He tried to tell them that any alliance with anyone would prove to be their shame and disgrace (30:5, 7) and would end in disaster (30:12ff). It was sin and evil in the sight of God.

But Isaiah's words were in vain. The people of Judah stood opposed to the Holy One of Israel (Isa. 31:2, 6). They were in revolt against their God. They preferred the sovereignty of another nation both politically and religiously to their allegiance to God. They knew from experience that Assyria, like the other nations, imposed its gods on those it conquered. Politics and religion were ruthlessly mixed, and the justice of Yahweh, the care of the poor, and the honor of God were ignored. The mix of politics, military might, and religious nationalism was the idol they turned to and worshiped. Isaiah told them that if they wanted to be saved from Assyria there was only one thing they could do: "For thus said the Lord Yahweh, the Holy One of Israel: 'Conversion and calmness would have been your salvation, quietness and trust your strength' " (Isa. 30:15). Instead, they chose the sword and to go to war.

Isaiah predicted that Assyria would fall by a sword, but one not wielded by the hands of men and nations:

> "Assyria will fall by a sword not wielded by a man. They will be devoured by a sword not held by a mortal. They will flee before the sword, their young men will be captured and put to forced labor. They will desert their post and the officers, in terror, will abandon the standard." It is Yahweh who speaks, whose fire is in Zion and whose furnace is in Jerusalem. (Isa. 31:8)

As the Christian Community Bible points out,[4] Isaiah's teaching is firm. Before getting involved in dangerous political games, the king must be just and the people faithful to the commandments. Then, all may rely on God, their Rock.

But when Sennacherib invades Jerusalem, Hezekiah sends messages, groveling before him. When Sennacherib demands money and the surrender of Jerusalem itself, Isaiah steps back in and tells Hezekiah to hold out. Jerusalem, under siege, digs in. Isaiah keeps telling Judah that God will deal with Assyria (Isa. 37:22–29), and, miraculously, it happens as Isaiah promises. The Assyrian army succumbs to disease, and Sennacherib is murdered by his own sons! Judah manages to survive; Judah is basically one of the many vassals of Assyria, but the people are alive. From 701 to 633 B.C.E. they exist, but they don't reform or change their stance. Judah's dealings with foreign powers are evidence of corruption and the betrayal of its covenant with Yahweh. The rulers and leaders go back to an economics of greed and acquisition, exploiting the poor, and their pride rises again. Judgment is inevitable. God will not be mocked.

Isaiah's renewed prophecy of doom is directed at "the hero and the soldier, the judge and the prophet, the diviner and the elder, the captain and the man of rank, the counselor, the wise man, the craftsman and the enchanter" (Isa. 3:2–3). He also attacks the haughty women of Zion (3:16–24). His detailed words turn upside down all their intents and frivolous waste of wealth. They will know "stench, baldness, sackcloth and shame." Isaiah pronounces Yahweh's declaration of guilt by using courtroom images: " 'You have devoured my vineyard. The spoil of the poor is in your houses. What right have you to crush the people and to grind down the poor?' declares Yahweh Sabaoth" (3:14b–15).

The parable of the Lord's vineyard in chapter 5 is a love song of God for his people. God knows what he must do, and it is a heart-wrenching task. He has done everything he can for the vineyard: dug it up, cleared the stones, planted the choicest vines, built a watchtower, hewn out a winepress, and waited for a crop of good grapes (Isa. 5:2). But the harvest consists of sour grapes. In response, God, the beloved, will dismantle all that he has previously done for the vineyard, piece by piece, until it is just a "wasteland" producing only briers and thorns (5:6). All of this will be done because God "looked for justice and found bloodshed; He looked for righteousness but heard cries of distress" (5:7).

All of the prophets are torn between judgment and mercy, between the justice and the forgiveness of God. God is also torn, torn between hope that his people will once again turn and be faithful and the necessity to judge justly and be truthful. Isaiah points this out to the people again and again: "Yet Yahweh waits to give you grace; he rises to show you compassion. For Yahweh is a God of justice. Blessed are all who wait for him" (30:18).

It is a thankless, never-ending task of cajoling, pleading, threatening, grieving, demanding, praying, and calling down the glory of the Lord. Isaiah sings of God his friend! Yahweh lays down the choice: "I myself will march against them. I will burn them altogether. Or if they come to me for refuge, let them make peace with me, yes, let them make peace with me" (27:4b–5). Choose!

But they will not. And so Isaiah is shattered by what happens to the people because of their terrible sin against God and against the poor; he is shattered by the grief and justice of God, who must act truthfully. God is pained and suffers alongside his people, even as he allows their destruction by others. Injustice in the land has destroyed their knowledge of God.

When Hezekiah falls ill, Isaiah goes to him and cures him. Restored to health, Hezekiah is visited by the envoys of Babylon, and he arrogantly shows off his wealth, his treasure houses, and all that he possesses. Isaiah's reaction and Hezekiah's response are recorded in 2 Kings 20:16 as well as in Isaiah 39:5–8:

> "Hear this word of Yahweh, the God of hosts: Behold the days are coming when all that is in your palace, and which your fathers have treasured to this day, will be carried off to Babylon. Nothing will be left. And some of your descendants, born of you, will be taken and will become eunuchs in the palace of the king of Babylon."
>
> Hezekiah then said to Isaiah. "The word of Yahweh which you have spoken to me is good!" For he thought: there will be peace and truth in my lifetime. (Isa. 39:5–8)

Even though Hezekiah has known the healing power of Yahweh and his kingdom has been saved from Assyria, he remains selfish, full of pride, and disdainful of his people and their future. He thinks only of his lifetime. Hezekiah's reign continues to be one of injustice, filled with suffering for the majority of the people, who are poor. They are caught in the effects of military campaigns and live through one ordeal after another. Although Israel is surrounded by enemies, her worst enemy is within, deep in her own heart. She makes herself the enemy of Yahweh God.

Hezekiah's son Manasseh comes to power and reigns for forty-five horrible years, persecuting the prophets, openly promoting idol worship, committing crimes against the people through greed, butchery, and wantonness. Later prophets will hold him immediately responsible for the fall of Jerusalem and the exile of the people, though he is merely a sign of the people's adamant refusal to worship God alone. It is the people who abandon Yahweh. In the end, Manasseh is murdered.

The next king is Josiah.[5] He is followed by his sons Jehoahaz and then Eliakim (also called Jehoiakim). Both continue in the footsteps of Manasseh. Jehoiakim dies in 597 B.C.E., and his son surrenders to Nebuchadnezzar, the king of Babylon. This begins the first exile, with the leaders and the wealthy and men of use in war — ten thousand in all — carried off to Babylon.

The next king of Judah is Zedekiah, who rules for eleven years and does what "displeased" Yahweh. In 587 Jerusalem is utterly destroyed along with the temple, and the second exile begins, with even the poorest driven in chains to Babylon. The sentence laid on Israel is now exacted (see 2 Kings 23–25). All of this is seen as the will of God, because of the evil wrought by the kings and the people.

This is what happened. This is the history that swirled around Israel and the prophet Isaiah. But Isaiah the prophet is also the poet and singer of the glory of God. His songs that echo down to us through history are larger than any nation, any dynasty, any era of politics, any time of war, or any political realigning of the earth's peoples. They tell of Isaiah's vision of God and offer a further revelation of who God is and what God's plan is for his people, in fact, for all the peoples of the earth. Isaiah's songs stand out as hope and wild expectation for all those caught in the whirlwind of war, killing, and mayhem. His songs will not be silenced:

> The people who walk in darkness
> have seen a great light.
> A light has dawned
> on those who live in the land of the shadow of death. . . .

> For the yoke of their burden,
> the bar across their shoulders,
> the rod of their oppressors,
> you have broken it as on the day of Midian.

> Every warrior's boot that tramped in war,
> every cloak rolled in blood,
> will be thrown out for burning,
> will serve as fuel for the fire.

For a child is born to us,
a son is given us;
the royal ornament is laid upon his shoulder,
and his name is proclaimed:
"Wonderful Counselor, Mighty God,
Everlasting Father, Prince of Peace."

To the increase of his powerful rule
in peace, there will be no end.
Vast will be his dominion,
he will reign on David's throne
and over all his kingdom,
to establish and uphold it
with justice and righteousness
from this time onward and forever.

The zealous love of Yahweh Sabaoth will do this.

(Isa. 9:1–6)

These are the poetry and songs of Advent, of every season that seeks peace, of every people that longs for a cessation of killing and an end to war and a time of justice, that longs for the Kingdom of God to come upon the world and reign forever. These are the dreams of humankind, the hopes of the poor, and the fervent prayers of the oppressed who seek God in the midst of wars and political and economic killings of the powerless.

Isaiah's words began with warnings about stumps and how they would be reduced to nothing, but Yahweh has another reversal — from the broken-down stump of his own people something incredible will arise:

From the stump of Jesse a shoot will come forth;
from his roots a branch will grow and bear fruit.

The Spirit of the Lord will rest upon him —
a Spirit of wisdom and understanding,
a Spirit of counsel and power,
a Spirit of knowledge and fear of the Lord.

Not by appearances will he judge,
nor by what is said must he decide,

> but with justice he will judge the poor
> and with rightcousness decide for the meek.
>
> (Isa. 11:1–4a)

The presence of this king, this leader, will inaugurate a new beginning, a reign of peace for all nations, all peoples; even creation itself will know the presence of the Holy One of God and the glory of God:

> The wolf will dwell with the lamb,
> the leopard will rest beside the kid,
> the calf and the lion cub will feed together
> and a little child shall lead them.
> Befriending each other, the cow and the bear
> will see their young ones lie down together....
>
> No one will harm or destroy over my holy mountain,
> for as water fills the sea
> the earth will be filled with the knowledge of the Lord.
>
> (Isa. 11:6–7, 9)

The vision is made public. The dream is planted in the hearts and souls of the remnant that will live on its hope and wait on God's time, remaining faithful and watching for the signs of the coming one. This message of Isaiah is the one that most of us know and respond to, but we should remember that these words are born of a terrible time for Isaiah's people; they are born of the shedding of innocent blood and the destruction of the poor. They are also born of the grief of God. God's sorrow brims over and is washed upon the world in tears of mercy that seek to cleanse us of our evil ways.

Isaiah is a prophet, but he is also an intercessor for his people. He prays for them, with them, in spite of them, on their behalf, hoping that his prayer will be enough to carry them through this time of loss and reckoning of their sin. He prays, in hope, this psalm:

> Let the righteous walk in righteousness. You make smooth the path of the just, and we only seek the way of your laws, O Yahweh.
>
> Your name and your memory are the desire of our hearts. My soul yearns for you in the night; for you my spirit keeps vigil.
>
> When your judgments come to earth, the world's inhabitants learn to be upright....

Yahweh, your hand is lifted up, but they fail to see that.
Let them see your zeal for your people, that they may be put
to shame.

Yahweh, please give us peace; for all that we accomplish is
your work.

O Yahweh, our God, other lords besides you have ruled us,
but it is your name alone that we honor. . . .

As a woman in travail moans and writhes in pain, so are we
now in your presence.

We conceived, we had labor pains, but we gave birth to the
wind. We have not brought salvation to the land; the inhabitants
of a new world have not been born.

Your dead will live! Their corpses will rise! Awake and sing,
you who lie in the dust!

Let your dew fall, O Lord, like a dew of light and the earth
will throw out her dead. (Isa. 26:7–9a, 11–13, 17–19)

This is the man who prays for his people, who hopes on their behalf,
and who will die because he speaks the truth to power and honors the
vision of the Holy One who called him to be a prophet in the temple in
Jerusalem. This is the prophet whose knowledge of God opened up a
way for a new thing to happen on the earth and who laid a foundation
for the wonders that will come for a people that obeys and believes in
God, whose name is Peace, as the only God.

We close this chapter on Isaiah the prophet and poet with the story
of another poet. This one was young, only thirteen years old. His name
was Jassim, and, like many street children in southern Iraq before the
1991 Gulf War, he sold cigarettes on the street. His home was in Basra,
which was bombed mercilessly in the war. Many of those missiles and
bullets were coated with depleted uranium (DU) waste from nuclear
industrial sites. It's been noted that, following the war, there was an
epidemic of cancer throughout Iraq, but in Basra it was "an explo-
sion." Basra was also the birthplace of Abraham, the land of Jonah,
and the starting point for the wise ones who followed a star that took
them to a child born on the outskirts of a city.

Felicity Arbuthnot, a reporter, met Jassim in a hospital. He was
suffering from a virulent form of leukemia. She described him: "He
was lying listlessly watching his small world of the ward through huge
dark eyes, made larger by the contrast with his beautiful, pale, almost

translucent skin. His thick, black, curly hair shone as if it had been polished, belying his precarious state of health."[6]

As soon as he heard that Felicity was a writer he was transformed, pulling out his Mickey Mouse decorated notebook. Inside, in beautiful Arabic script, were his poems. She found them "extraordinary in their craft and talent, with an insight far exceeding his years." This one is called "Identity Card":

> The name is love,
> The class is mindless,
> The school is suffering,
> The governorate is sadness,
> The city is sighing,
> The street is misery,
> The home number is one thousand sighs.

Felicity read his poems and lines of other writers that were scattered throughout his little journal, astonishing words such as: "Life does not take into consideration our passion." Like any budding writer, he wanted to know what she thought of his poems. She was stunned into silence. Instead, she told him that he must "fight as hard as you can and get well, because you are already the most astonishingly talented poet. If you can create art like this at 13, I cannot imagine what you will have achieved by the time you are 20. You are going to be part of Iraq's great, ancient literary tradition, in the country that brought the world writing."

She described him then as "glowing." Sadly, Jassim's very life depended on a European aid agency returning within ten days with the chemotherapy he needed. When Felicity left, she had his poems published in Europe and sent them with a friend to give to Jassim. But the aid agency didn't get back to Iraq in time. Jassim had fought hard and tried to hang on, but he died just days before the package of his poems arrived bound in a small book.

While Felicity visited with Jassim, she quoted for him a poem by James Elroy Flecker, which he carefully copied into his book as she repeated it word for word. Sadly, it has become his epitaph:

> Since I can never see your face
> And never take you by the hand
> I send my soul through time and space

To greet you. You will understand.
The way I shall not pass along

He asked a "friend, unseen, unborn, unknown"
To "read out my words, at night, alone:
I was a poet, I was young."

Felicity penciled in: "Just like you, Jassim." She ended her short
story about Jassim: "Rest in peace, little poem: 1985–1998."

Since the Gulf War, the people of Iraq have endured a slow and
painful death in the form of U.N. and U.S. economic sanctions. For the
children, the women, and the elderly it has been a modern slaughter
of the innocents. An infamous piece, an interview taped in May 1996,
appeared on CBS's *60 Minutes:*

> LESLIE STAHL: We have heard that a half-million children have
> died [as a result of economic sanctions against Iraq], more chil-
> dren than died in Hiroshima and Nagasaki. Do you think the
> price is worth it?
>
> MADELEINE ALBRIGHT: I think that is a very hard choice, but the
> price, we think the price is worth it.

Since that interview in 1996, three times that number of people have
died in Iraq from starvation, childhood diseases, cancer, and lack of
basic supplies. Medicine, on occasion, is allowed in, but not all of the
medicine, including chemotherapy, needed to save lives.

Economic sanctions are a failed policy and have become a weapon
of mass destruction. The church in the United States stands solidly
against the continuation of this shedding of innocent blood. Bishop
Joseph Fiorenza, president of the National Conference of Catholic
Bishops, has said: "To use sanctions as a political tool is wrong, cruel
and immoral — no just reason exists to continue the sanctions against
Iraq." Or, as Denis Halliday, the former U.N. Humanitarian Coordina-
tor in Iraq, says: "We are destroying an entire society. It is as simple
and as terrifying as that." It is striking how the backdrop for Isaiah's
warnings and threats and his pleas for the lives of the innocent and the
honor of God continues almost three thousand years later.

This policy of economic sanctions is just a small piece in a larger
policy of excess military spending seen as normative in the United
States. Current levels of military spending expected for the year 2000

top out at about $310 billion. We must remember that Iraq has a military budget of about $1 billion per year. Ben Cohen, the founder of Business Leaders for Sensible Priorities (also the founder of Ben and Jerry's Ice Cream), meets regularly with business and community leaders to question the enormity of the military budget and to advocate more appropriate spending alternatives. He spoke of these issues in a recent interview.

LAPIS: I know the thought is that we can eliminate 15 percent or approximately 40 billion dollars from the military budget without harming national security and that all these business leaders plus these military figures think that is a perfectly reasonable goal. Are there any thoughts about what the specific cuts might be?

BC: Essentially the basic reasoning for saying that the budget can be reduced is that there's no longer an enemy that has near the power that the Soviet Union had. [Now] the reality is that Iraq has a military budget of one billion dollars a year. There's no reason on earth why we should have to spend 270 times that amount in order to protect ourselves against them.... The Pentagon now describes as our potential adversaries a group they have dubbed the Rogues, that is, Iran, Iraq, Libya, Syria, North Korea, and Cuba, and between them all of those countries spend a grand total of $15 billion a year....

We currently have 12,000 nuclear weapons. If we cut that number in half, which would still leave us with more than enough to blow up the entire world, we save $17 billion a year, [and] we could add 425,000 teachers to reduce class size.... If you spend $10 billion a year in 10 years all the schools in the country are rebuilt.... The U.S. is the only industrialized country besides South Africa that does not provide health insurance for all of its kids, so we have 11 million kids in our country that don't have any health insurance. Well, for the price of two and a half Sea Wolf submarines, we could provide health insurance.... There are two or three of them currently rusting in port....

It's been said that a nation's true priorities are expressed by its budget, how it spends its money. It was Albert Einstein who said that you cannot simultaneously prevent and prepare for war.

[You make a] tremendous effort to either take care of people or kill people. . . .

I think basically what's going on is that our country, the last remaining superpower on earth, needs to learn to measure its strengths not in terms of how many people it can kill, but in terms of how many people it can feed, house, clothe, and care for.

I can't believe that there's so many people in our country that go to church or temple or mosque and believe in God and consider themselves to be religious and ignore the basic tenet of turning swords into plowshares.[7]

The American Roman Catholic bishops, working with Pax Christi USA, began a program called Bread not Stones in 2000 to petition Congress to substantially reduce military spending and redirect those funds to pressing social needs. Their statement reads in part:

The social needs of our nation and world are held hostage to military spending, making our world increasingly insecure. As the Vatican II document *Gaudium et Spes* pointed out years ago, "the arms race is an utterly treacherous trap for humanity, and one that ensnares the poor to an intolerable degree."

The Vatican's 1976 restatement of the United Nations Statement on Disarmament made this point even more strongly:

The armament race . . . is to be condemned unreservedly. Even when motivated by a concern for legitimate defense, it is in fact . . . an injustice. . . . [It] is in itself an act of aggression which amounts to a crime, for even when they are not used, by their cost alone armaments kill the poor.[8]

If Isaiah were with us today, he would once again stand in our streets and seek to remind us that what is necessary, what is essential to the practice of religion, to heartfelt worship, and to knowledge of God, is trust in God and the making of peace. For those who believe in the Prince of Peace we pray:

When at last the spirit is poured on us from on high, then will the desert become a garden, and this garden will be free as a fallow land.

Justice will dwell in the wilderness; and in the fertile land, righteousness. Justice will bring about peace; justice will produce calm and security forever....

How blessed will you be.... (Isa. 32:15–16, 20)

By the power, the might, and the glory of God, may it be so.

❧ SEVEN ❧

Lamentations and Ezekiel
The Pain and Hope of Exile

The people were routed from their promised land and sent into exile. Jerusalem, their beloved city, and the temple were razed. They were now slaves in an alien land, bereft of the presence of their God. Their God had allowed all this to happen because of their evildoing and unfaithfulness. It would be a time of repentance, of survival, of mourning the loss, and of grieving the death of their national dreams of grandeur. They were a people broken in spirit. It was the work of the prophets to hold the battered remnant together and to form them into a people who would be faithful once again and obey the new covenant that Yahweh would make with those who sought his mercy and cried out for his protection. It was a time of lamentation and of hope that once again they would return home and dwell in peace as a people. The exile would last seventy years.

Lamentations

The prophets of the exile include Jeremiah, Ezekiel, Second Isaiah, and the author of the haunting cries and prayers of the book of Lamentations. Perhaps Lamentations originated when, the exile over, the remnant that returned gathered to pray on the ruins of the temple, to wail their grief at the glory that was no longer and at all they had lost because of their sin before God. Or Lamentations could have taken shape in exile, while those who had been driven from homes and land and temple gathered as slaves in an alien land to mourn and recount their loss. These lamentations are not really songs of despair as much as they are of remorse for their sin, unfaithfulness, and evil. They are prayers that seek to remember a place, a life, a relationship, even an identity that was cherished and gone. Now they seek to cope with tragedy and inconsolable loss. The mood of the five lamentations fluctuates, soaring and dropping, repeating, reviewing again and again what happened and the consequences of their faithlessness.

Although the lamentations are often attributed to Jeremiah and many of his themes and images are found in the laments, it is now thought that they were penned by others. In the Jewish community, they have become part of the *Megilloth* (or the "Scrolls") which are read on Jewish feasts, including the midsummer celebration of the Ninth of Ab, which commemorates the fall of Jerusalem to the Romans and the devastation of the Herodian temple in 70 c.e. They evoke memories of the first temple and its destruction and of the last temple and the few pieces of it that remain, even to this day.

The lamentations are plaintive poems, written in Hebrew in alphabetic acrostics. Each chapter has twenty-two verses, and each verse begins with the successive letters of the Hebrew alphabet. The arrangement and style seem intended to go beyond mere words to express the depth and overwhelming feelings of horror for what is being described — the destruction of a world, a people, a relationship. These poems grip us with their emotions and exhaust us with their relentless grief.

Grief and exile. Weeping that will not stop. Eyes that stream with tears for the people's arrogance, for what human beings do to one another in their selfishness and greed. They are tears for loss, for stupidity, for remorse. But it is also God who weeps — for those who suffer, for the innocent who were the victims of injustice and inhumanity, for those who have been justly judged and condemned, and for the chosen and beloved people who did not repent, did not turn back to face their God. In the first lament we read:

> This is what I weep about,
> what makes my tears to well up.
> No one is near to restore my spirit,
> no one at hand to console me.
> My children are desolate,
> for the enemy has triumphed.
>
> (Lam. 1:16)

God weeps. Jerusalem, the place of God's dwelling, weeps. The people weep. The prophet weeps. The one who prays on behalf of and for the people weeps. Even in destruction and exile, the bond between God and those chosen has not been irreparably severed.

But the weeping is more than tears. It involves an awareness that what has happened was the result of sin and evildoing on the part of the people who broke the covenant and insulted the awesome grandeur of God, the Holy One. The lamenter also cries out: "Yahweh acts justly, for I have defied his order" (Lam. 1:18); "I cried for help to my lovers, but they betrayed me" (1:19); "My heart recoils within me: I know that I have been rebellious" (1:20b).

It is awareness that comes too late, after the fact, and it has a bitter taste. This God of glory now seems to be an enemy of those he once favored and protected. And so the one who laments describes a God who stands in opposition to the people and who can use history to make judgments and call to justice:

> He turns his hand against me alone,
> all the day long, again and again.
> He has worn away my flesh and skin;
> he has broken all my bones.
> He assails me and surrounds me
> with tribulation and bitterness.
> He leaves me to dwell in darkness,
> like those who have long been dead. . . .
>
> I could not even cry for help,
> for he has stopped my prayer. . . .
>
> Like a bear lying in ambush,
> like a lion waiting for its prey,
> he lunged at me, tore me to pieces,
> and left me alone and helpless.
>   (Lam. 3:3–6, 8, 10–11)

This God personally moves against the believer, who once again knows the reality of God through his painfully acute absence. This is homelessness in the world, no place to be secure, no place to rest, nowhere to know one's place. What has transpired is terrible, but it is a consequence of betraying justice, betraying faith, and betraying the holiness of the people's covenant with Yahweh. Those who languish in exile have learned deep in their very bones that to dwell in God is to be at home, to have a place.

One of the most familiar images for God in the Talmud is *Makom,* which means "place." God's place is the world, his domain, his kingdom. The tradition says:

> In this simple term is the implication that God is the very reverse of exile, for exile is to be removed from *Makom,* from place. To dwell in God is to be home. Though this will not chase away the displacements of the world, its earthly exiles, real disappointments, and trials, it does allow a deeper feeling of rootedness in the universe. God is the ground of being, granting some sense of never truly leaving home.[1]

Exile, though painful and empty, though a bitter and demeaning life of slavery in a foreign land, brought a deeper and truer sense of God's presence and of what home might be. Psalm 137 is the classic song of loss and longing:

> How could we sing the Lord's song
> in a strange and alien land?
>
> If I forget you, O Jerusalem,
> may my right hand fall useless!
> May my tongue cleave to my palate
> if I remember you not,
> if Jerusalem is not the first of my joys.
>   (Ps. 137:4–6)

But the people did sing again, with tears choking their words as they remembered and, finally, with hope and even unbridled joy. They took down their harps and resolved to hear again the word of Yahweh, to turn again toward Jerusalem and the glory of Yahweh. The foundation, the core of the lamentations, is found in this refrain from the third lament:

> But this, when I ponder,
> is what gives me hope:
>
> Yahweh's love abides unceasingly.
> His compassion is never consumed;
> every morning it is renewed.

And his love remains ever faithful.
"My portion is Yahweh," says my soul.
"On him shall I rely."

Yahweh is good to those who hope in him,
to souls who search for him.
It is rewarding to wait in silence
for the Lord's salvation. (Lam. 3:21–26)

This, then, is the lesson of the exile for those who endure and return home. The land is ruined. They are without a temple. Although the patterns have been destroyed, the presence of God is woven through every generation, every land, every experience of history, every moment of their lives. In exile, they remember! They remember God's steadfast and enduring love (*hesed*); they remember God's endless compassion (*rahamin*); and they remember that their God is ever faithful (*amunah*). These are the great words of the covenant. This is the way of God that leads the exiles to affirm the unexpected — hope in a future transformed by God's justice and mercy.

Restoration took place even in the exile, for it was during this period of sojourn in Babylon that the Talmud was written, that academies of learning within the Jewish community were first formed, and that a great golden age of learning was experienced. This period of studying the Torah and reverence for the word of God, written and inscribed on scrolls and in the people's heart, was the foundation of modern Judaism.

This anguishing period also saw the development of the notion that God went into exile with the people. David Wolpe describes it this way:

The fullness of exile is seen in the exile of God. For all the daring of the Rabbis in speaking about God, no concept was more astonishing than this idea that God Himself was in exile. When the people were cast out of their land, the Midrash claims, God (or more precisely, the *Shechina,* the Divine presence) went with them, suffering the same pangs of exile. For the Rabbis, God is so in love with humanity that He will submit Himself to a kind of homelessness in the universe, a self-exile, to empathize with His beleaguered people.[2]

A haunting tale from medieval Jewish tradition was told by Abraham ha-Levi, a *hassid,* a holy man and storyteller. He was also a hermit who studied the Torah and was thought to carry a spark of the soul of Jeremiah or of those who cried the prayers of the lamentations throughout history:

> Once upon a time there was a man who was sick unto death and the rabbi came to visit him. The rabbi didn't pray for him — rather he immediately began to instruct him. The rabbi told him: "Listen to me and if you do what I tell you, not only will you live, but you will live another twenty-two years! Promise me, right this instant, that you will get up off this bed you are lying upon and go to the western wall in the holy city of Jerusalem and, once there, you will lean your head against the stones and grieve, pour out your soul and shed your tears, for your own sin and for the injustices of our people. If you do this, I promise that you will be given a vision of the holy *Shekhinah* that will sustain you all the remaining years of your life. Promise!" Of course, the man did! And immediately he was cured.
>
> He rose from his bed and began to sell everything he had, for he was very poor and had to borrow money to make the trip to Israel. Arriving in Jerusalem he went straight away to the temple wall and rent his garments, wailing loudly, his head on the cold stones. And the *Shekhinah* appeared to him, just as she was described in Jeremiah and Lamentations, with her hair all disheveled, her garments muddied and torn, departing from her home in the Holy of Holies. She was weeping, in distress, shamed, and covered with dirt and refuse.
>
> When he saw her, he cried out and banged his head against the wall and fainted away in grief. While he lay on the ground he saw her again. This time the *Shekhinah* bent down and lifted his body into her arms, cradling his head like a baby's between her knees and wiping the tears from his face. She sang to him and consoled him! She told him: "There is hope for you and the people. You will return. You will come home!"
>
> He returned home and went to see the rabbi to tell him everything that had happened, just as he promised it would, and to try to describe to the rabbi the awful beauty and disfigurement of the *Shekhinah,* the glory of Yahweh in exile with his beloved people.

Rabbi Abraham told him, "You will live twenty-two more years because you have repented and you know the sorrow of the Holy One. In honor of the twenty-two letters of the oral Torah, and for the sake of the soul of Jeremiah the prophet and those who listened to the word of repentance, you must go among the people and call them home. You must help them to remember that the exile is eased, that the exile is subdued when you honor the Divine Presence among us. May the prophets help you in your task now."[3]

These lamentations can easily be translated into more contemporary modes to reveal the consequences of our own behaviors. We need only stand in the foyers of our schools, on the open space in downtown Oklahoma City, outside the walls of prisons during a death watch, or walk in the gates of military bases that store nuclear weapons to cry out at the horror and the loss that such places represent. Here are a couple of laments from a 1999 prayer service:

This is what I weep about, what makes my tears well up. Our young people are desolate, depressed, without hope. They kill one another in classrooms and libraries and on the streets, imitating what they see us doing around the world in Iraq and Kosovo. They have access to guns — I recoil and cry out against the killings and the disdain for human life. We lament all those who died violently and unexpectedly, cut down in anger, and our refusal to change laws or to get involved. . . .

Terror is our lot! Pitfall, ruin, and desolation. Great is the grief of our God over the hard-heartedness of the people. There is no relief, no compassion for the children, starving, eating out of garbage dumps, eating dog food, hungry all the time. The land has been ravaged and laid waste with cash crops, exported to the North. The water and ground have been salted with radioactive waste and turned into killing fields of the future. We lament all those who barely survive, who are slowly starving to death without basic necessities, without justice and without dignity, and we deplore our turning away from their cries of need. . . .

My soul is downcast when I recall what affliction we have perpetrated on others, how we have trampled underfoot the prisoners of the land. We build more and more prisons, enacting harsher laws, to penalize the poor, to bleed vengeance and punishment from human beings, denying them any rights or dignity in our hate and insecurity. We practice the art of killing in the death penalty and spend blasphemous amounts on arms, defense, and aggression rather than on human welfare. The Lord does not approve and is clothed with anger at our decisions. We lament this senseless misuse of money, of power, and of life and our own turning away from our responsibilities to one another.

The church has appropriated these lamentations to describe the horror of crucifixion and the tearing apart of the body of Jesus on Good Friday. Throughout the universal church, these laments deplore the destruction of the Body of Christ — the destitute, the suffering, and the innocents ravaged today. In these prayers, perhaps, like those driven into exile, bereft, and with nothing but a hope of returning, we too might arrive at compassion and a firm resolve to make restitution and atonement for our actions and inaction in our own history before it is too late. If we wait too long, all we will be left with is lamentation. In the face of sin and human evil, the book of Lamentations vows acknowledgment of responsibility and justice. Yet it sings:

> But this, when I ponder,
> is what gives me hope:
>
> Yahweh's love abides unceasingly.
> His compassion is never consumed;
> every morning it is renewed.
> And his love remains ever faithful.
> "My portion is Yahweh," says my soul.
> "On him shall I rely." (Lam. 3:21–24)

Ezekiel: The Seer of Visions

Ezekiel, a priest and prophet, a visionary and architect of a new Jerusalem in spirit, probably went into exile with the first group of Israelites driven out of Jerusalem in 597 B.C.E. This group was composed of nobles, priests, artisans, and wealthy persons, along with Jehoiachim, the young king, and they settled in encampments in Babylon. Jehoiachim's uncle, Zedekiah, was installed as a puppet king in Jerusalem. Judah was given a last chance to survive by living in loyal submission to the Babylonian empire. In 587, just a decade later, another rebellion against Babylon resulted in the absolute destruction of the temple and city, and an even larger group of people was driven into exile. The disasters prophesied for so many years by Jeremiah, Isaiah, Micah, and Ezekiel during the first part of his preaching (chapters 1–33) had finally come to pass. God had departed from his dwelling place, and the people and land were pillaged.

Ezekiel began having visions about five years after arriving in Babylon. His visions were composed of wild images, disconcerting warnings, and startling pronouncements, with lurid descriptions of idolatry and sexual indiscretions and dire threats and powerful depictions of the glory and the name of God.

A famous story about Ezekiel and the wheel from the Jewish mystic tradition, sometimes called "The Four Who Entered Paradise," gives us a look at Ezekiel's visions and their range of meanings then and now:

> Once upon a time there were four rabbis who were awakened by an angel who carried them off to the Seventh Vault of Heaven, where they saw the sacred wheel of Ezekiel! Each looked at it and then descended. The first rabbi, having seen such glory and splendor, didn't know what to do with such sights. His mind revolted and he went insane, wandering and blabbering through desert and ravine for the rest of his days.
>
> The second rabbi returned to earth, and when he remembered he grew bitter and cynical about what he'd seen. He rationalized that it was a dream, only a dream in which he imagined Ezekiel's wheel. Nothing happened. He didn't bring anything back with him to prove he was there or that that power and heaven really existed. He looked at everything cold-bloodedly and without soul.
>
> The third rabbi was enamored of the vision and memory and talked about it incessantly in sermon after sermon, writing treatises and tomes on each detail and sound, connecting it to every detail in life. He drew the wheel and analyzed its meanings, explaining everything in terms of it, and so betrayed his faith in Yahweh and heaven itself.
>
> The fourth and last rabbi was silent for a long time. Then he tried to put into words, in poem and song, what he had seen. He saw everything — his beloved wife and cooing daughter curled asleep, the blossoming branch and the sun departing, the decay-

ing mulch and broken bodies of the old, the stars of heaven and words on the scroll — and it was laced through with light, with transcendence, with the glory reflected in the wheel. He spoke and wrote song after song after song of the glory, of the praise and the beauty suffusing the universe, the emanations of the glory of the Holy One, blessed be His Name, everywhere. He alone lived a holy life in the shadow of the wheel.

The book of the prophet Ezekiel begins with such a transportive vision of the glory of God loose in the universe, and its effect on Ezekiel is lasting as it seeps through all of his prophecies, his symbols, and his life. The shadow of that light defines his words, his actions, and his very identity. The visions at the beginning of the book of Ezekiel are inaugurated with the words: "There the hand of Yahweh was upon me." The text continues:

I looked: a windstorm came from the north bringing a great cloud. A fiery light inside it lit up all around it, while at the center was something like glowing metal.
   In the center were what appeared to be four creatures with the same form; but each had four faces and four wings. Their legs were straight and their feet were like those of a calf, shining like polished bronze. Under their wings (and on their four sides) they had human hands. The wings of one touched those of the other. Their faces did not turn as they advanced, because they were able to go forward in any of the four directions of their faces.
   I saw they had human faces; but each one also had the face of a lion on the right, and on the left the face of an ox, and all four had the face of an eagle. . . .
   While I looked at the creatures, I saw a wheel on the ground beside each of them, glittering as if made of chrysolite. The four wheels had the same shape: indeed each was double — two wheels placed crosswise, so they could follow any of the four directions without turning as they went. Their rims were lofty and looked terrifying, and the four of them were covered with eyes all the way round. (Ezek. 1:3b–10, 15–18)

This is a small portion of the vision. It continues through chapter 2 and the first half of chapter 3. The image is of whirling motion in every direction, with fire, light, and metal flashing; there is also a sense of

universal power that covers the whole world, all air and space and
time. And there is sound, roaring, singing, multitudinous noise, with
water and air moving. In the midst of all this, Ezekiel sees a creature
like a man, like a human being. The description instills in him terror,
wonder, delight, and fear:

> I heard a noise above the platform over their heads. Above it
> was a throne resembling a sapphire and high on this throne was
> a figure similar to that of a man. Then I saw a light as of glow-
> ing bronze as if fire enveloped him from his waist upwards.
> And from his waist downwards it was as if fire gave radiance
> around him.
>
> The surrounding light was like a rainbow in the clouds after
> a day of rain. This vision was the likeness of Yahweh's Glory.
> On seeing it I fell on my face and then I heard a voice speaking.
> (Ezek. 1:25–28)

This will be the sustaining vision and image of God that Ezekiel
will carry within him and that will color all his words and symbolic
actions. This glory of God that has been disdained by the people and
clouded and besmirched by their injustice and sin is the glory that has
left the temple an empty shell to be burned and abandoned. This is
the God the people in exile must remember, learn to worship, and be
bound to once again. It is the God they took for granted, forgot in their
evil, and demeaned before the nations by their injustice and reliance
on other allies.

The distance between this God and Ezekiel, the human being, is
vast. It is God who bridges the gulf and summons Ezekiel to stand up
and listen as God speaks. But the summoning and sending of Ezekiel
are hardly comforting. He is going to address a stubborn and rebellious people who have sinned against God from the beginning. He is
to speak, and "whether they listen or not this set of rebels will know
there is a prophet among them" (Ezek. 2:5).

Ezekiel's first command is startling:

> "Open your mouth and take in what I'm about to say."
>
> I looked and saw a hand stretched out in front of me holding
> a scroll. He unrolled it before me; on both sides were written
> lamentations, groanings and woes.

He said to me, "Son of man, eat what is given to you. Eat this scroll and then go; speak to the people of Israel." I opened my mouth and he made me eat the scroll and then he said to me, "Eat and fill yourself with this scroll that I'm giving you." I ate it and it tasted as sweet as honey. (Ezek. 2:8b–3:3)

Ezekiel absorbs the words into his own flesh and becomes the word to the people. This word tastes sweet like honey, but it will sound bitter to the ears of his hearers who are hard-hearted and starved by their sin and injustice.

Ezekiel's face is unyielding. His forehead is made as hard as a diamond, harder than flint, so that he can stand against these rebels. Ezekiel's heart is for the Lord, for the glory of Yahweh. It is set against the people whose hearts are broken and who refuse to obey and submit to the law and tradition they were given.

Then the prophet is lifted up, transported in a trance as he hears the acclamations and praises of the creatures crying out: "Blessed be the Glory of Yahweh in his dwelling place" (Ezek. 3:12). Noise fills him and he is sick for seven days. Then the word comes again, and he is told that he is to be the watchman for Israel. In the first thirty-three chapters Ezekiel rages against the people and tries to force them to face the exile, the destruction of the temple and city, and the reality that both are gone and will not be returning soon. Ezekiel also seeks to instill in them the reality that the departure of the glory of God from the temple is their doing — they drove God away. Later, when the people finally accept that the fate of the temple is sealed and all is gone, he will turn to a message of restoration, hope, and revitalization of their covenant, their lives, and their very hearts.

Ezekiel's mission involves a number of bizarre gestures and symbolic actions, some that last moments and some that last years. He embodies the message in his very presence, but, faced with that presence, the people all fail to listen when he speaks or change their ways. They continue to think that there's a chance, that politics and rebellions and plots will help them recover lost territory and overthrow Babylon and return to their land and temple.

Ezekiel undergoes house arrest; he is shut up, literally and figuratively. He is bound with cords and also becomes mute. Only God will be able to open his mouth and loose his tongue. He is told to draw a picture of Jerusalem on clay tablets and then to act as if he is laying siege to the city, digging a trench around the figure of the city and setting a battering ram against it. Then he is told to lie on his left side, taking upon himself the sin of Israel and bearing it for the 390 days that he lies there. Then he is to lie down on his right side, bearing the sin of Judah for 40 days. During this time he will slowly waste away on severely rationed food — as will the city of Jerusalem and the land and the people. More is to come. He is to shave his head and beard and separate the hair in thirds — again, to symbolize what will happen. One-third of the people will die of the plague or starve; one-third will die by the sword outside the city; and one-third will scatter to the winds (Ezek. 4–5).

Then come the visions of the destruction of the people and the glory of God leaving the temple forever because of the abominations committed there and by the people who worship therein. The cherubim, the creatures described in the beginning of Ezekiel's vision-call, and the wheels lift up and carry off the glory of God, leaving the temple empty. Ezekiel is told to dig a hole in the side of his house with his hands and crawl through at night, leaving in the dark, carrying his baggage. He is to tell the people that this will be the fate of the king and all his nobles and that even though they will find themselves scattered among the nations, they will be pursued by a sword. Only a few will be spared to confess their abominations, so that wherever they go, "They will know that I am Yahweh" (Ezek. 12). But when the people taunt Ezekiel that his visions don't come to pass, God retaliates, saying: "There will be no further delay concerning my words: what I say will be done — word of Yahweh" (12:28).

The people are led by false prophets crying out "Peace!" when there is no peace and by women who prophesy using magic bands around their wrists and veils that ensnare souls. Ezekiel is sent against them with the word of God. His words resound but fall on deaf ears:

> I hate the wrist bands with which you ensnare souls like birds. I will tear your veils and free my people from your hands. No more will they fall into your hands and you will know that I am Yahweh. You have disheartened with lies the righteous whom I would never dishearten, and you have strengthened the wicked, that he might not turn away from his evil ways and so save his life. (Ezek. 13:20–22)

It all comes down to the one message: "For I want to take hold of Israel's heart, the heart of all those who have strayed from me"

(Ezek. 14:5). The people are compared to a useless vine that will be burned in fire. And, in blunt language that cannot be misunderstood, the people are reminded by the imagery of marriage of the bond they covenanted with Yahweh and of how they have appallingly abused the faithfulness of God by corrupting themselves, by acting as a harlot with other idols and nations, preferring them to their beloved God, doing what is detestable. The covenant will be upheld, and it is the people who will be shamed, not God.

Ezekiel's history of Israel is one of unmitigated failure, rebellion, desecration of the Sabbath, child sacrifice, criminal abuse of the poor, and mockery of God. This is why the sword in the hand of God — Babylon — will come against them. The way they tore apart the poor — devouring people, amassing treasure, and increasing the number of widows — will now be their lot. Similarly, the priests and prophets — who whitewashed the laws and spoke with lying visions, practicing extortion, oppressing the poor and the alien, and denying them justice — will know the wrath of God. It is God who tells Ezekiel: "I looked for a man among them to build a wall and stand on the breach to protect the land lest I destroy it, but I found none" (Ezek. 22:30). There is a hint of God's desperation, of God's hope against hope that the people will turn, but they do not.

Perhaps the most heartrending of his actions comes when Jerusalem is laid siege to and still the people hold out for a reprieve. The word of the Lord comes to him:

> "Son of man, I am about to suddenly take from you the delight of your eyes, but you are not to lament or weep or let your tears flow. Groan in silence and do not mourn for the dead; wear your turban, put on your sandals, do not cover your beard or eat the customary food of mourners."
>
> I spoke to the people in the morning and my wife died that evening. The next morning I did as I had been commanded. Then the people said to me: "Explain to us the meaning of your actions." I said to them, "The word of Yahweh came to me in these terms: 'Say to Israel: I am about to profane my sanctuary, your pride, the delight of your eyes for which you long. The sons and daughters you left behind will also fall by the sword, but you will do as I have done: you will not cover your beard or eat the customary food of mourners; you will keep your tur-

bans on your heads and sandals on your feet. You will not lament
or weep. Instead, because of your sin, you will waste away and
groan among yourselves. Ezekiel will be a sign for you. Do as he
did and when this happens you will know that I am Yahweh.' "
(Ezek. 24:16–24)

Ezekiel's personal loss, his sense of tragedy, his conduct were
God's word about the coming loss of Jerusalem. From the onslaught
of his visions and eating of the scroll he has *become* the embodiment
of the word of God among the exiles. They know him as prophet.
All the terrible acts of evil contradicted the glory of God's presence
and violated God's holy name. Justice would be rendered, not only on
Israel but on all the nations. Chapters 25 through 32 contain oracles
against the other nations that gloat over the fate of Israel, the nation
that has fallen before the face of God.

And then it happens: "On the fifth day of the tenth month in the
eleventh year of our exile, a fugitive arrived from Jerusalem to tell
me, 'The city has fallen' " (Ezek. 33:21). All the warnings and threats
have been given. It is done. Once again, Ezekiel receives a vision, a
call to be a watchman, and he is told what he must do and what the
people must do:

> "For your part, son of man, I have set you as a watchman for
> Israel, and when you hear my word, you must give them my
> warning. When I say to the wicked: 'Wicked man, you shall die
> for sure,' if you do not warn the wicked man to turn from his
> ways, he will die because of his sin, but I will also call you to
> account for his blood. If you warn the wicked man to turn from
> his ways and he does not do so, he will die for his sin, but you
> yourself will be saved. . . .
>
> "Say to them: As I live, word of Yahweh, I do not want the
> wicked to die but rather that they turn from their ways and live.
> Turn! turn from your wicked ways! Why, O Israel, should you
> die?" (Ezek. 33:7–9, 11)

This is God's will and intent. It couldn't be clearer or more heartrending. What follows is one of the most heartening parables of the
prophet as he seeks to turn the people's faces toward the future and once
again toward righteousness and a new, unthinkable bond with God. It
is the parable of the bad shepherds, a minihistory of the leadership of

Israel, telling of both a king and priesthood who fleeced the sheep for
personal gain, scattering them to the four directions, and ruling them
harshly rather than tending them, strengthening the weak, caring for
the sick, or searching out the straying or the lost (Ezek. 34:1–10).

Now there will be something new. God will move to reclaim his
own people and once again lead them himself! The text evokes the
ancient images of the shepherd King David, who was taken from the
flocks to tend the fledging nation of Israel, or the still-more-powerful
images of Moses the shepherd, carrying the lost and wounded sheep
out of bondage into the promised land:

> I myself will care for my sheep and watch over them. As the
> shepherd looks after his flock when he finds them scattered, so
> will I watch over my sheep and gather them from all the places
> where they were scattered in a time of cloud and fog. I will bring
> them out from the nations and gather them from other countries.
> I will lead them to their own land and pasture them on the moun-
> tains of Israel in all the valleys and inhabited regions of the land.
> I will take them to good pastures on the high mountains of Is-
> rael. They will rest where the grazing is good and feed in lush
> pastures on the heights of Israel. I myself will tend my sheep
> and let them rest, word of Yahweh. I will search for the lost and
> lead back the strays. I will bind up the injured and strengthen the
> weak, but the fat and strong will be eliminated. I will shepherd
> my flock with justice. (Ezek. 34:11–16)

There will be a new regime, a new life of justice, a new form of
leadership, a restored political and economic order. Hope is being re-
seeded in the exiles' hearts. The sentinel, who now senses the presence
of God with his people, will help God gather the people back under his
protection. The people will return home and be pastured with peace.
They will be restored, not so much with a new king or a newly built
temple but with a relationship of community and care. As the Spirit
lifted Ezekiel and stood him on his feet to face the vision of God,
now God will stand all his people again on their feet, to face God and
the nations with dignity. The God that was remote now draws close.
The God that is king of the universe is also a compassionate shepherd.
Majesty and mercy coexist. Once again God will adopt the people and
intervene and offer healing to those who have suffered. God makes a
covenant of peace with them that even the land itself and the animals

will honor (Ezek. 34:23–27). Finally, they will know that "you are my sheep, the flock of my pasture, and I am your God, declares Yahweh" (34:31).

Why? Why does God do this? Why does God turn and embrace once again a people that has rejected him and ignored his words and laws? Again, Ezekiel the prophet gives an answer that alters the people's idea of God and their relationship to him. He declares the word of Yahweh to them:

> It is not for your sake that I am about to act, but because of my holy Name that you have profaned in the places where you have gone. I will make known the holiness of my great Name, profaned among the nations because of you, and they will know that I am Yahweh when I show them my holiness among you.
>
> For I will gather you from all the nations and bring you back to your own land. Then I shall pour pure water over you and you shall be made clean — cleansed from the defilement of all your idols. I shall give you a new heart and put a new spirit within you. I shall remove your heart of stone and give you a heart of flesh. I shall put my spirit within you and move you to follow my decrees and keep my laws. You will live in the land I gave your forefathers; you shall be my people and I will be your God. (Ezek. 36:22–28)

God's revealing himself to the nations will make known his greatness, his goodness, and his justice. The destruction of Jerusalem and the deportation of the people are a mockery, an insult that shows contempt for the God of Israel. God's response is to restore the stricken people and to counter their despair with a seemingly unbelievable hope. Then Ezekiel has another vision, probably his most famous — the vision of the valley of dry bones.

He is transported to a valley whose floor is covered with dry bones. He walks among them, and the voice of the Lord asks him: "Son of man, can these bones live again?" And Ezekiel is told to prophesy to the bones! He obeys and cries out, "Dry bones, hear the word of Yahweh!" and then he hears noise and commotion. He watches as the "bones join together" and then sees sinews and flesh growing on them and skin covering them. But there is no spirit in them. Then Yahweh tells the prophet to summon the Spirit to come from the four winds and "breathe into these dead bones and let them live!" Ezekiel obeys the command, and breath enters them. "They came alive, standing on their feet — a great immense army!" (37:1–10). Then the word of Yahweh is given to the people of Israel:

> Son of man, these bones are all Israel. They keep saying: "Our bones are dry, hope has gone, it is the end of us." So prophesy! Say to them: This is what Yahweh says: I am going to open your tombs, I shall bring you out of your tombs, my people, and lead you back to the land of Israel. You will know that I am Yahweh, O my people! when I open your graves and bring you out of your graves, when I put my Spirit in you and you live. I shall settle you in your land and you will know that I, Yahweh, have done what I said I would do. (Ezek. 37:11–14)

Nothing can stand between God and his people. He has chosen them, and they will be his forever. No nation, no calamity, no event in history will undo the bond. Although the glory of God departed from the building of the temple, now the Spirit of God is sent into the very bodies of the people. The sound in the temple is that of wings and wheels — the motion of God's life returning to reclaim the people. He proclaims the word: "I shall make my home at their side" (37:27). God is moving in! First, he had to proclaim the unthinkable: "God is gone!" (10:18–22). The reentry of God is equally unthinkable; God is so near! In fact, their new city's name will be "Yahweh is there." God's holiness will reside within and among them.

Much of the remainder of the book of Ezekiel presents a glorious vision of the rebuilt temple of Jerusalem. The descriptions in chapters 40 through 48 are not precise enough to serve as blueprints because the imagery is meant to build a temple in the minds and memories of the people. Again, Ezekiel's imagery is stunning, fresh, and evocative. The temple has water flowing from its sides, and wherever it flows there is an abundance of living things — birds, fish, and crops. The flowing streams become a river of life for all. The scene is painted with hope: "Near the river on both banks there will be all kinds of fruit trees with foliage that will not wither and fruit that will never fail; each month they will bear a fresh crop because the water comes from the Temple. The fruit will be good to eat and the leaves will be used for healing" (47:12).

The prophet who has known deep in his own heart and mind, even in his bones, that God is holy, God is other, God is glory, also knows and passes on the knowledge that God is healing, God is restorative, God is goodness, God is life and everlasting justice and peace. God will do all this for a people who spurned him but who, after a long exile, have begun to listen to the prophets and to turn. This happens not because of their repentance but because it is the very nature of God to give life, to gather and heal, and to reveal his glory in human beings. In God, justice and mercy are merged — in a seemingly impossible paradox — and God seeks to share these paradoxical forces with those he has created and chosen.

The sages of the Jewish religion struggled long and hard with this paradox. After long discussion they decided that the name "Lord" refers to God's mercy, and the name "God" refers to his justice. They tell a story of how the two are combined:

> "When the Lord God made earth and heaven" (Gen. 2:4):
>
> Why is the expression "Lord God" used?
>
> This may be compared to a king who had some empty glasses. He said, "If I pour hot water into them, they will burst from the heat; if cold, they will snap." What did he do? He mixed hot and cold water together, and poured it into them, and so they remained.
>
> Even so, God said, "If I create the world on the basis of mercy alone, its sins will be great; on the basis of justice alone, the world cannot exist. Therefore, I will create it with a combination of mercy and justice, and may it then stand." (*Genesis Rabbah* 12.15)

Ezekiel faced the daunting tasks of condemning a people for their sins, of making them face judgment and terrible retribution, and then of turning them toward hope and a future reclaimed by memory and grace. He had to impress upon them both the glory of God's transcendence and God's holy and invincible love. He had to generate confidence in a people emptied of life and breathe fresh air into a people crushed by history. He had to remind a violent people who had also experienced the violence of others to rely once again on a God of peace. Although the destruction of the temple defined the people of Israel, even more so did the images of the good shepherd, the dry bones being set upon their feet, and the river of life running from the sides of the temple. This was to be their new awareness of God.

Ezekiel was skilled and adept, passionate and truthful, chanting and singing yet ignored, but his images have come down through the ages and have been taken up by every generation that stands in need of hope. Those who stand paralyzed with grief at horror and annihilation all around them resolutely cling to the hope that life will prevail, if only at a terrible cost. He is sentinel and singer, watchman and crier of warnings, desolate mourner of the delight of his eyes and the delight of his heart, dreamer who never returned to see the reality he sewed into the souls of a disconsolate people. Even his silence shouted at the people as if acting out symbolically what was to happen to them. Ezekiel ben Buzi saw wheels within wheels, myriad eyes of the cherubim, and the motion of God in every direction. Within the heart of such commotion and shining radiance was the figure of a man, the glory of God, the presence of God. Ezekiel eats of the mystery of the word of God and becomes the presence of the God of Israel in the midst of the people.

As Christians we pray often, sometimes daily, the words: "Our Father, who art in heaven, hallowed be your name!" Our very familiarity with the words can veil the deeper levels of meaning and the power we are asking to be let loose on the earth. God acts in Ezekiel's time for "the sake of his holy Name" because of his own nature, because of what it means to be God. Yet what the people have done has violated that name. What we must pray for is the will of God, the coming of justice, and the presence and power of God being let loose among us so that all the nations might see the holiness of God reflected in our behavior and in our obedience to God's code of holiness. Violence, the shedding of blood, unfaithfulness, betrayal, oppression, disregard for the poor, and the making of widows and war mar that name of God and smear his honor before the world. Yet God is still active, in motion throughout the world and in history, in the church, in those who are holy, and in those who suffer as sheep that rely on the Shepherd's care. The glory of God calls forth hope and a future of grace because that is God's will.

Today what does that hope look like? Rubem Alves, in his book *Tomorrow's Child,* speaks of hope:

> Let us plant dates, even though those who plant them will never eat them.... We must live by the love of what we will never see. This is the secret discipline. It is a refusal to let the creative act be dissolved away in the immediate sense experience,

and a stubborn commitment to the future of our grandchildren. Such disciplined love is what has given prophets, revolutionaries and saints the courage to die for the future they envisaged. They make their own bodies the seed of their highest hope.[4]

A pragmatic example of such a "seed" would be debt relief. In testimony before the Subcommittee on Foreign Operations, Export Financing, and Related Programs of the House Appropriations Committee, the spokesperson for the U.S. bishops, Francis Carlin, spelled out the church's concern with rebuilding countries devastated by war, drought, and starvation — countries like Liberia, Rwanda, and Bosnia. The bishops' motivation was "the gospel call to serve the least among us: we are guided in our work by fundamental principles of Catholic social teaching, which we believe apply equally to our nation and other members of the international community."[5] The bishop's testimony described how the world is becoming more and more indifferent to the poor, and yet the number of those in desperate need grows. "Every day a half billion people go hungry; three times that are chronically ill. Half the world's population does not have safe drinking water. A third are unemployed or underemployed, and at least that many lack shelter." Yet, in the face of these realities, a nation that continues to enjoy unprecedented prosperity gives meager amounts of aid, decreasing from year to year, to the most impoverished countries, specifically those in sub-Saharan Africa. Worse still is that half the aid is given for military and security purposes rather than for funding genuine assistance for people in need.

The U.S. bishops are clear about what is needed, what the law of human community demands:

> More than 40 of the world's poorest countries are bound in such a web of indebtedness that they have little hope for a better future. They will not be able to sustain their growth, much less invest in basic health care, primary education, and other services that are necessary to lift people out of poverty. In this Jubilee Year, we should all remember Pope John Paul's call for "reducing substantially, if not canceling outright" poor countries' debts.

The experience of life and survival in these forty poorest nations of the world mirrors the experience of the people of Israel who were destroyed and driven into exile. Today's victims, however, know this despair and oppression, hunger and slow death, in their own countries. They watch while First World nations, intent on profit, deplete their natural resources and offer inordinate loans that are contingent on austerity programs.

The bishops also call attention to the need to reflect on U.S. policies regarding refugees. Since 1993, the number of refugees admitted to the country has dropped by 41 percent. Since the Cold War, the United States has tended to "turn inward, increasingly abdicating its leadership role in protection, assistance and resettlement."[6]

The "problem" of refugees, which is central to the experience of the exile, is acutely contemporary. Statistics consistently reveal that at any time in history more than one-third of the world's population is on the move, as refugees, aliens, immigrants — that is, as exiled peoples. Elie Wiesel, a Jewish refugee and a survivor of the Holocaust, has written movingly of what it means to be a refugee in our time. He approaches the topic not from the perspective of politics but from the perspective of ethics:

> From the ethical perspective, it is impossible for human beings today, especially for my contemporaries, who have seen what people can do to themselves and to one another, not to be involved. We must be with those who have suffered, and we must be with those who have tried to prevent others from suffering. This is the real community: it does not deny the differences, but rather enhances and transcends them.[7]

He is interested in the concept and tradition of sanctuary. He speaks of the Talmud's understanding that sanctuary is linked to war and peace. Sanctuary (a word that connotes safety and even beauty — as we use the term "nature sanctuary" in saving wetlands, prairie grass, birds, and endangered species) is a result, an outgrowth, of violence. But Wiesel has discovered another sense of sanctuary that gladdens him:

> What is it? Here again I come to my Jewish tradition, and with delight I discover that when we speak of sanctuary in the Jewish tradition, it refers to human beings. Sanctuary, then, is not a place. Sanctuary is a human being. Any human being is a sanctuary. Every human being is the dwelling of God — man or

woman or child, Christian or Jewish or Buddhist. Any person, by virtue of being a son or a daughter of humanity, is a living sanctuary whom nobody has the right to invade.

What has been done to the word *refuge?* In the beginning the word sounded beautiful. A *refuge* meant "home." It welcomed you, protected you, gave you warmth and hospitality. Then we added one single phoneme, one letter, *e,* and the positive term *refuge* became *refugee,* connoting something negative.

What I hope this century will achieve before it reaches its end is to get rid of this species. No more refugees. Wherever people come, they should be accepted in every society with friendship, they should be given a new way and a new measure of hope by becoming citizens of that country, our brothers and our sisters.[8]

This was his hope. The new century and millennium are upon us and we have more, ever more, refugees. We see them as enemies, as interlopers, as numbers, as "them," as others coming to take what we have — our jobs, our homes, our security, our space. We have forgotten that we are all refugees from a garden long ago. Elie Wiesel tells us a story.

Who was the first refugee? Moses? No. Abraham? No. Adam. . . .

I remember how it happened, we all remember the day Adam fled; he committed a sin and he fled, at which point, God said to him, *"Aifo ata . . . "* which means "Where art thou? Adam, Where art thou?"

The specific story tells us that one day a great Hassidic master, the founder of the Lubavitch movement, was in jail. He too was a refugee. The warden of the prison came to see him and said to the rabbi, "I know that you know the Bible, maybe you can answer me. In the Bible it's written that God asks Adam, 'Where art thou?' Is it conceivable that God didn't know where Adam was?" And Rabbi Meyer Solomon answered: "God knew, Adam did not."

Do we know where we are? That is, do we know our place in history? Do we know our role in society? I can tell you my experience. . . . My place is measured by yours. In other words, my place under the sun, or in the face of God, or in my own memory, is measured by the distance it has from you. In other words,

if I see a person or persons suffer, and the distance between us
does not shrink, oh, then, my place is not good, not enviable.
Where am I? I am where you are, and if not, who knows
where or whether I am at all?

In conclusion, what is a sanctuary? The sanctuary often is
something very small. Not a grandiose gesture, but a small
gesture towards alleviating human suffering and preventing humiliation. The sanctuary is a human being. Sanctuary is a dream.
And that is why you are here, and that is why I am here. We are
here because of one another.[9]

Wiesel is eloquent, challenging, inviting, and his theology is rooted
in memory and in the history of Israel, a people that was driven into
exile. But the Bible speaks of sanctuary — God's sanctuary that was
once limited to the confines of the temple in Jerusalem. God, fortunately, takes sanctuary wherever he will. He went into exile with his
people, into their very hearts, and breathed new life into their dried
out bones and brokenness.

The God of Israel and the God of Jesus went into exile with us
in the mystery of the incarnation, leaving the glory of heaven for the
flesh of humankind. He now dwells and pitches his tent as a refugee
among us, not only asking for sanctuary but summoning us to be sanctuary for all the lost and straying sheep, all those wounded and driven
from home. The radiance Ezekiel saw in the temple was a figure like
a human being. Yahweh's house — God's dwelling place, the Holy
One's sanctuary — is now the body of every human being, especially
those who long for home, for refuge, for safety, for rest, and for a place
to pasture and to know God in joy and hope for their children.

Ezekiel would find much to say to the people of God in the year 2000.
Perhaps he would tell those of us in North America we have grown too
comfortable here, too attached to a place we have created, often through
greed, corruption, or selfishness, seeking to keep others out. Perhaps
we have lost a sense of longing, a sense of sanctuary, where the holiness
of God is at home among us. Perhaps we build our churches, our cathe-
drals, and forget that perhaps God would prefer to dwell elsewhere.

There is a story told in India aptly called "The Deserted Temple."
It is a vision, like Ezekiel's, of what reality is, whether we can see it
yet or not. A version of it can be found in Rabindranath Tagore's *A
Rich Harvest:*

Once upon a time there was a king who was approached by his servant and told: "Sir, your holy man never enters your temple. You can always find him out in the groves along the road leading out of the city. The people go to him there to hear him sing the praises of God and tell of visions, as the bees swarm to the white lotus. And your royal temple stands empty. No one lights the oil lamps or fills the honey jars or puts coins in the treasury." The king was angry and humiliated by the servant's words.

Immediately he set out to see if the words were true. And he found his holy man in the groves sitting in the dust, praying and preaching to the people. He approached him and questioned him: "Why do you stay out here in the fields and sing of the love of God instead of sitting in my temple with the golden dome?"

The answer was not what he was expecting: "Because God is not in your temple!"

The king was furious. "What do you mean, God is not in my temple? I spared no expense in building that temple. Why, there must be twenty million pieces of gold in those walls and roof, jewels uncountable in the ornaments and mosaics. Everything was done as was required in the texts to dedicate it with costly rites."

"Yes," the holy man responded. "I remember the time well. It was the year of drought, then the terrible rains and flooding came and after that fire destroyed homes and the people were without shelter. Thousands of your people knocked on your door, tried to get into the temple to sleep and to rest from exhaustion, and you turned them away. And I heard God say in the temple: 'This wretched man who calls himself a king will not even provide refuge for his people, will not even give them a roof, yet he wants to put one over me!' So God left and he went to stay with the people, with the destitute and those with only the canopy of sky over their heads. You can find him here under the trees, along the road, and on the borders of the city and your kingdom. That temple is as empty as your heart. It is a monument to your pride."

The king was livid. Enraged he started shouting at him, pulling him to his feet and threatening him. "Leave! Leave! Get out of my kingdom!"

And the holy man rose to his feet, bowed before him, and in peace said: "You are exiling me from the land that I have so loved, but you have already exiled my God and so I go, gladly to be with him once again." And off he went.[10]

May we see and internalize the visions of Ezekiel and know the place where the glory of God dwells. And may the nations know the glory of God in our holiness, our offering of refuge, our welcome to those in exile, and most of all in our justice and care for the presence of God among us in his sanctuary — in his people.

❧ EIGHT ❧

Second Isaiah

What is known as Second Isaiah or Deutero-Isaiah (that is, Isa. 40–55) is also called the Book of Consolation. Chapters 56 through 66, referred to as Third Isaiah or Trito-Isaiah, present a series of poems that announce a new Zion, a new people, a new creation, and the dawn of peace. We will look at Third Isaiah in conjunction with the other prophets of the return, Haggai and Malachi, as they seek to rebuild a temple and a people's identity.

The prophet Isaiah, who was called in 742 B.C.E., prophesied for over forty years, but the Isaian tradition of composition stretches out over at least two and a half centuries. The poems and prophecies of Second Isaiah, which were likely written by a poet-theologian of the "Isaiah school," perhaps 150 years after the prophet's death, have a clear setting in the late Babylonian Exile, from about 550 to 540 B.C.E.

The themes and promises of Second Isaiah form a universal vision of peace with justice that makes us long for its coming with an intensity and desire born of obedience to the word of God proclaimed among us. A story of Elijah called "The Fragrance of Paradise" can introduce us to the mystery and the lingering presence that the words of Isaiah instill in us:

> Once upon a time there was a devout and holy rabbi who loved the Torah. He studied the words, pouring over the scrolls diligently. He rolled the words around on his tongue, copied them carefully, and sought to penetrate their deeper meanings so that he could preach them to his people every Sabbath. He spent hours preparing his sermons and delving into the mysteries of the word of Yahweh.
>
> Now there was a belief in the Jewish community that on every Sabbath there was a gathering in paradise of the holy ones of Is-

176

rael: Moses, even Abraham, the prophets of old, Elijah himself, Jeremiah, Isaiah, and the great preachers and singers who gathered together to study Torah for the entire day. The rabbi had often dreamed of that gathering in paradise and wondered what it would be like to study Torah with the ancestors and faithful ones of Israel.

Well, God was pleased with the rabbi's faith, his devotion, and his desire and decided to reward him. He sent the prophet Elijah to him with a gift.

Elijah appeared in the man's study as the stars were coming out, signaling the beginning of Sabbath, and surprised the rabbi with the announcement that God was gifting him with one day, one Sabbath in paradise to study Torah with the elders and ancients of the Jewish people! He could not believe his ears and eyes.

Then he was whisked away and found himself in paradise. It took his breath away! Its beauty was unsurpassed, indescribable. There, gathered under the trees with birds darting about, the flowers blooming, and rainbows in the sky, were the giants of Israel: Abraham, Moses, David, Isaiah, Jeremiah — all of them — and Elijah led him into the group. They looked up and nodded, acknowledging his presence, and then bent down again to their books and study.

But the rabbi was distracted. He tried concentrating on the texts and the letters of the scrolls before him, but he kept drifting away. Paradise smelled so incredibly good. The fragrance was all around him. It exuded from flowers, bushes, trees, the creatures scurrying and walking about; even the dirt under his feet and between his toes was luscious smelling. He'd never experienced anything like it. He took great gulps of air, swallowing it, and breathing deeply, as he'd never done on earth. He couldn't get enough of it.

Of course the day flew by, and soon, all too soon, it was time to go. Elijah motioned to him and reluctantly he slipped away from the company still intent on the Torah before them and rejoined Elijah to return to earth. But before they left, he pleaded with Elijah: "Could I possibly take some of the fragrance of Paradise with me? I have never in my life dreamed that anything could smell so fresh, so good, so rich, and so delightful."

Elijah smiled and answered, "Of course, but you know that anything you take with you now will, of course, be taken out of your portion of Paradise in eternity."

The rabbi reconsidered. He couldn't bear the thought of losing any portion of his inheritance in eternity. So he sadly decided not to take anything with him. In seconds, he was back, in his own study on earth, and Sabbath was over.

He was forlorn, almost lost. He wandered from room to room, looking vaguely at his shelves of books, but everything somehow looked bleak, shorn of the radiance he had just experienced and tasted. As he moved about, he picked up a familiar smell, a scent. How could it be? Something smelled vaguely of paradise. It certainly wasn't as strong, but it was there, he was sure of it. He sniffed and inhaled deeply. Yes, it was the fragrance of paradise — but where? How? He had not taken any of it with him. And then he realized where it was — in his robe! He lifted his sleeve and smelled deeply. Ah, yes. He lifted the hem of his garment, his long caftan that he had been wearing, and the scent was stronger. His robe had dragged along in the dirt, been caught on bushes and flowers, and lain in the grass where he had sat. His robe was saturated with the fragrance of paradise!

Immediately he removed it and went into his study and lovingly wrapped it around his scrolls on his table. He would never wear it again. But he would stop every time he entered the room or even passed by and breathe deeply, catching its faint odor. And whenever someone needed comfort, was in despair, lost, or struggling with life's pains and tribulations, he would take them inside his study and bring them to the table with the scrolls and the robe and tell them to breathe deeply to catch a whiff of paradise. It never seemed to fade, or grow weaker. It was always there. The gift lingered and seeped through the room, its furnishings, and his clothes. The fragrance of paradise became the very air he breathed, and all his hopes were found in its scent.

The story is enchanting. It haunts. It makes *us* yearn for paradise, for a place, for a peace, a sense of gathering, a power of transformation and healing. And that is what the words of the prophet of Second Isaiah do to us. Their power has not been diluted and their imagery has not faded after thousands of years. They make us dream and hope, make music, and stake our lives on their veracity. They provide comfort. These are the opening lines: "Be comforted, my people, be strengthened, says your God. Speak to the heart of Jerusalem, proclaim to her that her time of bondage is at an end" (Isa. 40:1–2). It is the proclamation of liberation to a people who have suffered, borne guilt, and watched in vain for a glimmer of hope that would open the possibility of a future for them. But this word "comfort" does not designate just release or ease — it refers to strength for the way, for continuing to be faithful to God, even in bondage. But there is ample evidence that the prophet's message was not immediately believed or taken to heart; the people resisted, continuing to lament their position and their losses. "Yahweh has forsaken me, my Lord has forgotten me" (49:14).

The prophet announces: "A voice cries, 'In the wilderness prepare the way for Yahweh. Make straight in the desert a highway for our God'" (40:3). This is the prophet's call to the people, the rallying point for the return home. They are still captives in Babylon, but even this great city is nothing but dust in the eyes of God. All nations and all of history serve God's plan. God will move once again in Israel's history and raise up someone to do his will and obey him, even though he is an outsider, a pagan — the ruler Cyrus, who poses a threat to the rulers in Babylon. Once again God honors his people. The prophet commands them to remember:

> The grass withers, the flower fades,
> but the word of our God will forever stand.
> Go up onto the high mountain, messenger of Zion,
> lift up your voice with strength,
> fear not to cry aloud when you tell Jerusalem
> and announce to the cities of Judah:
> Here is your God! (Isa. 40:8–9)

This is "good news"! In fact, this is the first use of this expression in the Bible. Though the translation above blurs the term, other translations speak of a "messenger of good tidings." The exact words will appear again in Isaiah 52:7 in a blessing prayer: "How beautiful on the mountains are the feet of those who bring good news, who herald peace and happiness, who proclaim salvation." The prophecy of Second Isaiah is bound together by the reality of the word of God that lasts forever, that is not like any human word, but is fertile, rich, and nourishing; it makes truth a reality (55:10–11). The last lines of Second Isaiah sum up the words of the prophet and put an exclamation point on them — they will come true, for God's word is creative and intimate with the will of God for the earth and its peoples:

> For my thoughts are not your thoughts,
> my ways are not your ways, says Yahweh.
> For as the heavens are above the earth,
> so are my ways higher than your ways,
> and my thoughts above your thoughts.
> As the rain and the snow come down
> from the heavens and do not return
> till they have watered the earth,
> making it yield seed for the sower
> and food for others to eat,
> so is my word that goes forth out of my mouth:
> it will not return to me idle,
> but it shall accomplish my will,
> the purpose for which it has been sent.
>
> (Isa. 55:8–11)

The mystery of divine wisdom is about to move into the dark lands of desolation to burst forth, both on earth and in the hearts of the people. It begins with a reprieve, the forgiveness of all their sins, and the choice of a foreigner to send the exiles home. This going out of Babylon will be a new life-giving exodus, more life-giving and freeing than the first one. It is clear that Cyrus is obeying God and that, in the end, it is God who is bringing the people back and preparing the way for them.

But there is more — Yahweh is a God for all peoples and nations, a universal God, the only God. Israel's mission is to deliver the message and be God's witnesses in the world. Israel is to become "the servant of Yahweh." This servant image, which is found in four songs in Second Isaiah, can be read as referring to the prophet, the people Israel, or the one who will come to liberate and proclaim to all the countries the presence of God; or it can refer to all three. The God who will be revealed through Second Isaiah will be radically different from any earthly king. This God is the creator-maker of all things, "Thus says Yahweh, your redeemer, who formed you from the womb: I am Yahweh who made all things" (44:24). He is the sustainer and nourisher of all, especially the poor and weak. He is justice and peace personified, radiant and true. But he is also one who suffers — with the people, for the people, bearing their burdens and carrying their guilt and sin. He is redeemer and salvation.

The title of redeemer is repeated often. It is the Hebrew word *go'el,* which was a legal term for a person who was a relative or distant relation who would help you out. It referred to the person who bought you back if you had been sold into slavery to pay your debts or the person who paid your fines, took vengeance against your killer, or cared for your family in need. It was a relationship of closeness, obligation, and responsibility. Isaiah tells the people:

> For I, Yahweh, your God, take hold of your right hand and say to you: "Fear not, I am your assistance. . . . I am your redeemer, says Yahweh, the Holy One of Israel, your helper. (Isa. 41:13, 14b)

> This is what the Lord says —
> Israel's King and Redeemer, Yahweh Sabaoth:
> I am the first and the last,
> there is no other God besides me. (Isa. 44:6)

Yahweh is the comfort and the consolation of the people. This God wants his people to rejoice, to sing, to put on festive garments and dance. The tone of the texts above is similar to that in the four servant songs, which are found at 42:1–4; 49:1 6; 50:4–9; and 52:13–53.12. These songs offer a picture of the new Israel, the new community, the new way for every individual to worship and live in the world. The servant songs describe the presence of God among his own beloved children, whose love and service bring salvation. They embody a mysterious presence, a person who will come and bring forth the deepest hope and yearnings of all human beings. The first three songs are often used in Jewish worship (the last is not because of the centrality and distinctiveness of the person of Jesus for Christians that have developed over the centuries).

These Suffering Servant songs, pure poetry, all present a unique element — the suffering and death of this servant set the entire community free to live. He bears their guilt and iniquity, carrying them as it were to life and redemption, to freedom and joy. He has been described thus:

The vision of the sacrificial Servant leaves little trace in the rest
of Hebrew scriptures. There may be a link, as we shall see, in
Isa. 61:1–3, in Zech. 9:9 and 13:7–9, and in Dan. 12:3. It is in
the story of Jesus that it has seemed to come into its own, and
so has taken an immense part in Christian faith and experience.
In its Isaiah context, as we have seen, the figure is anonymous,
and whether past, present, or future can hardly be made out. It is
almost as if this servanthood were an idea — but a divine idea, a
revelation of Logos, creative person, in many a time, but which
has one supreme embodiment that sends its light of sacrificial
love to the beginning and end of the world, and recognizes all in
whom the light shines as its own.[1]

The first servant song describes a chosen one who delights God,
who carries the Spirit of God upon him. His work is to bring justice to
the ends of the earth, but he brings this justice with gentleness, with
care for the weak and wavering, tenderly watching out for those who
might perish even as he is moving about. He is faithful; nothing makes
him waver for even a moment. This is a description of a believer, of a
true son or daughter of Abraham, of Moses, of David:

> Here is my servant whom I uphold,
> my chosen one in whom I delight.
> I have put my spirit upon him,
> and he will bring justice to the nations.
>
> He does not shout or raise his voice,
> proclamations are not heard in the streets.
> A broken reed he will not crush,
> nor will he snuff out the light
> of the wavering wick.
> He will make justice appear in truth.
>
> He will not waver or be broken
> until he has established justice on earth;
> the islands are waiting for his law.
>   (Isa. 42:1–4)

This individual (or the community — the remnant that is faithful
even in bondage) is concerned with only one thing: justice. Later, in

the same song, it is Yahweh who declares: "I, Yahweh, have called you for the sake of justice ... and as a light to the nations, to open eyes that do not see, to free captives from prison, to bring out to light those who sit in darkness" (42:6). This is, of course, the work of the prophet in Babylon, and it is difficult work because there are many who settled in Babylon and decided to make the best of a bad situation. They stopped hoping and dreaming and certainly stopped singing or expecting to go home again.

The end of the poem is a demarcation point. It declares: "See, the former things have come to pass, and new things do I declare: before they spring forth I tell you of them" (42:9). This text is the gateway to new songs, resounding praise that joins chorus with nature, the wilderness, the seas and coastlands and all their inhabitants because now God is going to journey with and go before his people. Once again they are called: "You are my witnesses, says Yahweh, you are my servant whom I have chosen, that you may know and believe me and understand that I am He" (43:10). God is reasserting his sovereignty over his people, over the whole world. Once again there will be an exodus to freedom. The people are told not to dwell on the past but to turn: "Look, I am doing a new thing: now it springs forth. Do you not see? I am opening up a way in the wilderness and rivers in the desert" (43:18–19).

What they are to remember now is who they are! They are told "I will pour my spirit upon your race and my blessing upon your offspring.... One will say, 'I belong to Yahweh'; another will call himself by Jacob's name. On his hand another will write 'Yahweh' and take the name of Israel" (Isa. 44:3b–5). They must once again declare that they belong to God, that it is God who lays claim to them: "Remember this, Jacob, for you are my servant, O Israel, I have formed you to be my servant; Israel, do not forget me. I have blotted out your offenses as a thick cloud, your sins as a mist. Return to me for I am redeeming you" (44:21–22).

This is worth singing about and rejoicing over! God is doing this new thing, making for himself a new people, not because they have repented but out of God's goodness and very nature. The response must be repenting joy! Why continue to worship idols or empty expectations built on politics or economics? Why languish and continue to complain bitterly? Look around at earth, at the rising of the sun and its departure — this is the work of Yahweh. Yahweh is their God!

> I am Yahweh, and there is no other.
> I form the light and create the dark;
> I usher in prosperity and bring calamity.
> I, Yahweh, do all this.
>
> Let the heavens send righteousness like dew
> and the clouds rain it down.
> Let the earth open and salvation blossom,
> so that justice also may sprout;
> I, Yahweh, have created it. (Isa. 45:6b–8)

This is a new story of creation. Once again the word of God is spoken. The earth bears fruit, and justice and righteousness begin to spring up on earth. This is truly a new earth, a new season, a new environment, and it is God who does it all for his people. The prophet exhorts them to "come, gather together, and try to understand, survivors from among the nations." They are told to be careful not to be caught up in the idols and empty worship of Babylon — praying to gods who don't move, can't hear, and are made of wood and iron. "There is no other God besides me, a Savior, a God of justice" (45:20–21).

One day Babylon, too, will sit in the dust, toppled from its high place, and be no more — and it may happen suddenly, with no warning. To think for a moment that their gods have any power is folly, stupidity. If only the people had paid attention to God's commandments, then "your peace would have been like a river, your righteousness like the waves of the sea" (48:18). They must pay attention now!

The second servant song begins with this exhortation:

> Listen to me, O islands,
> pay attention, peoples from distant lands.
> Yahweh called me from my mother's womb;
> he pronounced my name before I was born.
> He made my mouth like a sharpened sword.
> He hid me in the shadow of his hand.
> He made me into a polished arrow
> set apart in his quiver.
>
> He said to me, "You are Israel, my servant,
> through you will I be known."

"I have labored in vain," I thought
"and spent my strength for nothing."
Yet what is due me was in the hand of Yahweh,
and my reward was with God.
I am important in the sight of Yahweh,
and my God is my strength.

And now Yahweh has spoken,
He who formed me in the womb to be his servant,
to bring Jacob back to him,
to gather Israel to him.
He said: "It is not enough
that you be my servant,
to restore the tribes of Jacob,
to bring back the remnant of Israel.
I will make you the light of the nations,
that my salvation will reach to the ends of the earth."

(Isa. 49:1–6)

Yahweh wants more than just a people who lean on him; he wants a people who speak for him, make him known, reveal him to the nations, and stand shining as a beacon of justice and truth before the world. He wants them to live in unity and to restore the honor of God among them. A new meaning with hope and a future has been introduced into their life and into their relationships with God and with one another. They are not only to envision a dream of community but to embody it for others to see and imitate. They have been God's since before they were conceived, and their name is always in the mouth of Yahweh. Although they dwell hidden now and their strength is waning, it will soon be time for the arrow to be removed from its quiver and sent into the heart of the world. They are arrows in the hand of the Holy One.

They must learn another way of looking upon God, another way of seeing themselves in relation to God and to the world, and it will not always be easy. The third song begins to speak of persecution, rejection, and endurance, but God is always present to rely on:

The Lord Yahweh has taught me
so I speak as his disciple
and I know how to sustain the weary.

Morning after morning he wakes me up
to hear, to listen like a disciple.

The Lord Yahweh has opened my ear.
I have not rebelled,
nor have I withdrawn.
I offered my back to those who strike me,
my cheeks to those who pulled my beard;
neither did I shield my face
from blows, spittle and disgrace.

I have not despaired,
for the Lord Yahweh comes to my help.
So, like a flint I set my face,
knowing that I will not be disgraced.

He who avenges me is near.
Who then will accuse me?
Let us confront each other.
Who is now my accuser?
Let him approach.

If the Lord Yahweh is my help
who will condemn me?
All of them will wear out like cloth;
the moth will devour them. (Isa. 50:4–9)

The poem continues with advice for the hard times to come: "Let anyone among you who fears Yahweh listen to the voice of his servant. Whoever walks in darkness and has no light to shine for him, let him trust in the name of Yahweh, let him rely upon his God" (50:10b). This is the way to live in the face of adversity, in the face of hardship. The next line is very revelatory and will perhaps connect us to what this might have meant for the exiles in Babylon: "Yet all of you who kindle flames and carry about burning torches, go into the flames of your own fire, into the sparks you have kindled" (50:11a).

The people had long been away from their land. Babylon was a massive empire, powerful, expanding, with strong gods and a culture that was materialistic and hedonistic. Isaiah knew that the people were being assimilated, which was the intent of their somewhat benign rulers, and he was urging them to resist. We know this from accounts of their captivity in the book of Daniel. The best and the brightest of Judean society and nobility were singled out and trained for Nebuchadnezzar's court. Daniel, Hananiah, Mishael, and Azariah were chosen; their names were changed (the first conscious loss of identity); and they were offered food and wine at the king's table. But Daniel begged the chief steward to give the four of them other food, food that would not defile the religious laws. So they lived on vegetables and water and appeared to be as healthy as those who ate the king's food. We are told, "God gave wisdom and proficiency in literature to these four youths, and to Daniel the gift of interpreting visions and dreams" (Dan. 1:17).

Nebuchadnezzar set up a golden statute and ordered everyone to worship as soon as they heard the sound of music, or else they would be thrown into a furnace. Everyone obeyed except Shadrach, Mishael, and Abednego (who are, of course, the three other men with Daniel after their name changes). They are thrown in the furnace, and by the grace of their God they are unharmed (Dan. 3). Later, Daniel is fed to the lions when he is caught praying to Yahweh for help (Dan. 6). The exiles, then, were continually pushed and goaded into obeying the king, worshiping idols, and appropriating the Babylonian way of life.

Second Isaiah fights against this assimilation. He tells the people: "Listen to me, you who pursue justice, you who go in search of Yahweh. Look to the rock from which you were hewn, to the pit from which you were quarried. Look to Abraham, your father, and to Sarah, who gave you birth. He was alone when I called him; but I blessed and increased him" (51:1–2). The people must remember God's deeds of old. They must repent and resist so that they can be a part of the new thing that God is doing. They must learn to fear God alone and not any nation or human being. Again they are reminded: "I, yes I, am your comforter. How then can you be afraid of man who dies, of the son of man who fades like grass?" (51:12). The people need all the encouraging and prodding that the prophet Isaiah can muster in images, prayers, songs, and declarations of God's intent and purpose.

The last chapter of Second Isaiah seems to be an exhortation to resist Babylon's culture, its food and drink and lifestyle, especially its idols and mockery of the God of Israel. He summons them:

Come here, all you who are thirsty, come to the water!
All who have no money, come!

Yes, without money and at no cost, buy and drink wine and
    milk.
Why spend money on what is not food and labor for what does
    not satisfy?
Listen to me, and you will eat well; you will enjoy the richest of
    fare.
Incline your ear and come to me; listen, that your soul may live.
I will make with you an everlasting covenant, I will fulfill in
    you my promises to David....

> Seek Yahweh while he may be found;
> call to him while he is near.
> Let the wicked abandon his way,
> let him forsake his thoughts,
> let him turn to Yahweh for he will have mercy,
> for our God is generous in forgiving.
>
> (Isa. 55:1–3, 6–7)

On one level, this is a call to the poorest, to those hungry, a summons that God will nourish them. It is an ancient version of the
"option for the poor." Isaiah seems to be telling them not to eat the
food of Babylon — the rich wines and lavish fare. It is a call not
to forget their heritage, their true names. They are not to live like
landed immigrants, getting rich and comfortable in exile. They are not
to sing the songs of the foreign land — they are, rather, to remember
the psalms they sung as they climbed the mountain of the Lord and
feasted on his commandments. As part of the return, of being ready to
leave, of their resistance to Babylon, they are to dwell on the memories of what God did for them in the Passover, in the Exodus, and in
Jerusalem. They are to feed on the visions and the good news of what
God is intending to do — "this new and wondrous thing."

They are to feed on the word of the Lord that comes through the
prophet. They are to feed on justice and righteousness and be a witness to their God. They are to cry out for freedom and hope once again.
They are to resist getting sucked into daily life in Babylon, referred to
often in Israelite literature as a "whore," because of its excess, decadence, and slavish obedience to its king and gods. Isaiah has been
given the word of Yahweh: it is food for the soul, nourishment for the
heart, a vision to keep them alive.

The final servant song (52:13–53:12) is about torture and disfigurement, what can be done to a human being by others. The servant is "despised, rejected, a man of sorrows familiar with grief, a man from whom people hide their face" (53:3). Yet the reason for his suffering is intimately bound up with the people, with all the people, with us. The reasoning is strong and unremittingly clear:

> Yet ours were the sorrows he bore,
> ours were the sufferings he endured,
> although we considered him as one
> punished by God, stricken and brought low.

> Destroyed because of our sins,
> he was crushed for our wickedness.
> Through his punishment we are made whole;
> by his wounds we are healed.
> Like sheep we had all gone astray,
> each following his own way;
> but Yahweh laid upon him all our guilt.

> He was harshly treated,
> but unresisting and silent,
> he humbly submitted.
> Like a lamb led to the slaughter
> or a sheep before the shearer
> he did not open his mouth.

> He was taken away to detention and judgment —
> what an unthinkable fate!
> He was cut off from the land of the living,
> stricken for his people's sin.
> They made his tomb with the wicked,
> they put him in the graveyard of the oppressors,
> though he had done no violence nor spoken in deceit.
>
> (Isa. 53:4–9)

This man suffered unbearably, with no consolation. He was utterly nonviolent in life and in the suffering that preceded his death. He was without deceit, truthful, righteous, and yet made an outsider, made other, by his tortures and anguish. He was not even buried with dignity, and not because of anything he had done. He was innocent, without sin, yet he bore all these horrors because of the people's sins. His body bore the visible effects of wickedness and injustice, and yet in his being crushed and wounded the people were freed. This is how we are healed, made whole, brought back. Somehow "he made himself an offering for sin" and "through him the will of Yahweh is done" (54:10–11). This just servant of Yahweh reveals the justice, the suffering, and the anguish of God clearly in his own body and terrible dying.

But the Suffering Servant will not remain cut off. This remarkable song speaks of what will happen to this man so treacherously broken and murdered: "he will have a long life and see his descendants.... [H]e will see the light and obtain perfect knowledge. [He] will justify the multitude; he will bear and take away their guilt" (53:10–11). How can this be? He is dead, delivered up, buried, stricken. How can he live a long life and see his descendants? God will grasp him from death because "he surrendered himself to death." Because he "was even counted among the wicked, bearing the sins of the multitude and interceding for sinners," he will "be given his portion among the great" (53:12).

The entire song is a mystery in which Second Isaiah seeks to give meaning to suffering, to death, to violence experienced by the innocent. No one will believe it. Hearers will stand speechless, silenced before such compassion, such an act of courageous love, such comfort given to a people — and at such cost to an individual. Somehow, there is redemption in submitting to violence, being persecuted unjustly, bearing sorrow and disfigurement without fighting back, without bitterness, enduring the evil that human beings can inflict upon one another, absorbing the sin of others into one's own flesh and soul. This is the ultimate obedience of the just — not to a God that demands such sacrifice but to what is truthful and holy about life itself. This feat, this act of sacrifice for and with others, saves all of us and makes us all human and capable once again of being holy. This holiness was unthinkable, unbelievable — but see, this is a new thing, "even a hidden thing you have not known before" (48:6b).

These songs overwhelm with beauty and power. Though they are inserted in various places of the book, they are what shape the message and the uniqueness of Second Isaiah. But there is one other image that is new. It is the image of compassion, of a God who is a mother nursing an infant at her breast, a woman whose child is part of her. Yet even this image from chapter 49, as close and intimate as it is, cannot adequately describe God's being bound to his own people:

> Can a woman forget the baby at her breast
> and have no compassion on the child of her womb?
> Yet though she forget, I will never forget you.
>
> (Isa. 49:15)

These few words reverse the laments and rejection of the long exile. The gracious comfort of God promised at the beginning of Second Isaiah is extended and deepened into compassion. The question is asked if a woman can forget the baby at her breast. Yes, she can, but it is not easily done. In dire straits, in extreme conditions, the child can be laid aside, but the mother will suffer, her milk will be wasted, and the child will be without nourishment.

The image, then, evokes a mothering God, but it also says that unlike any other mother, Yahweh will never forget, never lay the child aside, never hold back the compassion for the one she gave birth to and feeds from her own body. This too is a new thing that the prophet is announcing: God is saying that Israel is born of the womb of God's compassion and fidelity. The people will never be cut off from God's tender ministrations and nourishment. Somehow Yahweh has created a relationship of mutual need between himself/herself and the children who have been born of God's womb. This image is also found earlier in Second Isaiah:

> For a long time I have been silent;
> I have kept still and restrained myself,
> I moaned like a woman in labor,
> breathing and panting. (Isa. 42:14)

Here Isaiah proclaims that God was pregnant with Israel all the time that they have been in exile, and now God, moaning in labor, is giving birth to a new thing. It will be born! The new child will come forth. God will do this for his people. God, through Isaiah's mouth, keeps reminding Israel that they were formed "from the womb" by Yahweh their redeemer, who made all things (44:24).

But the image is not only of a mother. It is of a father as well. Yahweh puts more questions in Isaiah's mouth. "Woe to him who asks a father, 'What have you begotten?' or a mother, 'To what have you given birth?' " (45:10). It is the tradition of the Jewish people that

God is their parent, both mother and father. David Wolpe speaks of this parenting:

> It is the way of a father to be compassionate and it is the way of a mother to comfort. The Holy One said: "I will act like a father and a mother" (Pesikta de-Rav Kahana 19:3).
>
> For the Rabbis, God is quintessentially the parent of the human race. This is a recurrent image in the Bible as well. God is the parent and both Israel and the world are frequently called His child. "As a father has compassion for his children," writes the Psalmist, "so the Lord has compassion for those who revere Him" (103:13).
>
> Images of fatherhood emphasize the unity of the human race: "Have we not all one father? Has not God created us?" (Malachi 2:10). Human beings find ultimate community only in the parenthood of God. . . .
>
> Like any parent, God frets over the fate of His children, even when they are indifferent to Him: "I responded to those who did not ask, I was at hand to those who did not seek Me; I said, 'Here I am, here I am,' to a nation that did not invoke My name" (Isa. 65:1). The quality of Divine concern includes all shades of relation; it takes on that peculiar worry and regard known only to parents. . . .
>
> God cared for the human race from infancy through adolescence to adulthood. Here the image of mothering is important and apt: "You shall be carried on shoulders and dandled upon knees. As a mother comforts her son, so will I comfort you" (Isa. 66:12–13). . . .
>
> All of these actions are projected onto the Divine.[2]

Isaiah seeks to impress upon the people the all-encompassing nature of God: it is life-giving, nourishing, protective, sheltering, freeing, educating, and waiting for return. Second Isaiah attributes all human connections to God in an attempt to reveal the depth and breadth of God's presence, relationship, and concern. God loves his people. God loves the world. God loves all people. God loves the human race, together and individually, one by one by one, all six billion plus of us. We are "loved freely" (Hos. 14:5). God is endeavoring to draw closer and closer to his people, to lure them back with compassion. "With great tenderness [compassion] I will gather my people; . . . with everlasting love I have had mercy on you, says Yahweh" (Isa. 54:7–8).

Again, the images of women stand out: "Rejoice, O barren woman who has not given birth; sing and shout for joy, you who never had children, for more are the children of the rejected woman than the children of the married wife, says Yahweh" (54:1). Earlier the people had been told to remember Abraham and Sarah (51:2), who gave them birth. They had been born of a barren woman! Their history is one of barren women who conceive because Yahweh has compassion on them and opens their wombs. Now, Yahweh is giving birth again to a people conceived in justice and peace, born of compassionate promise and hope.

This notion of compassion overlaps religious traditions. The Buddhist image of the Bodhisattva is of a many-armed woman whose compassion is boundless. Her many arms reach out to those in need, those who cry out in desperation. She is the image of holiness, of divine maternal protection. A woman who not only speaks of this compassion but has sought to instill it in her people and who lives it is Aung San Suu Kyi, who has lived under house arrest in Burma for years because she has resisted a government that lacks justice and compassion and is oppressive and extremely violent. In 1997 she was asked to give a lecture in England. Her husband, in exile in England, delivered it for her. She described compassion as "the quivering of the heart in response to others' suffering, the wish to remove painful circumstances from the lives of other beings." Isaiah describes a God whose heart quivers in response to our suffering and who must respond, who must come to our aid and deliver us, who must interrupt history if necessary and intervene in our pain.

The book of consolation ends with a promise:

> Yes, in joy you will depart, in peace you will be led forth; mountains and hills will break into song before you, trees of the countryside will clap their hands.
>
> Instead of the thornbush, the cypress will thrive; instead of briers, the myrtle. This will make Yahweh famous and remain as an ever-lasting witness to him. (Isa. 55:12–13)

Once again, the people will know freedom, joy, peace, and a sense of worth. An English theologian, Mary Grey, tells of a woman's project that reveals Isaiah's sense of flourishing, a sense that is apparent in his imagery of a land that will blossom along with the returning people. Grey tells of a group of women who in a developing country chose to work on a rose-growing project — even though it would make no more money than other projects — because "the experience of working with roses was pleasurable and the scent of the roses stayed with them when they had finished."[3] They chose a form of development that nourished both body and soul. The power and evocativeness of the scent for the women are reminiscent of "the fragrance of paradise." The images bear the mark of Isaiah's poetry, which tells of the wild flourishing of newness in what God is doing. That poetry remembers what is vulnerable: the earth, all newborns, children, women, the old, and those who long for peace, for a chance at life.

Today we are in dire need of Isaiah's visions of the God of compassion and of the Suffering Servant who will die so that the people might live. And there are signs of such vision, such hope, such determination, and such nonviolent love. Winona LaDuke, a Native American woman who mixes dreams with reserves of spirit and righteous anger and works with her people to bring their children back to health and to save their lands, tells a powerful story:

> In the heart of the Mohawk nation is Akwesasne, or "Land Where the Partridge Drums." A 25-square-mile reservation that spans the St. Lawrence River and the international border between northern New York and Canada, Akwesasne is home to about 8,000 Mohawks.
>
> I'm riding the Akwesasne reservation roads with Katsi Cook, a Mohawk midwife turned justice activist. It's two o'clock in the morning. Her stamina is almost daunting. That may be the gift of a life-bringer, a midwife — all that power of birth and rebirth which stays in your presence month after month.... Katsi is alternating between singing and explaining to me the process of bioaccumulation of polychlorinated biphenyls (PCBs) in breast milk. A combination of Mother Teresa and Carl Sagan.
>
> Katsi Cook, Wolf Clan mother, finds that she must confront some large adversaries. Besides "catching babies," she finds herself in a stand-off against her adversary, one of the largest corporations in the world: General Motors (GM). At its Massens, NY, power train plant, GM has left a Superfund site — one with approximately 823,000 cubic yards of

PCB-contaminated materials. GM has tainted the land, water, and ultimately the bodies of the Mohawk people, their babies included.

"The fact is that women are the first environment," says Katsi. "We accumulate toxic chemicals like PCBs, DDT, Mirex, HCBs, etc. dumped into the waters by various industries. They are stored in our body fat and are excreted primarily through breast milk. What that means is that through our own breast milk, our sacred natural link to our babies, they stand the chance of getting concentrated dosages."

That is exactly what they found out in the 1980s. As a result, in 1985 Katsi started the Akwesasne Mothers' Milk Project to find out how the toxic contaminants move through the food chain. She and others studied how they moved from fish to wildlife to breast milk. They found that any of the new mothers who ate fish from the St. Lawrence River were contaminated at a level 200 percent greater than the general population. The fetal umbilical cords show the same results. If they were going to breastfeed their children, they had to stop eating the fish. The women are working at getting GM to clean up its waste and end such violations. And GM has been fighting them every step of the way.

In addition to fighting GM, the Akwesasne are fighting two federal governments, the United States and Canada, and two local governments, New York State and the province of Quebec. That's the outside fight. There is also an inner battle described by Katsi: "How are we going to recreate a society where the women are going to be healthy?" That initial environment affects the baby, the mother, the entire family.

After working for ten years against breast milk contamination, Katsi finally met with the head of the Environmental Protection Agency, named "the Great White Mother," asking mother to mother that the agency protect the water, the air, the soil, and the unborn Mohawks. Great White Mother didn't do much. But GM has had to "budge a little because of community pressure." In 1998–99 some cleanup began. GM dredged some of the contaminants out of the bottom of the St. Lawrence and shipped them off to "some unlucky community in Utah." But there is much more to do. She continues:

[I]ndustry, along with government officials and policymakers worldwide, must heed warnings that contaminated wildlife are sending before it is too late. The creation is unraveling and the welfare of the entire planet is at stake. As the Mohawks would say, when the turtle dies, the world unravels. Instead of letting that happen, the Mohawks are determining their history. They are facing down GM, the Environmental Protection Agency, and the big industries . . . and rebirthing their nation. From the first environment of the womb to the community and future generations, they are carrying on the principles of *Kaienarakowa,* the Great Law of Peace and the Good Mind.[4]

Katsi and Isaiah would be kindred souls. Both of them would qualify for the role of the Suffering Servant. They are polished arrows set apart in Yahweh's quiver, and their mouths are sharpened swords. Most certainly they know what it is like to be called from their mother's womb, their names pronounced and sung aloud before they were born. "May their labors not be in vain" (Isa. 49:1–4).

Another Suffering Servant appears in the story of Michel, a young Marianist brother I heard much about but never met in person. His regional superior in Colombia, P. Cecilio de Lora, wrote a short article about him. Michel was twenty-five years old on September 18, 1998. September 18 is the day the Marianists commemorate their three Spanish martyrs. Now they count one more, Miguel (Michel) Angel Quiroga Gaona:

> Michel, as we called him affectionately, was at a splendid moment in his life. Born on the 1st of October 1972, in Bogotá, he lived his Christian youth in our parish of Our Lady of Charity, where his Marianist vocation was born. He made his first profession on December 12, 1992. Last year he finished his degree in social sciences and, at the beginning of 1998, became a member of the Marianist community of Lloro, in the state of Choco.
>
> There with his beloved dark-skinned people, poorest among the poor of Colombia, he developed his mission, full of enthusiasm, creativity, and joy, characteristics that had marked his life.
>
> This morning, along with Father José María Gutiérrez, SM, and other members of the parish, he headed by boat to the community of Nipurdu on the Tumutumbudo River. About ten minutes outside of Lloro, a paramilitary group stopped them. They asked them for documents. José María identified himself

as the pastor of the area and asked them how they could ask for documentation since they themselves were illegal. They said they wanted to question one of the people traveling with them who did not carry documentation. Then Michel told them not to bother the people, and, right there, they fired at him and killed him. They did not let the group return to Lloro and forced them to continue upriver for some time.

Tomorrow, God willing, they will be able to bring him to Bogotá, where he will have a wake at his home parish in Socorro. . . . Michel died as he lived: defending the poor of the earth, passionate for peace and justice. . . .

As his friend told me, he died defending someone else who was in danger and became himself a victim of violence and injustice. He was a disciple of Jesus, cut off in his youth, his joy and devotion, but "he didn't shield his face" as he confronted those who would harm someone who was innocent. He was taken and surrendered himself to death, "interceding for another" (Isa. 50; 53). One of the quotes they printed on cards with his picture, standing with his hands behind his back, smiling gently, reads: "Yes, you are alive! Because your killers have dealt with you as sowers of seed: they have sown your life in the depths of the earth just as wheat is sown, so that it may itself grow and, along with it, many other grains might grow" (St. Ephraim).

Lastly, there is the little-known story of Anna Jarvis, who worked from 1907 to get Mother's Day established as a holiday in the United States. In 1914, Mother's Day was finally declared a holiday by Woodrow Wilson, the president. Later, Jarvis worked to repeal the holiday because she believed it had lost connection with any sense of who mothers are and what they stand and hope for. She believed that the holiday should be based on the "Proclamation for Mother's Day" written by Julia Ward Howe (1819–1910), a leader in the woman suffrage movement, and she didn't want the celebration to be lost in sentimentality or individual emotion. This was the proclamation:

Arise, then, women of this day!
Arise all women who have hearts, whether your baptism be that of water or of tears!

Say firmly: "We will not have great questions decided by irrelevant agencies.

"Our husbands shall not come to us reeking with carnage, for our caresses and applause.

"Our sons shall not be taken from us to unlearn all that we have been able to teach them of charity, mercy, and patience."

We women of one country will be too tender [toward] those of another country to allow our sons to be trained to injure theirs.

From the bosom of the devastated earth a voice goes up with our own. It says, "Disarm. Disarm!"

The sword of murder is not the balance of justice! Blood does not wipe out dishonor nor violence indicate possession.

As men have often forsaken the plow and the anvil at the summons of war, let women now leave all that may be left of home for a great and earnest day of counsel.

Let them meet first, as women, to wail and commemorate the dead.

Let them then solemnly take counsel with each other as the means whereby the great human family can live in peace.

And each bearing after her own time the sacred impress, not of Caesar, but of God.

Where would we find Isaiah today? This Suffering Servant would stand between us and death row, calling for a moratorium on "legally" killing another human being. He would say that killing is wrong. To cut off another from the land of the living, to so despise another human being, to reject any hope of repentance or of making restitution for his actions, to so harshly treat another is to become a killer oneself. This is abhorrent to our God, who is compassionate, a father and mother to all who are part of the human family. Second Isaiah would summon us all with the words:

> Listen to me, you peoples, hear me, O nations.
> I am to give you my law,
> my justice will be a light to the nations.
> Suddenly my justice will appear....
> Hear me, you who know righteousness,
> you who have my law in your hearts:
> do not fear the reproach of men
> or be terrified by their mocking....

> But my justice will last forever
> and my salvation for all generations.
>
> (Isa. 51:4–5a, 7, 8b)

And he would look for the remnant that refused to live by such injustice, the faithful disciples, the just servants of Yahweh who would resist the idols of death made of wood and iron, death by electricity and injection, and who would remind others of this new thing that God is doing: "I, Yahweh, have called you for the victory of justice; I will hold your hand and make you firm; I will make you as a covenant to the people and as a light to the nations, to open eyes that do not see, to free captives from prison, to bring out to light those who sit in darkness" (Isa. 42:6–7). Or in the words of Pope John Paul II, speaking to members of Pax Christi International in May 1995:

> Movements like yours are precious. They help draw people's attention to the violence which shatters the harmony between human beings which is at the heart of creation. They help to develop conscience, so that justice and the search for the common good can prevail in the relations between individuals and peoples. These are the foundations for lasting peace.[5]

✿ NINE ✿

Third Isaiah, Haggai, Zechariah, and Malachi

The Prophets of the Return

A famous Jewish story about when the Messiah will come also tells about dashed expectations, about things that don't work out exactly as we hope, and about waiting with some sort of integrity. It also looks at the interpretation of words, promises, and answers and delves into the hard and enduring reality of truth despite outward appearances. Though this story appears earlier in this book, it is appropriate for a number of other insights crucial to the prophets and their messages. Earlier it was told to focus on present change; now it focuses on the long-enduring wait in hope. Ah, what a story can give expression to and stir:

> Once upon a time Rabbi Joshua ben Levi was surprised to meet up with the prophet Elijah. They talked heatedly of theological issues and then the rabbi blurted out: "When will the Messiah come?"
>
> Much to his surprise, Elijah responded by asking him: "Why don't you ask him yourself?"
>
> He stuttered back, "How? Where?"
>
> And Elijah told him that he would find the Messiah at the gates of the city of Rome. In response to his query about how he would recognize him or pick him out of the crowd, Elijah said: "You will see him among the poor, the afflicted, and the diseased, binding up their wounds. However, while all the others bind an entire area covering several wounds with one bandage,

the Messiah dresses each wound separately, attentive to each small area that is diseased."

Immediately the rabbi left the presence of Elijah and set off for Rome. After a long journey he arrived and soon singled out the Messiah using Elijah's description of him. He was carefully tending the wounds of the poor, just as the rabbi had been told. The rabbi approached him reverently and bowed, giving the greeting: "Peace to you my master and teacher."

The Messiah responded, "Peace to you, Joshua, son of Levi."

The rabbi went straight to the point: "Master, when will you come and redeem us?"

He looked up at him and answered: "I will come today."

Rabbi Joshua went back home. It wasn't long until he met up with Elijah again and Elijah queried him on whether or not he had seen the Messiah and asked his question. The rabbi answered, "Yes, but the Messiah lied to me! He said that he would come today, that day, but of course, he didn't. He didn't come. He hasn't come."

"You should know better, rabbi," Elijah said. "What he meant was 'if only people would but hearken to God's voice, then I would come today'" (Ps. 95:7) (*Sanhedrin* 98a)[1]

Sometimes that last line is translated: "Would that today you would hear his voice!" You can almost taste the disappointment and the bitterness in the rabbi's voice. The Messiah didn't come. He hasn't come. The story brings into stark relief the experience of Israel — not only while it waits for the Messiah but during so much of its long history. Were the people waiting for a specific individual, a Messiah who would be leader, king, and prophet for Israel? Would his coming signal a time that would be everlasting, or were the prophecies intended to announce a messianic period of justice, with peace extended from Jerusalem out into the world? Neither materialized. When the remnant returned to Israel and to the burned-out rubble of the temple, they realized that there would be no exaltation or immediate return to the Jerusalem of the past. In fact, many decided not to return at all — it was too hard and dangerous. They were the next generation, those born in Babylon, without such close ties and memories to Jerusalem. Life in Babylon was good, certainly better than it had been in Jerusalem when the poorest of the people had struggled to survive

while their enemies moved in, confiscated land, and harassed those
left behind in Israel.

Third Isaiah

The prophet known as Third Isaiah returned to Jerusalem with the
remnant after 537 B.C.E. He was part of the original Isaian family and
circle of disciples described earlier in Isaiah:

> Yahweh added: "Bind this testimony and seal it in the midst of
> my disciples." So I will wait for Yahweh who hides his face
> from the people of Jacob. I will hope in him. Here am I and the
> children he has given me. We are signs and portents in Israel
> from Yahweh Sabaoth, who dwells on Mount Zion. (8:16–18)

The ten chapters (56–66) known as Third Isaiah convey a sense of
weariness. The temple has not been rebuilt as the political situation
makes it too dangerous, and the people are struggling to survive. None
of the wild dreams of First Isaiah has come true, although the people
have been allowed to return. They arrived in a land that is nothing like
what was so glowingly described and sung about in Babylon.

The story about the rabbi and the Messiah, which comes from the
first part of the third century, reveals the ambiguity of the feelings of
those who have long waited for a glimpse of the Messiah or for times
that augured justice and peace for the Jews. It also reveals a number
of crucial insights into the Messiah that are found in Third Isaiah.
First, the Messiah is already here! He can be easily found among us.
He binds up the wounds of the sick, outcast, and poor of the earth,
those on the fringes of the cities of power. He already shares in the
sufferings of the people. His work and presence are one of healing,
comfort, and solidarity.

When is he coming? He is coming today! Immediately! Now! If
only people would obey the commandants and attend to the word of
God — if only . . . The Messiah's appearance is like a magnet that at-
tracts the people who do the work of justice, live in obedience to God,
and are attentive to being holy among the nations. The answer given
to a bitter and tired people who want to know what the Messiah is
waiting for is the answer passed on from the old to the young in the
Jewish community today, "He's waiting for you, my child."

And so Third Isaiah begins:

> This is what Yahweh says:
> Maintain what is right
> and do what is just,
> for my salvation is close at hand,
> my justice is soon to come.

Blessed is the mortal who does these things, and perseveres in them, who does not defile the sabbath and who refrains from evil. (Isa. 56:1–2)

In this opening chapter the universalism of hope, of following the way of God, is once again reiterated: "I will bring them all to my holy mountain and give them joy in my house of prayer, . . . for my house will be called a house of prayer for all nations. Thus says the Lord God, Yahweh, who gathers the exiles of Israel: There are others I will gather besides those already gathered" (Isa. 56:7–8). The message is still one of comfort and peace to a people weary, both from doing wrong and its consequences and from coming back to so little. The prophet encourages them:

> "But from now on I will console,
> I will heal and fully comfort him,
> — all those of his people who mourn.
> I will bring smiles to their lips. Peace!
> Peace to him who is far and to him who is near.
> I will indeed heal you," Yahweh says.
>   (Isa. 57:18–19)

The people struggled to live in a ravaged land. The land was poor, and the beauty of paradise had not returned with them. What did the prophecies mean? How much longer would it take? Isaiah provides the answer: there is no peace without justice. The people must prepare; they must open up a way and remove all the obstacles. They must be humble and live with contrite hearts (57:14–16). But, once again, there is a need to be specific and to question whether what the people do outwardly is indicative of what they are thinking and feeling in their hearts. God knows what they do. He sees their fasts and penance, but he sees also what they do to the poor, to their day laborers, and to their neighbors. That is not the ritual fast he desires. He wants their hearts — still!

Is it true that they seek me
day after day, longing to know my ways,
as a people that does what is right
and has not forsaken the word of its God? ...

Look, on your fast days you push your trade
and you oppress your laborers.
Yes, you fast but end up quarreling,
striking each other with wicked blows.

Fasting as you do
will not make your voice heard on high. ...

See the fast that pleases me:
breaking the fetters of injustice
and unfastening the thongs of the yoke,
setting the oppressed free
and breaking every yoke.

Fast by sharing your bread with the hungry,
bring to your house the homeless,
clothe the man you see naked
and do not turn away from your own kin.

Then will your light break forth as the dawn
and your healing come in a flash.
Your righteousness will be your vanguard,
the Glory of Yahweh your rearguard.
Then you will call and Yahweh will answer,
you will cry and he will say, I am here.

(Isa. 58:2, 3b–4, 6–9)

This prophet still sings and uses images of light, of intimacy and justice. He is still trying to capture the hearts of the people for their God Yahweh while they are sliding back into their old ways of self-ishness, greed, hoarding, and unjust treatment of their neighbors and families. The contrast of light and dark is rooted in each person's heart, in their actions, in the practice of what they believe. "If you do away with the yoke, the clenched fist and malicious words, if you deprive yourself for the hungry and satisfy the needs of the afflicted, your light will rise in darkness, and your darkest hour will be like noon" (Isa. 58:9b–10; NJB). Yahweh wants to rebuild their dwelling places and their life together, but it is they who resist, blocking the work of Yahweh, blocking his glory from returning in its full splendor. He pleads, using poetry, trying to tell them what he would do for them if they would only respond:

> Then your light will rise in the dark,
> your night will be like noon.
> Yahweh will guide you always
> and give you relief in desert places.
> He will strengthen your bones;
> he will make you a watered garden,
> like a spring of water
> whose waters never fail.
> Your ancient ruins will be rebuilt,
> the age-old foundations will be raised.
> You will be called the Breach-mender,
> and the Restorer of ruined houses.
>
> (Isa. 58:10b–12)

There is always the "if." The relationship is still lopsided. God is attentive and faithful, but the people are slow, dragging their feet and hardening their hearts with the practices of evil. He would like to change their names again — not as the Babylonians once took away their names as the children of Yahweh, but to give them new names that will aptly describe what God is doing for them once again. But the people are going their own way, ignoring the Sabbath for their jobs, speaking with malice (58:13–14).

Third Isaiah uses an image of God's interest in them — God's arm is not too short to reach them nor are his ears too dull to hear them. It is their sins that veil their faces so they cannot see the presence of God. Justice lies beyond reach because of their lying, their "hatching viper's eggs and snakes," their rushing out to do evil. Once again, God is grieved. The people need to confess their iniquities. God will justly judge, but he will also remain with them and with their children and their children's children, forever and ever. The people so quickly forget what has happened in the past and how their injustices have brought down misery upon them (Isa. 59).

But Third Isaiah is undeterred, as is Yahweh, whose message breaks out like the sun coming up again and again over the whole world, not just upon Israel's people. This is a song of advent, of coming, of approaching goodness, of what will be:

> Arise, shine, for your light has come.
> The Glory of Yahweh rises above you.
> Night still covers the earth
> and gloomy clouds veil the peoples,
> but Yahweh now rises
> and over you his glory appears.
> Nations will come to your light
> and kings to the brightness of your dawn.
>
> Lift up your eyes round about and see:
> they are all gathered together and come to you,
> your sons from afar,
> your daughters tenderly carried.
> This sight will make your face radiant,
> your heart throbbing and full.
>
> (Isa. 60:1–5a)

The people's responses are lackluster to what God wants to do and is doing for them, bringing them home and starting over again. They must learn and remember. He seeks to move them, to make them look into the future when foreigners will rebuild the walls, when the gates of the city will never close, when there will be no violence in the land, and when Yahweh God himself "will be your everlasting light and your God will be your glory" (Isa. 60:19b). They are reminded again that "I Yahweh will do this, swiftly, in due time" (60:22b). It is God's plan, but the people are essential to its coming.

Yahweh will visit his people, altering their destiny. His presence will echo back through the ages to give substance to the ancient prophecies. The description, couched in bridal imagery and rejoicing, is borrowed from Isaiah's earlier words about the just servant of Yahweh. For Christians, the core of Jesus' synagogue proclamation is that in him the word is fulfilled and the time has come:

> The Spirit of the Lord Yahweh is upon me,
> because Yahweh has anointed me
> to bring good news to the poor.
> He has sent me to bind up broken hearts,
> to proclaim liberty to the captives,

> freedom to those languishing in prison;
> to announce the year of Yahweh's favor
> and the day of vengeance of our God;
> to give comfort to all who grieve; . . .
> and give them a garland instead of ashes,
> oil of gladness instead of mourning,
> and festal clothes instead of despair.
>
> (Isa. 61:1–3)

Isaiah reminds them that God has already done much of this for them. They once were slaves in Babylon, and now they have been allowed to return home and rebuild their lives, their temple, and their dreams, to again worship their God Yahweh and become his witnesses before the nations. God wants to do even more for them, making the earth a garden again, with seeds and grasses springing up along with justice and praise. God wants to make Jerusalem and his people a "burning torch" of salvation so her holiness will shine forth like the dawn and give her a new name: "My Delight and the land Espoused. For Yahweh delights in you and will make your land his spouse" (Isa. 62:1–5).

Isaiah has a hard time of it. Again, he tells the old stories, the beginning in Egypt, the stay in the desert, the entry into the promised land; how God stayed with them, carrying them, giving them sanctuary, and, yes, in anger judging them and punishing them by leaving them to a fate of bondage at the hands of other nations. But Yahweh has taken them back again. He is holding out his hands to a rebellious people, letting them find him even though they never went looking for him (Isa. 64–65). God wants to create something new of them and for them and to turn their sorrows into joy. He wants them to turn around. The Hebrew word *shuv* means to repent, to change direction, and to move into something new. Now they can learn from their experience of the exile; they can get past being guilty and, instead, let their faces be radiant so that the nations can see the forgiveness of God in their lives. This is what God dreams for his people:

> I now create new heavens and a new earth, and the former things will not be remembered, nor will they come to mind again.
> Be glad forever and rejoice in what I create; for I create Jerusalem to be a joy and its people to be a delight. I will rejoice over Jerusalem and take delight in my people.

The sound of distress and the voice of weeping will not be heard in it any more.

It will no longer know of dead children or of a grown man not completing his days. He who reaches a hundred years will have died a mere youth, but he who fails to reach a hundred will be considered accursed.

They will build houses and dwell in them; they will plant crops and eat their fruit. No longer will they build houses for others to dwell in; no longer will they plant for others to eat the harvest. (Isa. 65:17–21)

If that isn't enough to give hope to the people, the earlier dream is brought back to bear its weight:

Before they call, I will have answered; while they were yet speaking, I will have heard.

> The wolf and the lamb will feed together,
> the lion will eat straw like the ox....
> They will not destroy nor do any harm
> over all my holy mountain says Yahweh.
> (Isa. 65:24–25)

God has dreams and hopes for his people, even if their hearts are cold and their vision dulled. He is not interested in a temple — his resting place is heaven, and earth is his footstool. What he does want is worship. He wants people who are "meek and contrite of heart, who tremble at my word" (Isa. 66:2). In response to meekness, contrite spirits, and a people who are attentive to his word given through prophets, in commandments, in psalms, and in practice, there will be a new Jerusalem. For the first time, one can sense that the new Jerusalem is not necessarily the city of Jerusalem but any place where God's beloved people dwell with his glory. Once again Yahweh will give birth to something that will belong to all peoples, anyone who seeks God:

> Long before being in labor,
> she has given birth;
> before having birth pangs,
> she has been delivered of a son.

Has anyone ever heard of such a thing? Has anyone seen the like of it? How could a land spring forth in one day? How could a nation be formed in a moment? . . .

Rejoice for Jerusalem and be glad for her; all you who love her. Be glad with her, rejoice with her, all you who were in grief over her, that you may suck of the milk from her comforting breasts, that you may drink deeply from the abundance of her glory.

For this is what Yahweh says: I will send her peace, overflowing like a river; . . . and you will be nursed and carried in her arms and fondled upon her lap.

As a son comforted by his mother, so will I comfort you. At the sight of this, your heart will rejoice; like grass, your bones will flourish. For it shall be known that Yahweh's hand is with his servant, but his fury is upon his enemy. (Isa. 66:7–8, 10–14)

This reality will be offered to all the nations of the earth. It is the mission, the honor, and the responsibility of Israel, of the people of God, "to proclaim my glory among the nations" (66:20).

The book concludes with a vision of the world in which those who adore Yahweh come into the temple and those who refuse are annihilated — a sign of God's invincible justice. It is as though the book ends with an unwritten command: wait, wait on Yahweh's time, and in the meantime "maintain justice, do what is right until the justice of God comes to reign on the earth." This prophet of Third Isaiah is as radical as his forerunners. The transcendence of God is matched by his compassion and care for the outsider and the oppressed. The very integrity of his being demands integrity in worship, fasting, and penance that promotes freely given justice and compassion in imitation of their God. God waits to respond with unbounded fidelity, new life, forgiveness, and a universal mission to show forth his glory to the whole world.

A bright golden thread runs through all sixty-six chapters of Isaiah, telling of the servant who is just, obedient, and faithful even in the face of inhuman cruelty and death. This innocent servant will be the bearer of peace, the gift of Yahweh to his people. This servant will shout by his presence and sing by his compassion of the nearness of God among his beloved children.

Thousands of years later, a man, Martin Luther King Jr., influenced by these songs of truth, of justice, and of God, wrote:

"Truth crushed to earth will rise again."
How long? Not long, because "no lie can live forever."
How long? Not long, because "you shall reap what you sow."
How long? Not long:

Truth forever on the scaffold,
Wrong forever on the throne,
Yet that scaffold sways the future,
And, behind the dim unknown,
Standeth God within the shadow,
Keeping watch over his own.
How long? Not long!
Because the arc of the moral universe is long
But it bends toward justice.[2]

Haggai

Haggai and Zechariah were contemporaries late in the sixth century. Both prophesied around 520 B.C.E., although neither of them mentions the other in his writings. The book of Ezra refers to both prophets as supporting the work of Zerubbabel, the governor of Judah, and Joshua, the high priest, to rebuild the temple in Jerusalem. The people were encouraged to return to Israel by Cyrus, the Persian ruler, whose policy was to allow his conquered peoples to retain their own religions as long as they stayed loyal to him. In fact, those who wanted to go back were aided financially and helped to rebuild their sanctuaries. As noted earlier, only a remnant returned; the largest number opted for a certain known security in Babylon.

The Israelite remnant returned to find that their hated enemies, the Edomites, had moved into southern Judah. There was friction with the Edomites over borders, as well as dissension among those who returned. The land had been ravaged, homes burned, fields gone to seed, groves and vines destroyed. In comparison to the visions of Isaiah and Ezekiel, the reality was grim. Although the temple provided an image, an identity, a gathering place that reconfirmed that they were once again in their own land and free to worship Yahweh, they were slow to rebuild the temple, and they knew that it would not resemble the towering magnificence of Solomon's temple. Haggai was single-minded, pragmatic, and determined to get the people to rebuild the temple as a priority before anything else could happen in their lives.

The people were reluctant, for economic reasons — they were intent on building their own houses first and working on their lands again. As an excuse, they used a fundamentalist interpretation of their period of punishment as prophesied in Jeremiah 29:10. The seventy-year period had not yet been completed; technically they had three years to go. In the day-to-day struggle of starting from scratch, they had lost any sense of urgency about the temple. The foundations had been laid in 538 B.C.E., but then work had stalled and nothing was done for the next fifteen years. Finally, Zerubbabel, Joshua, and Haggai set in motion the rebuilding of the temple and the solidifying of the people back into a community. Haggai began with guilt, self-interest, and reminders of why they were called home:

> So says Yahweh of hosts: This people claim that the time to rebuild the House of Yahweh has not yet come. Well now, hear what I have to say through the prophet Haggai: Is this the time for you to live in your well-built houses while this House is a heap of ruins. Think about your ways: you have sown much but harvested little, you eat and drink but are not satisfied, you clothe yourselves but still feel cold, and the laborer puts the money he earned in a tattered purse. . . . You expected much but it turned out to be very little. I blew away what you had piled up. Why? Because my House lies in ruins while each of you goes running home. Therefore the heavens have withheld rain, and the earth has not produced anything. I sent drought upon the valley and hills, upon the wheat and the vines, the oil and whatever the soil produces, upon people and animals, and upon any work of your hands. (Hag. 1:2–6, 9–11)

It worked. Together with the governor and the high priest, the people began work on the temple. Haggai's prophecies, delivered in the form of oracles over a period of four months, pushed the people toward restoration. This was his sole preoccupation. As they were rebuilding, they realized that the new temple would be nothing like the former temple, which took decades to build. Their structure was referred to as "a very little thing." But the people were encouraged to work, because "I am with you, says Yahweh. Do not be afraid, for my spirit is in your midst" (Hag. 2:3–4). Haggai's God exclaims that he will shake the heavens and earth and fill the temple with his glory and "within a short while" will shake all the nations and bring in the treasures of the whole world. "The renown of this Temple will be greater than before, and in this place I will give peace" (1:9).

Haggai's third oracle regards the uncleanness of the builders and their offerings to Yahweh and their lack of holiness in cultic practices. There is no mention of justice, of integrity, of right dealings with one's neighbor. Everything is in regard to the temple structure and its correctness. This is Haggai's only concern. Perhaps issues of morality and justice will surface after the temple is completed.

The atmosphere is tense with political intrigues, with unrest and revolution brewing in the provinces. In this context, Haggai's pragmatism stands out in stark contrast to the visions of his predecessors. Haggai uses this situation to foretell a bright and rosy future for the governor. Zerubbabel is told by the prophet, echoing Yahweh's words, that when the killing and the overthrow of kings are complete, "On that day I [Yahweh] will take you, Zerubbabel, my servant, the son of Shealtiel, and for me you will be like a ring on my finger with my initials on it. For I have chosen you, says Yahweh of hosts" (2:23). The image of the signet ring is strong: Yahweh will use Zerubbabel to seal officially the work on the temple and his place in the kingdom. Unfortunately, Haggai misreads the future and how God will work in Judah, for Zerubbabel disappears. History swallows him up with no mention of what happened to him. Haggai, however, has laid the base for the next stage of Israel's response to Yahweh through the rebuilt temple — in cult and in worship under the authority of the priests in the temple.

Zechariah

Zechariah began to prophesy just months after Haggai's oracles ended. Most likely he was a priest returning with the exiles. His writings, which consist of eight fantastic visions, were composed over a two-month period. The visions occurred at night, and usually an angel explained them to the prophet, who then recounted them to the people. Zechariah's major concern was repentance, and he reminded the people of how the words and warnings of the past prophets had come true, visiting judgment upon their ancestors: Yahweh "has treated us just as he had determined to do, according to our ways and deeds" (Zech. 1:6).

The first vision is of men on horses who patrol the earth, and the second is of four horns that represent the nations that had abused Israel while they were in bondage. It is time for God's judgment on those who punished Israel so badly. The third vision is of a man with a measuring line; he marks out the boundaries of Jerusalem and pronounces that it will be so expansive that it will be without walls. It is a time for rejoicing because God is coming once again to make his dwelling among them. It is in this vision that Israel is first called "the holy land" (Zech. 2:16).

Zechariah's fourth vision is of the high priest Joshua, clothed in dirty garments, being accused by Satan of impurity. Satan appears as a functionary of the heavenly court rather than an adversary of the human race. Joshua is cleansed, dressed in ritual festive garments, and given a promise: "Listen further . . . : I am going to bring my servant the Branch" (3:8). This is, again, a promise of one who will bring peace and prosperity to Jerusalem.

The next vision is of a lampstand, a bowl, and two olive trees that refer to Joshua and Zerubbabel, who will carry the hopes and the glory of God into the future with the people. This will be done "not by might nor by power, but by my Spirit" (4:6).

The sixth vision depicts a huge scroll flying through the air, and on it are listed all the evildoers, those who lie, swear falsely, and steal and what will happen to them! The scroll is much like a public confession that will lodge in the sinner's own house to convict him. The seventh vision is of a bushel basket that contains the guilt of the people in the form of a woman. Two other winged women lift it and carry it off to Babylon. The last vision is of four horses: red, white, dappled, and black, who with their four chariots set off to patrol the earth in all directions and bring back those scattered.

The remaining chapters of the first part of Zechariah reiterate the basics of morality: "Render true judgment, be kind and merciful to each other. Do not oppress the widow or the orphan, the alien or the poor, do not plot evil in your heart against another" (7:8). Yet the people are described as making their hearts as hard as diamonds so as not to hear the law or the words God spoke to them through the earlier prophets.

But this generation of Israelites must be different. They have been brought back by Yahweh, and they have laid the foundation stone of the new temple. God is determined to deal kindly with his people. He tells them: "I am sowing peace. The vine will give its fruit, the earth its produce, the heavens its dew, and to the remnant of this people I will give all these things" (8:12). In the tradition of Micah, he tells them what they need to do in one line: "This is what you must do: Speak the truth to one another; let those who judge give peace through honest sentences and do not plot evil in your heart against one another" (8:16). This one line lays the base for much that is treasured in Judaism:

> Rabbi Simeon ben Gamaliel (mid-second century C.E.) had a favorite saying: The world is established on three things: justice, truth and peace. All three, he noted, were found in a line in Zechariah 8:16: "Speak the truth to one another, render in your gates judgments that are true and make for peace." Rabbi Simeon then went on to say "The three are, in fact, one. For when justice is exercised, truth is attained, and peace is achieved." (*Pesikta de Rav Kahana, Piska* 19.6; see also *Mishna Avot* 1.18)[3]

If the children of Israel do this, they will behold miracles in the future: "Yahweh, the God of hosts assures you. 'In those days ten men of different languages spoken in various lands, will take hold of a Jew by the hem of his garment and say: We, too, want to go with you for we have heard that God is with you' " (8:23).

The writings attributed to Zechariah end here. Chapters 9 through 14 are attributed to a number of others who may have written perhaps even a hundred years later. One portion, however, reveals a major revelation into the mystery of the Messiah, the king who will come to Jerusalem and to the world. It is easily recognized because it is the reference behind Jesus' entrance into Jerusalem before his death:

> Rejoice, greatly, daughter of Zion!
> Shout for joy, daughter of Jerusalem!
> For your king is coming, just and victorious,
> humble and riding on a donkey,
> on a colt, the foal of a donkey.
> No more chariots in Ephraim,
> no more horses in Jerusalem,

for he will do away with them.
The warrior's bow shall be broken when he dictates peace to
the nations.
He will reign from sea to sea
and from the River to the ends of the earth. (Zech. 9:9–10)

This is a startling image. Although donkeys were regularly used for royalty, this is in stark contrast to the usual Mideastern model of power based on war horses, chariots, and battle gear. The new Jerusalem, the new temple, the new people will follow the one who "dictates peace to the nations" and reigns "from sea to sea."

The remainder of the images, which are scattered, deal with the purification of the nation of Judah, of other nations, and of the messianic one who will cease hostilities and inaugurate a season of peace. These later writings came at a time when there had been no king in Israel for two hundred years, yet hope still lived that the monarchy would be restored, and that restoration would depend on a remnant of the poor and lowly who were faithful. There would be a cosmic battle, slaughter, and Yahweh would dawn over Israel once again. There would be leaders who would be dependable, described as a cornerstone, a tent peg, and a battle bow (10:4–5). Once again there would be an ingathering of all the nations, a return so vast that the first exodus would pale in comparison.

Chapters 11 and 13 include sayings that have become associated with the person of Jesus as the Suffering Servant, stricken and rejected, paid off with thirty pieces of silver. While Christians have interpreted this as a reference to Judas, the rabbis interpreted it to mean that when the Messiah comes he will dictate thirty principles or precepts that will lay the foundation for the new kingdom. Chapter 13 contains intimations of doom, the end of prophets and prophecy (13:2–6). The demise of the prophets here refers to false prophets, those who lie and do not speak in Yahweh's name. It is worth noting that this historical period ushered in a time when the priests were the ruling authority in Israel in lieu of kings or prophets.

In fact Haggai, Zechariah, and Malachi signal the end of prophecy in the Jewish canon. They are seen as the final voices in rabbinic thought. With their deaths, prophecy as we have known it is over. The tradition teaches that there were many prophets, some unknown and lost to history, others unnamed and unheeded (1 Sam. 19:20; 2 Kings

2:3; Jer. 29:1). It is believed that in the days that are coming God will "resurrect them and will publish their prophecies" (*Midrash Song of Songs Rabbah* 4.11.1).[4] All those who have spoken or written in the Lord's name will be associated with the glory of God and will know him on that day when God comes forth from his hiding place and claims all of creation as his own.

Malachi

No one is sure who Malachi actually was. His name comes from the Hebrew word *mal'ak,* which means messenger or angel or one sent on an errand. His name thus means "my messenger." He was a postexilic prophet who preached around 465–460 B.C.E. The new temple had been completed for more than fifty years. The nation of Israel was still in a pitiful state, economically depressed, scattered, with a people who were selfish and utterly disheartened. They had expected so much from the dreams and visions of their ancestors, and they had inherited a struggle to survive and a temple that was a faint shadow of past glories.

Malachi's oracles have the structure of a dialogue between the prophet and the people. The prophet announces God's word and the people respond, usually with a question. Then God's concluding argument or judgment is rendered. There seems to be a low level of hostility, as though members of the assembly, priests, elders, and others are testing the prophet. Yet, clearly, Malachi must have had some stature in the community as a prophet of Yahweh.

He is faced, as all the prophets were, with combating the abuses that have developed over time. Many of the abuses are connected to temple worship and to the practice of marrying foreign women. Foreign marriages are seen as diluting the worship of Yahweh because the foreigners engage in religious fertility rites with other gods. Malachi also addresses the lack of respect among the priests, who seem to be more interested in their personal gain than in the honor and glory of the Lord of Hosts. The undercurrent is always the same: injustice, insensitivity to the poor among them, and giving second-rate offerings to God.

No matter what Malachi speaks in the name of Yahweh, the people question his words with a certain tone of derision. The book opens with a direct statement of the love of Yahweh for his people:

An oracle. These are the words that Yahweh directed to Israel through Malachi.

When Yahweh says, "I love you," you reply, "How do you show that love?" So Yahweh asks you, "Was Esau not Jacob's brother? Yet I loved Jacob and hated Esau. See how I left his mountains desolate and abandoned his land to the jackals of the desert. If Edom decides to rebuild its ruins, after having been destroyed, Yahweh of hosts says: They may rebuild, but I will demolish.... You will see this with your own eyes, then you will exclaim: The power of Yahweh goes beyond the borders of Israel." (Mal. 1:1–5)

The country is still besieged by the Edomites, who are trying to hold on to land appropriated during the exile. As usual, the complaints of the people begin with what others are doing to them. The debates have the tone of adolescents arguing with a very patient parent. Next to complain are the priests, who act with disdain toward God. God asks them: "Now if I am a father, where is the honor due to me? If I am your master, where is your respect for me?" (Mal. 1:6). The priests respond: "How have we despised your name?" It's as if they are saying, "Prove it, make a list, be specific." Of course the prophet obliges. The list includes offerings of animals that are blind, lame, or stolen and food they wouldn't feed to any official. None of them takes his ministry seriously, and the old language of insult comes to the fore:

I will curse you for none of you takes your ministry seriously. Right now, I am going to break your arm, throw dung in your face, the very dung of your animals, and sweep you away with them. And you will realize that it was I who threatened to put an end to my covenant with Levi, your ancestor, says Yahweh.

My covenant with him spoke of life, and peace, and I gave him these; it also spoke of respect and he respected me and reverenced my Name. His mouth taught true doctrine and nothing evil came from his lips; he walked in accord with me, being peaceful and upright, and brought back many people from their wickedness. The lips of the priest speak of knowledge and the Law must be found in his mouth, since he is the messenger of Yahweh of hosts.

> But you, says Yahweh of hosts, have strayed from my way,
> and moreover caused many to stumble because of your teaching.
> You have broken my covenant with Levi. (Mal. 2:3–8)

The priests now rule in lieu of kings, and, as the abiding authority in the land, they will take the brunt of the ire of God and the prophet. The old saying "familiarity breeds contempt" seems to apply to what has happened with the priests and their temple duties. Malachi is ruthless in condemning the priests for their contemptible service that is harming the people's faith. Part of this betrayal of the covenant belongs to those in the nation who have married foreigners. Surprisingly, Malachi's description of marriage is startlingly beautiful and steeped in covenant imagery that develops a theology of marriage beyond any relationship of financial or familial need. In fact, breaking of a covenant with one's wife is seen as equivalent to breaking covenant with God and profaning the temple. Relationship and worship are braided together in the same image:

> It is because Yahweh has seen how you dealt with your first wife, the wife of your youth. You betrayed her although she was your companion with whom you made a covenant. Has God not made a single being and given him breath? And what does he seek but a family given by God? Do not betray, then, the wife of your youth.
>
> I hate divorce, says Yahweh, the God of Israel, and those who are actually covering their violence. Be very careful, and do not betray. (Mal. 2:14b–16)

The words reveal by tone that these people know exactly what they are doing. They seem to taunt God, saying: "Where is the God who does justice?" What follows has a tone of immediacy — of someone coming with power, with fury, to purify and clear the way of debris and blockage. The messenger will make sure that the land and its inhabitants once again do know the God who does justice:

> Now I am sending my messenger ahead of me to clear the way; then suddenly the Lord for whom you long will enter the sanctuary. The envoy of the covenant which you so greatly desire already comes, says Yahweh of hosts. Who can bear the day of his coming and remain standing when he appears? For he will be like fire in the foundry and like the lye used for bleaching.

> He will be as a refiner or a fuller. He will purify the sons of
> Levi and refine them like gold and silver. . . .
> When I come to you to do justice I shall demand the immedi-
> ate punishment of the sorcerers and the adulterers, of those who
> swear false oaths, who oppress the wage-earner, the widow and
> the orphan, who do not respect the rights of the foreigner. They
> do all this and have no fear of me, says Yahweh. (Mal. 3:1–3a, 5)

Once again Malachi is dealing with a stiff-necked and belligerent
people, who are intent on continuing what they are doing and defending their position that there is no good reason to obey God because
there is no benefit for them in it. "Why do we have to return? . . . Those
who do evil succeed in everything; though they provoke God, they
remain unharmed" (Mal. 3:7, 18).

Their bitterness is rooted in their observation of history, in seeing the practices of even the priests and their neighbors, and so they
too succumb to doing evil. The age-old persistent question is stated
bluntly: Why do the evil prosper and those who obey God appear
to languish? Malachi's answer posits exactly where God stands and
where those who trust him must stand. They must stand and believe
and wait for "that day to come":

> Yahweh listened and heard what they said. He ordered at once
> that the names of those who respect him and reverence his Name
> be written in a record.
> And he declared, "They will be mine on the day I have al-
> ready set. Then I shall care for them as a father cares for his
> obedient son. And you will see the different fates of the good
> and the bad, those who obey God and those who disobey him.
> (Mal. 3:16–17)

The description of "the day I have already set" surges into first-century
Palestine. The rest of the book has been bound by Christians to the
person of John the Baptizer, the prophet, the forerunner and the one
called from his mother's womb:

> The day already comes, flaming as a furnace. On that day all the
> proud and evildoers will be burned like straw in the fire. They
> will be left without branches or roots. On the other hand the sun
> of justice will shine upon you who respect my Name and bring
> health in its rays. (Mal. 4:19–20a)

The book of Malachi is the last of the minor prophets in the Christian Bible, and so its last lines are a bridge to the books of the testament of Jesus. The massive figure of *the* prophet of Israel's liberation and law, Moses, and the ancient figure of Elijah, who disappeared into the heavens, once again leap off the page and into the present for those who can hear. The books of prophecy end fittingly with a strong warning and a promise of hope to come:

> Remember the law of my servant Moses, the laws and ordinances I gave him at Mount Horeb for the whole of Israel. I am going to send you the prophet Elijah before the day of Yahweh comes, for it will be a great and terrible day. He will reconcile parents with their children, and the children with their parents, so that I may not have to curse this land when I come. (Mal. 4:22–24)

These last lines, which appear to have been added later, serve as connective tissue between the law and the prophets. The pairing of Moses and Elijah at the end of these books argues that all the words of the prophets are to be seen as the fleshing out of the Torah given to Moses and the people at the beginning of God's revelation and covenant. It is a reminder to the people that God's election, God's love, and God's dwelling with Israel are all of a piece. There is a wholeness and integrity to Israel's history when remembered in light of the event that birthed and formed them in the beginning: the exodus out of bondage and oppression and toward freedom and justice. They are still held in the grasp of Yahweh, who fervently hopes that his glory will shine through them into the whole of creation.

Contemporary Issues

Over time the focus of the prophets has shifted away from kingship in Israel to rest squarely upon the temple as the place of worship in the land of Israel. Hope now lies in the coming of one who will be a source of universal peace, who will bring justice for all, and who will dwell first with the poor and the downtrodden of the land. He will cause the sun to bless their faces, and fidelity will reign as he brings his glory home to his people. That people will be a remnant characterized by meekness, humility, obedience, and peacefulness. This land without borders will even welcome foreigners.

The context of the prophets' messages brings to mind two contemporary situations in the Middle East that cry out for justice. When the first temple was destroyed, the rebuilt temple was a mere shadow of the former glory. That second temple, in turn, was destroyed by the Romans in 70 C.E., and what remains is a small portion of its western wall. In more recent times, it has been and still is the site of horrific clashes of violence and the focus of a narrow nationalism that is no longer based on religious worship (except for a small minority in Israel) but on Zionism, the right of Israel to exist as a political state created by the Allied nations after World War II. The deeding of the land of Palestine to the Jewish community after the Holocaust ignored the millions of Palestinians — Arab, Muslim, and Christian peoples — who had lived there for many generations. Throughout history, but especially in the last fifty-some years of Israel's occupation of Palestine, the place the prophets claimed for the residence of the glory of God has been marked primarily by blood-letting, slaughter, hate, and struggles for dominance. Even as we enter the twenty-first century, two issues — the fate of Jerusalem and the fate of the Palestinian refugees — seem to defy resolution.

The dispossession process of moving Palestinians from their land in 1948 and 1949 was equivalent to the forced march into exile of the Israelite nation that took place under the Babylonian forces. Also similar was the fact that many of those forced to flee their homes and possessions thought that it would only be a matter of days before they would be allowed to return. Since 1950, the hundreds of thousands of refugees from the dispossession process and later from the 1967 war have been the only large group of refugees not handled by the U.N. High Commission for Refugees. For half a century they have lived in ever-deteriorating and ever-worsening conditions, without even the basic necessities of water, shelter, jobs, or human dignity. People, some now elderly, in the camps of Lebanon, Syria, the West Bank, and Gaza still hold in their pockets the keys to their long-abandoned houses. They are despairing of ever returning or being compensated for their massive losses or of receiving an apology from the world community for their shoddy treatment.

The hope and the demand for justice on the part of all these people are expressed in one phrase: the right of return (U.N. Declaration #194) — whether or not they ever do decide to or are actually able to return. Like the ancient peoples of Israel, these people also have the right to return, to go home to the land of their ancestors and birth. If not, they should be compensated in some way for the distress of these last decades and for being forced to live in camps all these years. As reported:

> As more than one refugee told us, if Jews are now getting cash payments for their losses and their slave labor in World War II, why should Palestinians not be compensated in similar fashion?...
>
> When the price for Israeli relocation of settlers down from the Golan Heights may be $15 billion or more from the U.S. government, how can the long-standing claims of Palestinians be ignored? The political complexity of reaching a suitable plan for compensation under U.N. #194 will be exceeded only by the blunt impossibility of securing adequate funding to afford the payments that should, in law and justice, be made.[5]

Equally thorny is the question of the city of Jerusalem and its boundaries. Under a strict interpretation, the "city" refers to the temple environs and the Old City of history. But since the 1967 war, Israel has been moving the boundaries out by annexing Arab villages and Palestinian lands so that now the "city" boundaries encompass a land area more than one hundred times its size in 1967. Recent visits make it apparent that there is a concentrated effort to destroy any remaining landmarks or signs of Palestinian occupancy and a rush to redesign and build in such a way that there is no space for the Palestinians. While tourists are still allowed free access generally to the city, military checkpoints throughout the city deny that same access to Palestinians living on the West Bank. The same rule holds true for places of worship: outsiders are allowed into all places of worship, but not local non-Israelis — even if they have lived there all their lives.

Religiously, the basis for a "shared Jerusalem" open to peoples of all faiths, especially Islam, Eastern and Western Christianity, and Judaism is found throughout the Hebrew Testament and in all the books of the prophets. It is not just to exclude the original residents who were forced out militarily either in the first displacement of 1948 and 1949 or again in 1967. Jerusalem and all the peoples of the world must open their ears to the words of the ancient prophets that cried "Peace," that cried "Glory," and that cried out for the protection and defense of the refugee, the poor, the oppressed, and neighbors and foreigners treated unjustly in the land. Even before the earlier testament of ancient Israel ends, the true desecration of the temple is found in what human beings who claim to be chosen by Yahweh do to one another.

In a remarkable book on the message of the prophet Haggai, Marc Girard gives a list, pages long, of contemporary "temples" that demand rebuilding. His list culminates in the very earth itself, lying in ruins at the end of the twentieth century. These temples have been "created in the image and likeness" of the Holy One, Yahweh of hosts (Gen. 1:26). They form a litany of those beloved of God, precious in his sight in the writings of the prophets: refugees; the poor — the majority of human beings on the earth condemned to subhuman living conditions by the unfair distribution of resources and finances; children who are slave laborers or are driven into being children soldiers; children who are drugged, kidnapped, and sold into prostitution; political prisoners of conscience; all those caught in long-standing wars of racism, nationalism, and ethic cleansing; whole peoples caught, because of political decisions, with no rights, no land, no homes or livelihoods; widows, orphans, and the old dying from starvation and destruction of water and soil; and those who are the victims of biological and nuclear warfare between marauding nations who care nothing for either their soldiers or civilians.[6]

The temple in Jerusalem and the city itself are the seeds of hope for future peace with abiding justice and harmony between all peoples, even the wild creatures of the earth and the storm clouds, rains, and planets that seek to be in communion with the glory of God. Before debating and negotiating the treacherous roads of politics and nationalism, we must remember the Holy One's intent for this temple, this city, this land, and all that was created to show forth the goodness of God.

A short piece of poetry in the tradition of the prophets captures this well:

> Some things lead into the realm beyond words...
> it is like that small mirror in fairy tales:
> you glance in it and what you see is not yourself;
> for an instant you glimpse the Inaccessible...
> and the soul cries out for it.[7]

TEN

Nahum, Habakkuk, Obadiah, Jonah, Nehemiah, Ezra, Daniel, Joel

The Prophets Not Included

For a number of reasons, including that of length, several minor prophets are deliberately not included here. Because they are traditionally included among the prophets in Christian Bibles, it seems fitting to include some short comments about their messages or their times.

Nahum

Nahum is short but not sweet. A biblical scholar, Samuel Sandmel, has described Nahum's work as "a hymn of hate," a judgment that may have been justified by the history of his time — the turmoil of the seventh century B.C.E. Basically, the entire book is an oracle against Nineveh, the seat of Assyrian power, which had enslaved Israel and many others nations. The captives now shared only one thing: hate.

One long verse is directed toward Judah: "See, there on the mountains, the feet of one who brings good news, one who proclaims peace" (2:1). The wicked have been destroyed at last, and Yahweh can now restore Jacob's former magnificence and splendor. The prophet's vehemence slides far too easily into gloating nationalism. Understandably, the nation of Israel was far from practicing tolerance or forgiveness in regard to their enemies, yet today the bile-filled words seem incendiary. Perhaps words from another prophet can serve as a counterbalance:

But there is something that I must say to my people who stand on the warm threshold which leads to the palace of justice. In the process of gaining our rightful place we must not be guilty of wrongful deeds. Let us not seek to satisfy our thirst for freedom by drinking from the cup of bitterness and hatred. We must forever conduct our struggle on the high plane of dignity and discipline. We must not allow our creative protest to degenerate into physical violence. Again and again we must rise to the majestic heights of meeting physical force with soul force.[1]

Habakkuk

Habakkuk appeared just as Nebuchadnezzar rose in power and set in motion the historical events that would lead to the destruction of the temple and the bitter exile of Israel. His opening cry sets the tone for the three short chapters. His question is universal and is uttered by everyone who has any sensitivity to the suffering of the world and the power of evil to destroy and dishearten: "Yahweh, how long will I cry for help while you pay no attention to me? I denounce the oppression and you do not save. Why do you make me see injustice? Are you pleased to look on tyranny? All I see is outrage, violence and quarrels" (Hab. 1:2b–3).

In light of the depth of agony and the breadth of horror, the answers given by Yahweh seem almost simplistic, unless you stake your life on the existence of Yahweh and you are steadfastly committed to faithfulness as a single-hearted way of living. Yahweh's response is in the form of a vision that Habakkuk is told to inscribe on tablets so that all can see it, confident that the vision will come true in its time. The word of the Lord will not fail. Overriding any of the specifics, the answer stands alone: "But Yahweh lives in his holy Temple: let the whole earth be silent before him!" (2:20). God is God, and God's ways, to echo Isaiah, are not like ours at all; neither is God's time of judgment dependent on our insistence. Justice will be done, and the prophet is assured that in the meantime, "the upright ... will live by his faithfulness" (2:4b).

The prophet responds with a prayer to be sung to the tune of a dirge. At the end of the prayer/song is a curious note to the choirmaster of the temple to accompany it with stringed instruments, thus emphasizing all the power and might of the past that God has shown to Israel.

Habakkuk pleads to Yahweh, "in your wrath even, remember mercy" (3:2b). The prophet bends humbly before the majesty, the otherness, and the mystery of the God he serves. He concludes with an unqualified acknowledgment of God's goodness and his own trust that God will take note of his servants, no matter what happens around them. It is a prayer worth learning by heart:

> For though the fig trees blossom not,
> nor grapes be on the vines,
> though the olive crop fail
> and the fields produce no food,
> though the flock be lost from the fold,
> and the herd be gone from the stalls,
> yet in Yahweh will I rejoice,
> in God my savior will I exult.
> My Lord Yahweh is my stronghold;
> he makes my feet as fleeting as the hinds;
> he steadies my steps upon the heights.
>
> (Hab. 3:17–19)

Obadiah

Obadiah, the most terse of the prophets — with only twenty-one lines in all — didn't fare well, even with the Jewish rabbis because like Nahum it is mostly a diatribe against Edom, the longtime enemies of Israel. Obadiah's prophesy is a terrible vision of what Yahweh will do to the Edomites because of how they have contributed to the suffering of the exiles and acted in collusion with Babylon. His anger bleeds into curses against other nations and a defiant announcement that one day "deliverers will ascend Mount Zion to rule over the mountains of Esau [Edom], — then Yahweh will reign" (21). The text is primarily a stinging hope for destruction of Israel's enemies and for revenge in the name of God.

Jonah

The story of the reluctant prophet to the great city of Nineveh is very familiar. It has even been the subject of children's books, with the tale told from the vantage point of the whale and the poor shriveled-up plant that gave Jonah respite from the heat. It is almost comical if we forget Jonah's mean-spiritedness, his refusal to obey, and his childish pouting when his enemies repent and God's mercy is accorded to them. He does not want the city to repent — so he can gloat over its demise and watch while Yahweh inflicts punishment on its vile pagans. At the same time, the story is glorious because it reveals unerringly a universal God of mercy and justice and because it pokes holes in the self-righteousness of those who think themselves religious while blaming others for the evil in the world and taking pleasure in their suffering.

If the tale were told today, it might well be directed at great nations like China and the United States. Jonah would be sent off to preach to the largest nation in the world, notorious for its persecution of those who seek to practice their religion and its abuse of human rights. Jonah, an American Christian prophet, would be annoyed when every living being — from the highest officials of the government down to the millions of chickens and goats, even panda bears and monkeys — repented of their evil ways and began to practice protecting and encouraging the practice of all religions, free speech, political options, and personal freedoms! Jonah and the American Christians, displeased and indignant at this turn of events, might then whine as Jonah had: "I knew that you are a gracious and merciful God, slow to anger and full of love, and you relent from imposing terrible punishment" (4:2).

Jonah was so angry at Yahweh's mercy that he wanted to die, knowing that the turn of events would ruin his credibility at home! He was even angry when the plant that was sheltering him died. For this, Yahweh rebuked him, expressing his concern for the people of Nineveh: "Nineveh has more than a hundred and twenty thousand people who cannot distinguish right from left. . . . Should I not be concerned for such a great city?" (4:11). This morality tale ends with that question, which is meant to be taken to heart. Should not we, a nation of hundreds of millions who "cannot distinguish right from left," also learn mercy and graciousness, become slow to anger and full of love, and relent from imposing harsh penalties in our self-justification?

What if the Chinese sent to us a Buddhist prophet who lamented our insistence on the right to manufacture and keep on "ready-alert status" millions of nuclear weapons, defense missile systems, radioactive and depleted uranium bullets, and land mines? What if the prophet declared that our weapons and our covert low-intensity war policies at home and around the world were destroying any possibility of world harmony and that within forty days we would all be destroyed? Suddenly Jonah's position isn't so laughable but is, rather, worthy of a serious call to examine our national conscience.

Nehemiah and Ezra

The accounts of the "minor" prophets Nehemiah and Ezra are part of the historical section of the Christian Bible, immediately following 1 and 2 Chronicles. Present during the first return of the exiles, around 539 to 400 B.C.E., they are memorable because of their call for a return to holiness and the practices of justice outlined in the book of Deuteronomy. Both were deeply concerned with the moral life of Israel.

Both had positions of some standing: Ezra was a scribal priest and Nehemiah was cupbearer to the Persian king (an extremely important though dangerous position, as poisoning was a common method of assassination). As the Israelites returned to Judah, both were given government appointments in Judah, with Nehemiah serving as governor.

Ezra was concerned with the laws of marriage and sacrifice and with racial and religious purity at a time when Israel was sorely tempted to become absorbed into Babylonian culture and religion. His story is found in both his own account, the book of Ezra, and in Nehemiah. Ezra is remembered primarily for his appearance in the book of Nehemiah, where he assembles the people "in the square before the Water Gate and they ask Ezra to bring the Book of the Law of Moses, which Yahweh had given to Israel.... [He read it aloud] from early morning until midday" (8:1b-ea). The reading continued unabated for seven days and culminated in the celebration of the feast of Sukkoth, which commemorates the giving of the law to Moses. Because of this first public reading, Ezra is considered the father of Judaism and is thought to be the final editor of the Torah, the first five books of Moses.

Nehemiah is remarkable for a number of reasons. First, he was not technically called by Yahweh but considered himself called. As the notes in the Christian Community Bible explain, he is the epitome of any believer deeply moved by the suffering of people because of historical events: "He is an example of all those who are able to recognize the voice of the Lord through events and who do not wait for a special call to get to work."[2] He prayed passionately not only for himself but for all the "sins of the children of Israel" (1:6) and begged God to listen and to help him as he sought to honor God's name.

Then Nehemiah took the initiative, asking the Persian king to give him letters so that he might travel back to Jerusalem. Once there he inspected the walls of the city, which were in ruins, and the burned gates. He recounted to the returnees how God was with him, even using the king in Babylon to help. He encouraged them to join him in the work of rebuilding, even though he encountered opposition, derision, and accusations of treason. Rebuilding the walls was only the outward symbol of what his real work was: rebuilding the moral and ethical life of the ruined people. The common people went to him with their complaints about the economic realities of poverty and the practices that were creating a permanent underclass in the society. They spoke of unpayable debts, children and wives who were being sold into slavery, and the real horror that these situations were not caused by outsiders, but by Jews themselves. Nehemiah reproached them: "Why do you not have compassion on your brothers?" (5:8).

Nehemiah's actions go beyond the usual call of a prophet. Without referring to the Deuteronomic code or the call to Sabbath justice or the Jubilee Year, he sets in motion reforms by using his own money and food and those of his neighbors to be a catalyst for the whole nation. Along with Nehemiah, they respond by canceling and writing off each other's debts:

> "What you do is not good. Should you not live in obedience to our God lest we be put to shame by our pagan enemies? My brothers, my relatives and I have also lent money and wheat. Now then, let us forget everything they owe us, returning to them at once their fields, vineyards, and olive groves, and canceling their debts in money, wheat, wine and oil." They answered me, "We will return these and demand nothing from them. We will do as you have said." (Neh. 5:9b–12)

This is the Holiness Code of the Torah, and Nehemiah is working single-handedly to keep it alive as a practice and not just as a theoretical ideal. Above all, Nehemiah is advocating an ethic of resistance to greed and selfishness and to any systemic practice that can result in the creation of an underclass of the poor within the community. Before the priests and people he shakes out his mantle in a prophetic gesture, saying: "So may God shake out of this house and his inheritance all who do not fulfill this word, and may he be so shaken that nothing is left of him" (5:13). The entire assembly shouts "Amen!" and praises Yahweh.

Even though King Artaxerxes had appointed him governor of Judah and he and his household and servants work untiringly on the walls over the next twelve years, he is maligned, threatened, set up, denounced to the king, and slandered in letters — all in an attempt to discourage him from the work. Finally, the walls are up, the gates finished, and the doors in place. It seems to be at this point that Ezra arrives to read the law aloud and to proclaim the fulfillment of the people's obedience.

This scene harks back to the scene in Deuteronomy 29 when Moses summoned the people before entering the promised land, telling them the story of exodus and challenging them to live the covenant God has made with them in the land they are about to enter, calling on them to choose life for themselves and their descendants. The connections are intentional: "The secret things belong to Yahweh, our God, but what he made known to us belongs to us and our children forever. So we have to put into practice all the provisions of this Law!" (Deut. 29:28).

Today, the same platform of action is put before us in the call to cancel the debts of the fifty poorest nations of the world. The choice is more a religious matter than an economic or social issue. This demand for economic justice can be found not just in Jewish law and Christian texts but also in writings from many other religions. We are called to take heed and to practice what is God's demand among all peoples. Avvaijay, a Tamil sage who attacked social ills through poetry in the first century c.e., wrote:

> There are only no castes but two if you want me to tell,
> One, the good men who help the poor in distress,
> The other, that will not so help.

Daniel

The book of Daniel, while certainly the writing of a prophet, also belongs to the genre of literature termed "apocalyptic." This is the form of biblical writing that offers long-range predictions of what will come to pass in the "end times," times of upheaval, of political, moral, and economic collapse, and even of the destruction of the world, or the world as the authors knew it. The book of Daniel, which was probably written around the time of the Maccabees (167–164 B.C.E.), tells of the time of the exile in Babylon, a time of testing that will one day become the basis of judgment and vindication for those who were faithful to Yahweh.

The book of Daniel is similar to only one other book in the Bible — the book of Revelation, which draws heavily upon Daniel for symbols, terminology, and intent. Because of the amount and density of material in the book and its complex relation to Christian theology, as well as questions of its dating and genre, there is not space here to deal justly with it. However, because of recent interest in apocalyptic literature, there are a number of excellent books on Daniel to recommend. Perhaps the best, and most controversial, would be Daniel Berrigan's *Daniel: Under the Siege of the Divine.*[3]

Joel

And so we come to the last of the "minor prophets," Joel, who probably prophesied around 400 to 350 B.C.E. The people have returned home; the temple has been rebuilt; the priests are in authority; and there is, relatively speaking, political and religious peace. The people are very involved liturgically in the rites of the temple, in sacrifice, and in listening to the law — we know this because when Joel calls for a fast, everyone responds. And then the people are plagued with locusts that eat the crops, the fig trees, the vines, unlike anything the people have seen before or heard of in the past. The plague is seen as akin to the plague upon the Egyptians when pharaoh would not allow the people to go and worship their God.

Joel announces that this is the prelude to the dreaded and feared "day of the Lord," "a day of gloom and darkness, a day of clouds and blackness" (2:1b). The only way to respond is with a fast that turns the people's hearts, their feet, and their deeds toward Yahweh. The famous lines "Rend your heart, not your garment. Return to Yahweh, your God — gracious and compassionate," have become the rousing theme of Lent, the springtime of the human soul. And the call to fast follows in chapter 2, encouraging the people to shift their focus as a group toward the face of God, so that perhaps "God will relent once more and spare some part of the harvest from which we may bring sacred offerings to Yahweh" (2:14). If they do not have food, they will have no offerings to the Lord.

The call to the people to rend their hearts, to fast, and to think of nothing but God is followed by a call to exalt and rejoice, for Yahweh will act magnificently, providing them with food, rousting their enemies, and giving them years that compensate for the ones of drought, locusts, and poor crops (Joel 2:18–27). And then Yahweh will gift his people again — this time with his own Spirit that will be poured out on all, from the youngest to the elders. This outpouring is for Jews only, to be followed by a battle that is universal, where Yahweh stands for the cause of Israel and reverses the promise of Isaiah: "Proclaim the holy war, call the warriors, let men of war advance! Hammer your plowshares into swords, your sickles into spears! Let the weak say: I am a warrior! And the meek: I too will fight! . . . and Yahweh will announce: 'Jerusalem will be a holy place, and foreigners will never pass through there again.' Israel will rise and the other nations will fall" (4:1–19).

Again the prophet is caught up in the spirit of nationalism. Even the return to the Lord begins with the blast of the *shofar,* the ram's horn which also signaled the advance of the army (Joel 2:15). The people do battle to rid the land of the locusts, and one day the land will also be rid of foreigners, and the people will have the land to themselves — it "will drip wine and the hills will flow with milk" (4:18). The meaning of history is read through narrow nationalistic pride and independence as much as through the word of Yahweh calling them to righteous worship.

There is ostensibly no reference to justice, to the care of the poor, to righteous living — instead righteousness is seen in the narrow focus of liturgical practice, fasting, and sacrifice. This became the bane of the prophet's message. Just as the kings had deviated from the law, so too the priests would slide away and lead the people with them.

The book of Joel, probably more than any other Old Testament book, reveals how Christians have appropriated selected texts — in this case, the call to fast used for Ash Wednesday and the announcement that there would be an outpouring of the Spirit of God. Joel has had a strong impact on the book of Revelation as well. But Christians go considerably further in their interpretation of Joel, adapting its meaning in a way never intended by its author. The book, however,

without overlays of later interpretation, is best seen as a heavily nationalistic and vengeance-minded text written to fill a need at a certain
stage of Jewish history. Its message lacks the fullness of the developed
thought of Isaiah, Jeremiah, and Ezekiel. In these prophets, not only
shall Israel and its faithful remnant be gathered from the nations where
they were scattered but Jerusalem will become a signal for all nations
and all peoples who seek God with open hearts.

The word for "spirit" in Joel 3:1 is the same word (*ru-ach*) used in
the account of Moses, and the word for "prophecy" (from the root letters *Nun-Bet-Aleph*) is the same. It is easy to see how this text became
a source text for the coming of the Spirit in Acts and a foundation for
the universal experience of the gifts of the Spirit, especially prophecy,
in Christian tradition. But Christian tradition uses only the first two
verses of Joel 3, because the context in the next two verses is a warning of "wonders in the heavens, and on the earth blood and fire and
columns of smoke. The sun will darken and the moon turn to blood at
the approach of the great and dreadful day of God. Then all who call
upon the name of Yahweh will be saved" (3:3–5). The coming of the
Spirit upon the people of Yahweh is bound to the coming of that day
of judgment and vindication.

The concept of the Spirit in Christianity develops quantitatively,
exponentially, because of the Spirit's intimate connection to the Father
and to Jesus the Christ in the Trinity. What follows is a reference to
what this Spirit is and how it works from the writings of Hildegard of
Bingen in the Middle Ages, summed up by Elizabeth Johnson:

> The Spirit is life, movement, color, radiance, restorative stillness
> in the din. She pours the juice of contrition into hardened hearts.
> Her power makes dry twigs and withered souls green again with
> the juice of life. She purifies, absolves, strengthens, heals, gath-
> ers the perplexed, seeks the lost. She plays the music in the soul,
> being herself the melody of praise and joy. She awakens mighty
> hope, blowing everywhere the winds of renewal in creation.[4]

The dynamic of the divine Spirit not only has moved out indiscriminately among all peoples of the world but has saturated the entire
universe. The Spirit of God is, as it were, loose everywhere, waiting
and attentive to anyone who seeks its presence and power. Reinterpre-
tation of the writings of the Earlier Testament takes quantum leaps in
Christian theology.[5]

❧ ELEVEN ❧

Contemporary Prophets

"Would That All Yahweh's People Were Prophets!"
(Numbers 11:29)

A Jewish Midrash says that when God spoke and revealed himself on Sinai there was "a miracle of God's word" and that each person who has ever lived or will live heard that voice as it echoed through the universe. But each heard it in the way they could absorb it and integrate it into their lives and world. In his book *The Healer of Shattered Hearts,* David Wolpe invites us to "imagine a voice and message as diverse as humanity." He goes on to share some of the rich nuances of the word:

> To the zealous, God fashioned each utterance like a resolute call, in the clipped and urgent tones of command. To the reflective, God calmed His voice, and in a softer, slower cadence urged words of thoughtful devotion. For those who understood revelation with their minds, God presented an intricate puzzle, teeming with intriguing variations and possibilities. For those who sought to understand with their hearts, God spoke words of passion, presenting revelation not as insight but as intensity. To some, God's voice was shattering, to others, soothing. To some, a tornado, to others, a tranquil wind. All at once, in infinite echoes, the sound of God's Spirit filled every unique yearning soul.[1]

After this lyrical opening, Wolpe writes that many people today have trouble hearing the voice. There are, however, also many for whom the voice still permeates every fiber of their being and drives them in every season to speak out on behalf of God's glory, on behalf of their neighbors, especially those who suffer injustice at another's hand, and on behalf of the land itself. He notes that the roots of this marvelous universality of revelation are found among the stories of Moses as he prepared the people to enter the land they had sought for forty years.

One revealing story is found in the book of Numbers, chapter 11. Moses, it seems, is exhausted. The whining and complaining of the people have worn him out. Throughout the arduous escape from Egypt and the long years in the desert Moses alone has borne the responsibility of being the liaison between the rebellious people and the Holy One. When Yahweh instructs him to choose seventy older men upon whom God will confer shared authority, Moses questions God on how he will provide so many people (six hundred thousand) with meat for a whole month! God's reply is cryptic: "Is Yahweh's arm shortened? Now you will see whether or not my word is true" (Num. 11:23). The text continues:

> Moses then went out and told the people what Yahweh had said. He assembled seventy men from among the elders and placed them round about the Tent. Yahweh came down in the cloud and spoke to him. He took some of the Spirit that was upon him and put it on the seventy elders. Now when the Spirit rested upon them, they prophesied. But this they did not do again.
>
> Two men had remained in the camp; the name of one was Eldad, the name of the other Medad. However, the Spirit came on them for they were among those who were registered though they had not gone out to the Tent. As they prophesied inside the camp, a young man ran and told Moses, "Eldad and Medad are prophesying in the camp." Joshua, the son of Nun, who ministered to Moses from his youth, said, "My lord Moses, stop them!"
>
> But Moses said to him, "Are you jealous on my behalf? Would that all Yahweh's people were prophets and that Yahweh would send his Spirit upon them!" (Num. 11:24–29)

We are told that Moses was unique among the prophets, having walked with God and seen him face-to-face, that he was beloved by God, and that there would never be another like him. This was Moses' fervent dream for his people and for his God's honor: that all might be prophets and that the Spirit of God would rest on them all, making them zealous for justice, for obedience to the law, and devoted to the word of God.

Only two of the seventy are named, Eldad and Medad, and they did not enter into the Tent of Meeting with the rest. Jewish tradition says that they are remembered by name because they alone of the seventy were humble and asked: Why us? According to the tradition, their prophecy came immediately from God alone and was a permanent gift, while the other elders were able to prophesy only for a short time. And, according to the tradition, they were considered young men, not old ones, and of all the people the Spirit came upon that day, they alone entered the promised land.

From Moses on, there will be people touched by this Spirit of God, which is often described as the Spirit rushing upon them. Just before the people enter the promised land, Yahweh, through Moses, promises that prophets will be with them to give them access to and understanding of the will of God:

> I shall raise up a prophet from their midst, one of their brothers, who will be like you. I will put my words into his mouth and he will tell them all that I command. If someone does not listen to my words, when the prophet speaks on my behalf, I myself will call him to account for it. But any prophet who says in my name anything that I did not command, or speaks in the name of other gods, that prophet shall die. (Deut. 18:18–20)

And so goes the history of Israel, interpreted through the prophets, through the word of Yahweh their God. Today, thousands of years later, this concept of the prophet can be found on every continent and in nearly every religion. This chapter will look at contemporary prophets who are still single-heartedly concerned with the worship and honor of God, with God's insistent call to justice and the care of the poorest, and now with even the ravaged earth itself. Since the beginning, the prophets have seen these three issues as one — a demanding, holistic ethic and response to the presence of the other.

The stories that follow speak a word of hope, a demand for justice, and a call to see ourselves as one, a community of diversity in which we are all one. And note carefully that the word of hope is closely linked to the warning that if we do not take this imperative to heart we will all die.

Trees

Among native peoples in the Americas and among many other indigenous peoples, trees are known as "the tall standing ones." Anyone who knows and speaks the language of the trees is considered to be highly blessed and an essential speaker for the community. The trees are also referred to as "silent witnesses" because they alone remain as histories collide and time passes. In this century we are seeing for the first time massive deforestation over a large part of the earth. In a staggering one-page letter, entitled "Earth to World Leaders," that appeared in *Lapis* magazine, Robert Muller, former assistant secretary general of the United Nations, depicts a series of questions the Earth directs to the leaders:

The Earth would ask:

Why Each Minute:

1. do you destroy 52 acres of my tropical forests (38 million acres a year) after having destroyed most of the forests in your "rich" countries?

2. do you let 50 tons of fertile soil be blown off my cropland?

3. do you add 12,000 tons of carbon dioxide to my atmosphere — a staggering total of 6.3 billion tons in 1997?

Why Each Hour:

1. do you spend 120 million dollars on military expenditures — a trillion dollars a year?

2. are 55 people poisoned and 5 killed by pesticides?

3. are 60 new cases of cancer diagnosed in the US alone — over 5,000,000 cases each year?

Why Each Five Hours:

1. do you let a species die out on this planet? This means a loss of 84,000 species in the next 50 years.

Why Each Day:

1. do 25,000 people die of water shortage and contamination?

2. are 10 tons of nuclear waste produced?

3. do 250,000 tons of sulfuric acid fall as acid rain in
   the Northern hemisphere, killing lakes and devastating
   remaining forests? . . .

Why During a Human Life:

1. do you dump so much garbage and waste on me? While
   the average person in a poor country leaves behind 150
   times their weight in waste over a lifetime, why does the
   average American leave behind a mountain of waste 4,000
   times his own weight?

Yes, why, why, why . . . [2]

Earth's letter to humankind is much longer, but these short verses
are more than enough to make us stop, at least for a moment, to reflect
on what we are doing and what our legacy will be to our children's
children down to the seventh generation. Coupled with these statistics
is a prayer from the book of Revelation that hopefully will not only
make us stop in our tracks but cause us to turn in an opposite direction.

> *We thank you, Lord God,*
> *Master of the universe,*
> *who are and who were,*
> *for you have begun your reign,*
> *making use of your invincible power.*
> *The nations raged*
> *but your wrath has come,*
> *the time to judge the dead*
> *and reward your servants the prophets,*
> *the saints and those who honor your Name —*
> *whether great or small —*
> *and destroy those who destroy the earth.*
>
> (Rev. 11:17–18)

The trees of the earth are silent witnesses, prophets who stand
against us. With their deaths, their decay, and their disease they call
us to halt our unfettered pursuit of greed, our materialistic waste of
natural resources, and the literal fouling of our own nests with the excess of our waste on our way to unlimited profits. Bound to the trees
are prophets — people who know the language of the trees and how
they serve as weathervanes in a vast bioculture called earth.

Rodolfo Montiel and his compadre Teodoro Cabrera have been in a high-risk prison in Mexico, in a special "social re-adaptation center" in Iguala, since May 1999. They are trying to recover from torture that stopped only when they signed blank sheets of paper — their confessions. Both are accused of being traffickers in narcotics, but Rodolfo defines himself this way: "I am something even more dangerous to them. I am an *ecologista*. A *campesino ecologista*." Their story, told in the July/August 2000 issue of *Sierra* magazine,[3] begins with Boise Cascade, an Idaho timber giant that moved operations south of the border to the Sierra Madre range because of environmental demonstrations and restrictions on logging in the Pacific Northwest coastal range. Boise Cascade decided the million or so acres of white and sugar pine of the coastal Sierra Madres were their next target. The company was aided by the 1994 North American Free Trade Agreement (NAFTA), which encourages U.S. companies to do business with the farming groups and indigenous groups that together hold title to 80 percent of Mexico's native forests. The farming groups, called *ejidos,* which were once interested in land reform, now work in tandem with local bosses, the *caciques,* and with the military and U.S.-based corporations to squeeze dry the poor campesinos and the land itself. The area in question lies on the coast between Acapulco and Zihuatanejo, resort cities that cater to American and European tourists.

Rodolfo, a poor man with only a corn patch, watched as the logging and the resulting drying up of the rivers tolled the death knell of what little subsistence farming was possible in the poor villages of his area. So the poor decided to organize to stop the logging. Their group chose a name as long as their vision for the future: The Ecologist Campesinos of the Sierras of Petatlan and Coyuca de Catalan, which included the areas they came from. They were immediately labeled as a front for drug traffickers and guerrillas. On February 20, 1998, they took a stand at a narrow road where the logging rigs had to pass to get to the Boise mills, and they turned back the trucks — forty-three on the first day alone. The group of 104 persons sent word that they wanted to negotiate with Boise. Instead, the military arrived.

Then people started disappearing: some were hung in trees and others turned up dead in the countryside. Men and women and soon whole villages up and left to try to escape the military. Both Rodolfo and Teodoro, along with their families, were hunted, arrested, and tortured. They are still in jail, but Boise Cascade pulled out of Mexico in June 1998. They have now moved their Latin American operations to Chile, with plans to build a "near billion-dollar chip mill on the shores of a pristine bay near Puerto Montt."[4] But logging continues in Mexico, led by Mexican companies and U.S.-based Westwood Forest Products. A giant new plywood mill has been built outside of Zihuatanejo, and troops are still camped out in the area and hounding the people. Juan, one of those who remains and another contemporary prophet, was interviewed: "We do not know what they want. Sometimes they come down and ask us about the *ecologistas*. We're all *ecologistas* here — we defend our *ocoteros* [pitch pine stands]. They bring us life. They even accompany us in death when they give us the wood for the coffin."[5] Juan's seventeen-year-old brother, Romualdo, who was shot down by the local military, lay in his own pine box just a few feet away as Juan spoke.

Rodolfo Montiel is dangerous because he told the truth. He spoke simply and without any investment except survival and love for his land and his own people. He stated the issue clearly:

> When someone kills many people, he is guilty of genocide. Someone who kills a lot of trees is guilty of ecocide. The two crimes are related; trees bring us water and water brings us life. When I see a tree cut down, it wounds me inside. It feels like one of my own children has been murdered. . . . If I get out of here I'm going right back to the sierra to defend the forests.[6]

Communities all over Mexico and throughout other parts of the Third World are struggling with international companies and the globalization of markets that they promote. For these people, this is an endeavor to simply survive. Such conflicts often result in the death of those who speak out against injustice, greed, and destruction. This was true of Chico Mendes in the Amazon and Ken Saro-Wiwa in Nigeria. Usually, the issues are as much about human rights as they are about ecological concerns, as was pointed out in the article in *Sierra:*

> The Jesuit-run Miguel Agustín Pro Human Rights Center has taken up the defense of the *campesinos ecologistas*. "The charges against Montiel and Cabrera are a pretext," says Digna Ochoa, the center's legal director. "They are really in jail because they disturbed the economic interests of local and

transnational timber companies." The defense of the forests, she asserts, is a human-rights issue: "The right to a healthy environment is fundamental. Human rights are not just limited to the abuses of the judicial system — although in this case they are flagrant. Human rights are integral. They are environmental, cultural, social, economic. We must look at them as a whole."[7]

The issue is global, but it is especially acute and widespread in the poorer countries of the world that still have large areas of resources coveted by the First World, although even these areas are being quickly depleted. The same article notes that "Mexico's forests are as abused as its citizenry. Half of the country's tropical and temperate forests have been lost in the past forty years, and its last great reserves are under siege. The Lacandon jungle in Chiapas has been reduced from 5,000 square miles to less than 2,000, and loses another 125 square miles every year."[8]

Amnesty International and the Sierra Club have linked up to speak out on behalf of Montiel and Cabrera, who, despite being in jail, were just awarded the Goldman Prize for environmental activism. Supporters can write to the Mexican president and demand that these men be released immediately and that the allegations of torture be investigated, along with the environmental consequences of logging in Guerrero.[9] Supporters can also contact Alejandro Queral at the Human Rights and the Environment Campaign.[10]

Recently Shell Oil took out a double-page spread in national newspapers and magazines using the Shell logo overlaid on many faces of human beings saying: "None of our business? Or the heart of our business?" The small print speaks of "human rights not being the usual business priority" for a multinational corporation. It goes on to say that Shell is "committed to support fundamental human rights." However, a recent article in *Sierra* notes:

> Meanwhile in oil-rich Nigeria, where Shell and other oil companies have substantial investments, unrest over land and oil rights in the Niger Delta has expanded. Four years after the November 1995 execution of activist Ken Saro-Wiwa, Nigeria's environment minister accused Shell and other multi-nationals of "heinous environmental crimes" and alleged that their activities ultimately caused Saro-Wiwa's death.[11]

The arrogance and dishonesty of such advertising seem to have no
bounds.

Salmon

Back in Idaho, the home of Boise Cascade, near the city of Lewiston, the Selway and Lochsa Rivers eventually merge with the Snake
River, one of the largest tributaries of the Columbia River. This area
was mentioned in the Lewis and Clark journals as being "crouded
with salmon." The rivers are still awesomely beautiful, but they are
now utterly empty of salmon. A writer in *Northern Lights,* a regional
journal, tells of what we've lost:

> But the spirits are gone — the great spirits of salmon, whose
> bodies made this country, whose nutrients form the vascular
> tissue of the oldest trees in these parts, whose presence in
> the lives of the people who once lived here — even at this
> distance from the ocean — was profound beyond the reach
> of words.... [A]lways more than just food, salmon supplied
> spiritual nourishment as well as nutrients to the body. The reg-
> ular, cyclical appearance of anadromous species in rivers and
> streams signaled that these fish were in touch with powers out-
> side of human comprehension.... Their miraculous arrival was
> a mystery that required explanation, and the explanation came
> in the form of legends, stories and creation myths in which
> the shape-shifting Salmon interacted with other magical fig-
> ures: Raven, Coyote, Fog Woman, Eagle, Bear. The natural, as
> always, possessed supernatural origins.
>
> The great abundance of salmon seemed to have a counterintu-
> itive effect on the people who depended upon them. Rather than
> taking these life-giving animals for granted, humans adopted an
> intricate set of rituals whose existence suggested an ongoing fear
> that if things did not go right, these fish, no matter how numer-
> ous, would not return. In fact, it was thought, humans played
> an important role in bringing salmon back into the spawning
> country, making salmon feel welcome enough to return home.[12]

These creatures range over thousands of miles of coastal lands,
ocean areas, and inland communities in Korea, Scotland, Ireland, and
Norway; their lives are intimately connected with the tribes of the

Ainu of Hokkaido Island, Japan; the Ulchi of Siberia; the Tlingit of Alaska; the Makah of Washington State's Olympic Peninsula; and many other peoples. All these ancient peoples believed that the salmon chose to return in abundance or scarcity. The salmon watched humans to see if their lives and rituals demonstrated sufficient reverence toward life and expressed harmony. These ancient groups, thus, considered the salmon "people." These groups still express their reverence for the salmon in various "ways." One of the most important "ways" is called the "First Salmon Ceremony." When the first fish is caught, all fishing stops. The fish is carefully cleaned and cooked and fed in small pieces to all the youngest children. The ceremony is meant to honor the fish and their coming and to hasten their way through the rivers to the spawning grounds. There is singing, dancing, and prayers, and a portion of the first fish is returned to the river. During these days no one is allowed to fish, thus ensuring that the first and largest run of salmon gets through to replenish stocks for the future.

Don Snow writes of what these rituals reveal of the humans involved:

> These careful rituals suggest a profound moral orientation towards the natural world. The first salmon ceremony is an encapsulation of the idea of "right action," and the affirmation of the relationship between moral behavior and good livelihood. The salmon simply would not return unless they were welcomed and treated with proper reverence. Right action involved careful observation, sacrifice, precise behavior, humility, duty, and a sense of shared destiny: as the salmon goes, so go the people. The abundant, life-giving fish were the animal representatives of an endless cycle of living. Humans participate in this cycle; they aid it along; and if they fail in their responsibilities, then the cycle may fail, too. . . . We are finally ready to see native wisdom evolved into a sophisticated conception of reciprocal stewardship. You take care of us, and we — incompetent humans — will try our best to take care of you.[13]

But now the salmon are almost gone, not only in the American and Canadian and Alaskan Northwest but also in Scotland and many other parts of the world. We have traded them for farm-raised fish (which must be fed with an enormous amount of other wild fish), for kilowatts and turbines. Wilderness areas dwindle and are replaced by large industrial farms and sprawling developments. Snow ends his article with the question: "Is the restoration of the salmon possible without the restoration of reverence?" That is the core of the issue, the heart of the moral debate.

Salmon are now protected in the United States under the Endangered Species Act in an attempt to save some of these mythic fish. The story of the dwindling supplies of salmon worldwide is symptomatic of a crisis: the seas are running out of fish. As is the case with trees and logging, oil reserves and drilling, and so many other exploitable resources, the issue of food — of fish — is one of globalized arrangements between governments in the First World and Third World. It is usually the local and indigenous communities that are caught in the middle. From Senegal and Mauritania to Australia and Scotland, the story of the salmon is repeated with tuna, shrimp, snapper, whales, sharks, sea bass, swordfish, marlins, and cod.

The World Trade Organization often refuses to acknowledge the depletion of whole species of fish or to encourage precautionary principles to save fish stocks already in dire shortage. Or, as protesters have written on their signs: "Corporations have always relied on governments to conduct their fishy business." Terms of trade, unfortunately, rule even the seas as industries desperately look for more and more fish stocks. Perhaps we must become impolite diners and protest how our fish is caught, where it comes from, and how healthy it is, let alone become more involved with regulation of fishing. The four largest "fishmongers" in the business are Mitsui, Mitsubishi, Marubeni, and Heinz (this last includes StarKist, John West, Petit Navire, and Greenseas). Seventy percent of the planet's marine stocks are fully exploited or overexploited already.[14]

Rice

India — along with many other countries, such as Pakistan, Indonesia, Malaysia, Singapore, China, and Japan — lives on rice. "The" rice of rice is the basmati, one among more than a hundred thousand varieties of rice evolved by Indian farmers. It is the women who are the "seed-keepers and seed breeders" and who begin every planting season with prayers and dances. They then offer the diverse seeds to the village deity and share the seeds among their neighbors. It is the annual festival of Akti, which binds together the rice, the land, the water canals, the water buffaloes, and the people. "Akti" means "survival," but it also has the same meaning as "religion" — to bind or tie together.

The rice-consuming parts of the world are very disturbed by a new development in large corporations called seed patenting. Vandana Shiva, of the Research Foundation for Science, Technology, and Ecology in New Delhi, writes:

> The basmati rice which farmers in my valley have been growing for centuries is today being claimed as "an instant invention of a novel rice line" by a U.S. corporation called RiceTec. The "neem," which our mothers and grandmothers have used for centuries as a pesticide and fungicide, has been patented for these uses by W. R. Grace, another U.S. corporation.
>
> ... Intellectual property rights on seeds are, however, criminalizing this duty to the earth and each other by making seed saving and seed exchange illegal. The attempt to prevent farmers from saving seed is not just being made through new IPR [International Property Rights] laws, it is also being made through the new genetic engineering technologies. Delta and Pine Land (now owned by Monsanto) and the USDA have established a new partnership through a jointly held patent [for seed] which has been genetically engineered to ensure that it does not germinate on harvest, thus forcing farmers to buy seed at each planting season.
>
> When we sow seed, we pray, "May this seed be exhaustless." Monsanto and the USDA on the other hand are stating, "Let this seed be terminated, that our profits and monopoly be exhaustless."
>
> There can be no partnership between this terminator logic which destroys nature's renewability and regeneration and the commitment to continuity of life held by women farmers of the Third World.[15]

Women and Trees

Another modern-day prophet is Wangari Maatthai of Kenya. The first woman to receive a doctorate in Kenya, she has chosen to walk a remarkably prophetic path:

She taught for a while, but then began to focus on the actions of the corrupt government, particularly in its alliance with American industries to clear-cut much of Kenya and overwhelm the people with "cash" crops instead of food crops... — all of which caused massive soil erosion and even more hunger and poverty. Wangari is one of the wonderful rare folks who doesn't know you can't do the impossible. She hit upon a plan to encourage Kenyan women to plant trees. By now, she has 80,000 women involved in a very strong organization called the Green Belt Movement and together they have planted 20 million trees throughout the land on private property. They are now taking on the government itself. Wangari was herself a candidate for the Kenyan election in 2000 that re-elected the current president Moi. She is also a nominee for the Nobel Peace Prize.[16]

Kenyan politicians operate on the premise that all public land belongs to the government (rather than the people), and in addition to making it available to foreign industries, they are using it as gifts to buy personal power and prestige. Wangari and her women (and others) oppose such actions. Jailed, beaten, and greatly maligned, Wangari is an extraordinarily strong, gracious, gentle woman with an awesome perspective.[17]

The long history of alliances between women and trees tells a story that is both dangerous and life-giving. In India in 1730 a young woman, Amrita Devi, founded what was called the Chipko Movement. From a small village in Rajasthan, she and other women tried to prevent the Maharaja of Jodhpur's soldiers from cutting down the trees surrounding her village by wrapping their arms around the tree trunks. The word "Chipko" actually means "tree-hugging." She and 363 women from her village of Bhishnoi were cut to ribbons. A children's book that tells the story does a terrible disservice to her and the movement, which is very strong in India today, because it tells a story that ends "happily ever after." A small note at the end mentions that Amrita Devi and the others were chopped up along with the trees they sought to protect. In a recent visit to India I read and encountered many women's accounts of their participation in this group and their involvement across the entire Himalayan region.[18]

These intertwining issues of trees, water, land, salmon, rice, and other food staples are contemporary moral issues that are being addressed by contemporary prophets. It is striking that these same issues were known and addressed early on in Christianity, even as early as the fourth century, as is shown in this passage from St. Ambrose:

> Why do the injuries of nature delight you? The world has been created for all, while you rich are trying to keep it for yourselves. Not merely the possession of the earth, but the very sky, air and the sea are claimed for the use of the rich few. . . . Not from your own do you bestow on the poor man, but you make return from what is his. For what has been given as common for the use of all, you appropriate for yourself alone. The earth belongs to all, not to the rich. (*De Nabuthe Jezraelita* 3, 11)

From the beginning, Yahweh, the prophets of old, and early followers of Christianity reiterated the intimate connections between rich and poor, people and land, faithfulness and freedom, prosperity for all and reverence and gratitude to the creator. They foretold the ultimate destruction of all when there was no faithful response in rightful living among people. Today we are even more all of a piece, and the calls to justice today link us all. Earth, air, water, food, and all that is created are seamlessly bound into one patchwork quilt. Because it is all of a piece, it will also unravel together. The prophets' cries today are no different than those in the centuries before Christ. They are perhaps more complex and intricate, delicate and interwoven, but the sin, the injustice, and the evils are still the same: arrogance, ego, violence, disregard and disdain for creation (including human beings), racism, and nationalism.

The Other Side, a prophetic monthly magazine, usually includes a short report called "Short Takes." Here are two announcements that could have come from the prophets of the Hebrew Scriptures: "240,000 people could be fed for a year with the food Americans waste each day," and "The U.N. estimates that universal access to basic education, healthcare, food and clean water would cost an additional 40 billion per year — less than 4 percent of the combined wealth of the world's 225 richest people." People cause these injustices that befall the victims, including the earth and all its creatures. But, as Thomas Merton writes, "Courage comes and goes. Hold on for the next supply." The supply comes in people like those mentioned above and in all who follow in the footsteps of the prophets.

"The Bees": Bishop Ruíz and Chiapas

"The Bees," or Las Abejas, as they are known in Spanish, is a group of more than four thousand poor people from twenty-four villages from Tzajalchen, high in the Sierra Madres of Chiapas, which is home to many indigenous peoples. Many of these Mayan Indians are refugees of the paramilitaries of the wealthy landowners and of the PRI-istas, the army of the longest ruling government in Mexico's history, a government just recently voted out of power. The village of Atcteal, located in this region, was the site of a brutal massacre in December 1997 of forty-five people, mostly women, children, and the elderly. The slaughter lives on powerfully in the people's memories and hearts. The people found themselves caught between the military forces of the government, the landowners, and the Zapatistas. They spoke for themselves in an article in *The Plough:*

> "We are in absolute agreement with each and every cause in the Zapatista struggle, and we cannot let go of these flags [i.e., the Zapatista flags that proclaim revolution, freedom, justice, and dignity]. All the same, we cannot agree with the chosen method, that of taking up arms." So when the leaders of the Zapatista movement asked of the nation's civil society, "If there is another way, show it to us," they, The Bees, in radical honesty, took it upon themselves as a challenge.... Because of their stand they have been unjustly accused of being "neutral."
>
> Today we must shout: By no means are they neutral! Their option is very clear and radical! They are neither a "third group" in the conflict nor cowards! They are simply people who have believed without wavering that the struggle for life is waged with armaments of life. They were not afraid of holding a rifle, they simply preferred to run the risk of believing to the end that the Gospel was refining them in their hearts.
>
> They said: "We are prepared to die for this cause, but not to kill."
>
> ... The Bees are by no means a weak and defenseless group, though they may have been seen that way by their paramilitary attackers; neither is any group armed only with the force of truth. This massacre [at Atcteal], even if seen as a brash abuse of power, was not without reason coldly and carefully calculated. A group like this, armed only with love and truth, is the most dangerous and threatening to defenders of the system, because it more ef-

fectively unmasks their injustice. For this reason its elimination is the more urgent.[19]

Father Oscar Salinas of San Cristóbal de Las Casas preached at Mass on December 28, 1997, the feast of the Holy Innocents, about the massacre in Atcteal, which became a turning point in the struggle of the indigenous peoples against the Mexican government and the wealthy landowners. It was not just a tribute or a memorial. It was a call to imitate and take hope from the choices made by The Bees: "The innocent martyrs of Atcteal are saving us from our confusions and cowardice. Interceding they died. Fasting they died. This was the death they chose, praying and fasting for all of us. We can see it. With them has been planted the seed of peace."[20]

Folks like these villagers didn't arise out of nowhere. They were born and nurtured in Chiapas over the last twenty-five years by a remarkable man and those who worked with him, Bishop Samuel Ruíz, up until very recently the bishop of San Cristóbal de Las Casas, Chiapas. He is a man in the tradition of Bartolomé de Las Casas, their first bishop, who sought freedom and dignity for the indigenous people in the face of their slavery and treatment at the hands of their Christian conquerors. Ruíz, appointed in 1960, initially didn't notice anything amiss. In an interview in *The National Catholic Reporter,* he said: "I traveled through villages where bosses were scourging debt-slaves who did not want to work more than eight hours a day, and all I saw were old churches and old women praying. 'Such good people,' I said to myself, not noticing that these good people were victims of cruel oppression."[21]

Then Ruíz began to learn the languages of his people, mostly Mayan dialects, and stayed with the poorest of the poor. In 1974, he asked the people to speak, and he listened. At root they wanted justice, the right to survive without fear, their land, education, health care, the right to organize and to go and come from markets where they could sell their products — nothing extraordinary. But they wanted these rights in a land where the powerful for generations had treated them as slaves at best (there are over 1.5 million poor in Chiapas). All the hopes and demands of the people would surface twenty years later in the Zapatista manifesto.

Ruíz explained that all he did was encourage the growth of the gospel in Mayan culture and that, sadly, it was five hundred years too late. Bishop Ruíz explains what he saw:

What all world cultures have is a revealing presence of God, what the Greek and Latin Fathers called the seeds of the word — *semina verbi* — hidden in those cultures. In consequence, evangelization (and inculturation) is not — forgive the expression — an attempt to determine how many goals from your culture you can score in the indigenous culture, how much of Western culture the indigenous culture can tolerate. The objective is rather to recognize the presence of a salvific process, an Old Testament like that of the Jewish people, an Old Testament of this cultural group, through which God has revealed himself. Recognition of this presence of God means that this is a salvific process that continues forward to the explicit encounter with Jesus Christ announced and testified to by the church.[22]

He explained that because the Mayan people were brutalized, conquered, and forced to accept a Western version of cultural Christianity, they never had the chance to meet Jesus Christ. At the same time, they lost any sense of their own identity as a people and as a culture. They are now in the process of reclaiming and recovering, even rediscovering, who they are, from their past histories, their pre-Columbian religions, and their land. "And their unity will not flow from their Christian identity but from a cultural identity, even if understood very differently. And this is what is uniting the indigenous peoples."[23] This process — or revolution, because of its radicalness and thoroughness — is happening across the continents of the Americas and universally among oppressed and colonized peoples. Once the church recognizes the essential nature of these peoples and honors the seeds of the word already there, they and we can make this presence of God a critical element of both their culture and their future.

Bishop Ruíz honored the people, respected their cultures, and enabled them to regain a vision and sense of themselves. He spoke of over eight thousand catechists who are aware of the situation of their people: some having never been evangelized by Western Christians, some who were exposed to the concepts of Christianity by force and robbed of their own culture and sense of dignity, and some who are struggling to re-vision their own cultures in light of their present belief in Christianity. This transformation, only at the beginning stages, is strong and spreading. Dom Samuel, as he is called, became from the beginning the voice, the echo, and the cry of his people for justice, for recognition, for freedom, and for a chance to practice and live their Christianity with integrity. He clearly used the language of the prophets:

> The church, when faced with [this] violence of the "established order," cannot remain silent lest it condone by its silence the sin of the world. With the energy that the spirit of the prophets has given us, and with the power of the gospel, we have called — in season and out of season — for the conversion of persons and of social structures. But it would seem that we have been "a voice crying in the wilderness."[24]

He began with the indigenous languages and a system of catechists, who may not be able to read or write Spanish but are known and respected in their villages and who serve their people without pay. Service freely given gives the catechists authority in the community, and it is the people who select and judge their catechists, a third of whom are women. After training by the diocese, they are involved with cooperatives, agricultural education, health care, and literacy programs as well as with teaching religion, counseling, and presiding at liturgical services in the absence of a priest. Their catechism, *We Are Seeking Freedom,* written by their own catechists in the 1970s, could come from a book of one of the prophets of old:

> It is God's will that we get rid of everything that oppresses us. The word of God tells us that as a community we should set out in search of freedom. If we seek improvement and freedom, God will accompany us. . . . We have to build up strength in our hearts and fight and suffer for a long time still. We have to fight against poverty, hunger and injustice.[25]

Along with his work training catechists and building ministry and structures based on cultural traditions and indigenous customs and values, Ruíz founded the Fray Bartolomé de Las Casas Human Rights Center in March 1989. One of the first tasks of the center was to make public the list of injustices the people were subject to: assassinations, tortures, wrongful imprisonment, theft of titles to land, and repression of protest marches. Further, in the ancient traditions of the prophets, the center condemned the *caciques,* the political bosses of municipalities, for harassment. As MacEoin says:

Given this partisanship, this preferential option for the poor, it is not surprising that Dom Samuel is the most hated and the most loved man in Chiapas. He is hated by those who benefit from and seek to maintain an unjust system of exploitation. He is loved by the poor for his lifetime of commitment to their rights and for his accompaniment of them in their struggle for food and dignity.[26]

Presently retired, Bishop Ruíz continues his work, now on a more international level, on behalf of indigenous communities, as negotiator between the Mexican government and the Zapatistas. He also continues to be the voice of those who seek to incorporate Christianity into their culture, their traditions, and their lives, to enrich the Body of Christ with the unique expressions of their "seeds of the word" that God originally sowed in their land and souls. They are seeking their own response to the call "Follow me" that they hear Christ saying in their language, as one of them.

Like others who have gone before us in faith, they echo the words of the prophets and call on the words, the dreams, and the actions of the prophetess Myriam, the mother of the prophet Jesus of Nazareth. They know through their own experience, in their deaths and crucifixions, the possible effects of living out this gospel. But they are part of the "poor, the meek, the remnant" of the gospel. They rally to the truth as it is expressed in those who speak on their behalf, like Dom Samuel or Monseñor Romero. In a homily in 1980, Romero said:

> In the Magnificat when Mary sings about God lifting up the humble and the poor, the political implications resound. She says, "God has filled the hungry with good things, and the rich, He has sent empty-handed away." Mary also says a few things that today could be considered downright seditious. "Throw the mighty from their thrones" when they are a disturbance to the people's well-being! This is the political dimension of our faith. Mary lived it, and Jesus lived it. Jesus was a real patriot in a nation of people who lived under foreign domination. Doubtless, it was his dream that his people would be free![27]

Matzo

The Jewish community tells a marvelous story to teach the underlying implications of the prophet Micah's most famous line: "It has been told thee, O Man, what is good, and what the Lord requires of thee: only to do justly, and to love mercy, and to walk humbly with thy God." Rabbi Samuel Stahl says, however, that that isn't exactly the most correct rendering of the text. Instead, he says, it should read: "Human beings have told you what is good, but what does God require of you?" The emphasis is on the word "require," referring to ethical behavior, how we treat one another, and whether or not we treat one another humanely. These are the criteria that God uses instead of our practice of religious rituals, though that is important because it reminds us of who God is. Rabbi Stahl tells a marvelous story of what that means today and every day:

> A few days before Passover, the late Rabbi Israel Salanter, founder of the ethics-based Musar movement in Eastern Europe, gathered together a group of his students. He was about to send them out to inspect a local matzo-baking factory to certify that its products were indeed "Kosher for Passover."
>
> One of his students asked him, "Rabbi, is there anything in particular we should be on the lookout for?"
>
> Rabbi Salanter answered "Yes, definitely! When you get to the factory, you'll see an old woman baking matzo. The woman is poor and has a large family to support. Make sure the owners are paying her a living wage."[28]

Sean Devereux

David Hodges, a Trappist monk and poet, lives on a remote island off the coast of Wales. One of his poems describes Sean Devereux, a UNICEF worker assassinated in Somalia in 1993. This short excerpt from the poem tells the story of this modern prophet:

> Sean had a mission.
> He died for truth,
> for speaking out the truth
> often at the point of a gun,
> helping to get the food through,
> among "his children"
> in the Africa he loved.
>
> Spoke out against the arms trade
> who supplied the guns,

then apologised and gave them food
while they shot each other for it.
Who did the killing? You and me.

He walked in Truth
"while my heart beats
I have to . . . 'help.' . . . "
"While there is life there is hope."

Jesus spoke up for the Truth:
"I am the Way, the Truth, and the Life."
He said "I was born for this,
to bear witness to the Truth
and all who are on the side of truth
listen to my voice."[29]

Foreign arms trade was once a matter of strategic interest, but now it is principally about money and politics and the sale of conventional weapons — from small arms to helicopters, from bombs and antipersonnel mines to sophisticated fighter planes. Since 1993 the United States has delivered more than $53 billion worth of arms to the developing world, with 80 percent going to nondemocratic countries. "These are the weapons that fuel ethnic and territorial conflicts, undermine democratic forces and destabilize entire regions of the world."[30] The big companies are household words in the United States: Lockheed Martin, McDonnell Douglas, Textron, Raytheon, Northrop, and Boeing. "Because the taxpayer has already paid for the research, development and creation of production lines, every sale abroad of a plane, a tank, helicopter or machine gun is pure gravy for the manufacturer."[31]

Along with many other prophets who seek to remind us of our acute and immediate need for conversion to nonviolent resistance to evil and aggression, the Dalai Lama says: "What's the use of anger, what's the use of hatred? Problems are bound to happen, we must find a way to overcome them without using violence." That way has been presented to us: Come, follow me, in the way of truth, of peace, and of life. As with the ancient prophets, the call is for the nations to embrace peace as the only remedy and our only hope.

Another "Woods"

A Dominican theologian, Richard Woods — in the tradition of the mystic-prophet Meister Eckhart, preacher, dragon-slayer, and writer — speaks and writes often about the connections between spirituality, justice, and the earth. In 1999 he wrote of what connects all the people in this book — the prophets and their constituencies:

> [S]everal factors connect Revelation, impending ecological catastrophe, and spirituality, and in particular a concern with social justice. For all these links ultimately converge on *poverty* — first, the growing impoverishment of the Earth itself as the source of all natural life; second, the increasing destitution of the majority of the world's peoples resulting from an inescapable escalation of material, cultural, and spiritual oppression; and third, the possibility of voluntary poverty, a radical detachment that can at least minimize environmental destruction and social catastrophe on the greatest scale in human history.
>
> As a way of living in and for the world, any spirituality for a possible future must be constituted by a positive responsibility for the natural world, a preferential concern for the victims of social and natural misfortune, and a compassionate and inclusive love for all human beings, creation itself, and the God of both. In short, it will be *ecological,* it will be concerned with *social justice,* and it will be *mystical* at its core and *prophetic* in application.[32]

Woods is clear about both the escalating environmental damage and the message of Christianity for dealing with this human-made nightmare. His answer to how to face it, courageously alter it, and redeem it lies in two great resources — "Christianity's mystical heritage and the ascetic discipline of voluntary poverty so frequently associated with it."[33]

Such a global and ecological spirituality must begin with its two-dimensional mystical element, the first dimension being "an insight into the unity of all human beings, deep within the divine field that grounds all existence."[34] We are living in a world that is absolutely transparent, and God is shining through it all the time. If we abandon ourselves to God and forget ourselves, we see it sometimes — maybe even frequently. God shows God's self everywhere, in everything —

in people and in things and in nature and in events. The only thing is that we don't see it. This mystical sense erupts into a religion of justice, a vision to seek out and extend to the very least the benefits belonging by rights to all. Woods posits that the "other" aspect of mystical spirituality involves theory and has resulted in an altogether altered understanding of the world. This theoretical dimension means that scientists like "Kepler, Copernicus, Pascal, Einstein and Teilhard de Chardin were mystics. They saw the wholeness and unity of the world from the perspective of scientific insight and experiment as well as from that of faith."[35]

This vision has developed consistently into an ethics of ecological and global responsibility. Theologians like Jürgen Moltmann, Hans Küng, Rosemary Ruether, Thomas Berry, Sallie McFague, Leonardo Boff, Sean McDonagh, Gerard and Patricia Mische, Carolyn Merchant, and others have delved seriously into what role the church should play in the work of restoring and protecting creation.

We can glimpse what this spirituality might be as a shared prophetic vision and praxis:

> A spirituality for a possible future will differ from previous forms of asceticism by primarily focusing on the common good of all the world's peoples, rather than upon the particular, often peculiar, individualistic, and private concerns of a religious elite. Practically and specifically, the members of the affluent nations who have been the primary beneficiaries of the industrialization that has despoiled the Earth must now voluntarily reduce their consumption of scarce and costly resources, especially those used to manufacture luxury items. Such a voluntary renunciation of a lifestyle of ostentation and waste can be a powerful signal to developing nations that their welfare does not depend on emulating the destructive habits of unlimited industrialization and patterns of wasteful consumption.[36]

These words cross the borders of religion, nationalism, economics, social structures, class lines, and science. There are echoes of many saints and mystics in them. Simone Weil wrote: "Instead of developing techniques for maximum profit, try to develop those that will give the maximum of freedom: an *entirely* new approach." These words came from a brilliant and compassionate woman who slowly starved to death working in a factory with the poor while struggling with the philosophy of the cross. And the poet William Blake wrote: "More! More! is the cry of a mistaken soul." And there are the Lummi native peoples who believe that "a person's wealth is measured by what he gives away, not by what he keeps."

Woods, in the style of a Dominican preacher, concludes with a call to transformation, a call to conversion, even a call to sacrifice and atonement:

> The undeniable fact that Earth is being systematically rendered unfit to sustain life today is a blasphemous affront to the Creator of life and thus constitutes a profound challenge to both Christian theology and spirituality. In the coming decades, any spirituality that does not address itself actively to the healing of the earth on both the individual and corporate level, to the alleviation of the suffering of the wretched of the earth by works of social justice, and to the unification of the human family and the world of nature in love and compassion, will to that extent become irrelevant.
>
> A spirituality for a possible future can only be a redemptive, prophetic spirituality that preserves, saves, protects and enhances life in all its manifestations, even at the cost of suffering and self-sacrifice, especially in the service of the powerless and the needy. It will also be a mystical, sanctifying spirituality that recognizes, advances, and celebrates the holiness, the divine wholeness of the world — both natural and social, the body together with its Head, the Word of God made flesh and raised in glory for the salvation of the *whole* world.[37]

Millennium Trees

The image of a tree or trees or a forest — what originally covered so much of the earth's surface and can still be glimpsed in shrunken pockets of old growth — reminds us of the grandeur of creation and the original intent of the maker and keeper of all things. We were meant to dwell in a garden — a rich, luscious undergrowth and canopy that all could enjoy. We have come so far from the garden. Grace, the power of the Spirit, and the reality of resurrection say we cannot go back to the garden, but we must make a new city, a new place, a new creation. The poet Wendell Berry says it best:

Invest in the millennium. Plant sequoias.
Say that your main crop is the forest
that you did not plant,
that you will not live to harvest.
Say that the leaves are harvested
when they have rotted into the mold.
Call that profit. Prophesy such returns.
Put your faith in the two inches of humus
that will build under the trees
every thousand years. . . .
Practice resurrection.[38]

In the end, the last word belongs to God. It appears in the last chapter of Revelation, the last book of the Bible. It is God's intent, God's dream, God's will, and God's design that we are invited, called, and begged to share in making this come true:

Then he showed me the river of life, clear as crystal, gushing from the throne of God and of the Lamb. In the middle of the city, on both sides of the river, are the trees of life producing fruit twelve times, once each month, the leaves of which are for the healing of the nations.

No longer will there be a curse; the throne of God and of the Lamb will be in the City and God's servants will live in his presence. They will see his face and his name will be on their foreheads. There will be no more night. They will not need the light of lamp or sun for God himself will be their light and they will reign forever.

Then the angel said to me, "These words are sure and true; the Lord God who inspires the prophets has sent his angel to show his servants what must happen soon."

"I am coming soon! [Blessed] are those who keep the prophetic words of this book." (Rev. 22:1–7)

The words of these contemporary prophets may not sear and burn our souls, but what they say is poetry, promise, and dire warning — whether couched in mystical, theological, even scientific language. They witness to the truth in word, in deed, in association with the poor, and in the call for religion to be practiced with justice and compassion. Their words echo and fall into the rich tradition of the word made flesh who pitched his tent among us and remained.

We end with the words of a prophet who simply responded to the cries of his own people in their struggle for justice, life, and dignity and who was murdered for speaking that truth in a violent world:

> The prophetic mission is the duty of God's people. So when I am told, in a mocking tone, that I think I am a prophet, I reply, "God be praised! You ought to be one too." For every Christian must develop a prophetic awareness of God's mission in the world and bring to that world a divine presence that makes demands and rejections.[39]

And so we pray: O God, whose name is Justice, Truth, and Mercy, raise up truth-tellers, prophets, and voices that resound throughout the earth with your own cry for compassion on behalf of all those who seek to live with human dignity. May your Words sing through the flesh of those you call forth and send out to declare your presence among us — insisting that we live together in peace with justice — or else! For your truth will prevail among us. May that day be soon. Amen. Amen. Amen.

Notes

Introduction

1. See David J. Wolpe, *The Healer of Shattered Hearts: A Jewish View of God* (New York: Penguin, 1991), 100.

2. Ignacio Ellacuría, "Discernir 'el signo' de los tiempos," *Diakonia* 17 (January–April 1981): 57–59.

3. Ignacio Ellacuría, "The Crucified People," in *Mysterium Liberationis* (Maryknoll, N.Y.: Orbis Books, 1993), 592.

4. Ibid., 580–604.

5. Jon Sobrino, *The Principle of Mercy: Taking the Crucified People from the Cross* (Maryknoll, N.Y.: Orbis Books, 1994), 49.

6. Jon Sobrino, *Jesus the Liberator: A Historical-Theological View* (Maryknoll, N.Y.: Orbis Books, 1993), 270.

7. Sobrino, *Principle of Mercy,* 53.

8. Abraham Joshua Heschel, *The Prophets: An Introduction* (New York: HarperCollins, 1962), 5; subsequent page numbers cited in the text.

9. Some of these ideas appear in an article Puleo wrote a few years before her early death, "The Prophetic Act of Bearing Witness: The Word of Sebastiao Salgado," *ARTS* (1999).

10. "The Council of the Elders," in *The Dream Assembly,* ed. Rabbi Zalman Schachter-Shalomi and Howard Schwartz (Nevada City, Calif.: Gateways Books and Tapes, 1989), 174–75.

11. Quoted in *Catholic Near East.*

Chapter 1. The Prophet

1. Abraham Joshua Heschel, *The Prophets: An Introduction* (New York: Harper & Row, 1962), ix.

2. Ibid., xiii.

3. Ibid.

4. Ibid.

5. Kathleen O'Connor, "A Pinch of Salt," *Salt Magazine* (September 1990): 11.

Chapter 2. *Moses: The Prophet-Liberator*

1. Dorothee Sölle, "Moses, Jesus, Marx: Who's Winning? Who's Losing? Where's God?" *The Other Side* (March–April 1992): 22–26.
2. *Sanhedrin* 39b; from Chaim Pearl, ed., *Theology in Rabbinic Stories* (Peabody, Mass.: Hendrickson, 1997), 161.
3. Bruce C. Birch, in *Sojourners* (March 1994): 31.
4. Quoted in Pearl, *Theology in Rabbinic Stories*, 19.
5. David J. Wolpe, *The Healer of Shattered Hearts: A Jewish View of God* (New York: Penguin, 1991), 41.

Chapter 3. *Elijah and Elisha: The Prophet and His Disciples*

1. See Richard McLean, *Zen Fables for Today: Stories Inspired by the Zen Masters* (New York: Avon, 1998).
2. Christian Community Bible (17th ed., 1991), footnote to 1 Kings 16:29–34, p. 474.
3. Louis Ginzberg, *Legends of the Jews,* 7 vols. (Philadelphia: Jewish Publication Society, 1967), 589–90.
4. Peninnah Schram, from an interview in *Jewish Book News,* 14.
5. From Nahum N. Glatzer, ed., *A Jewish Reader: In Time and Eternity* (New York: Schocken Books); reprinted in *Parabola Magazine* (spring 1998): 45.

Chapter 4. *Amos and Hosea: The Northern Prophets*

1. Thomas Merton, *Run to the Mountain: The Journals of Thomas Merton,* ed. Patrick Hart (San Francisco: Harper, 1996).
2. Much of this background material can be found in Robert B. Coote, *Amos among the Prophets: Composition and Theology* (Philadelphia: Fortress Press, 1981).
3. Ibid., 16.
4. Arthur Jones, *National Catholic Reporter,* June 7, 1991.
5. Norman Gottwald et al., eds., *God and Capitalism: A Prophetic Critique of Market Economy* (Madison, Wis.: A-R Edition, 1991).
6. Jones, *National Catholic Reporter,* June 7, 1991.
7. Henri de Lubac, *The Splendor of the Church* (San Francisco: Ignatius Press, 1999), 183.
8. David Fernández, "Threats," *Company* (summer 1997): 16.
9. Global Exchange, 2017 Mission St., #303, San Francisco, CA 94110; 415-255-7296; e-mail: *gxe-info@globalexchange.org.*
10. Ibid.

11. A form of this story, called "Plant Mulberry Trees," can be found in *Sagacious Wisdom: Chinese Folktales* (n.d., n.p.).

12. Abraham Joshua Heschel, *The Prophets: An Introduction* (New York: Harper & Row, 1962), 47.

13. Ibid., 59.

14. See ibid., 60.

Chapter 5. Jeremiah and Zephaniah: The Long March to Jerusalem — the Temple Destruction and Exile

1. For a book-length treatise of this story, see Shigeyuki Nakanose, *Josiah's Passover: Sociology and the Liberating Bible* (Maryknoll, N.Y.: Orbis Books, 1993).

2. Abraham Joshua Heschel, *The Prophets: An Introduction* (New York: Harper & Row, 1962), 103.

3. Ibid., 114.

4. Ibid.

5. Ibid.

6. See David J. Wolpe, *The Healer of Shattered Hearts: A Jewish View of God* (New York: Penguin, 1991).

7. Walter Brueggemann, "Making History," *The Other Side* (1986): 24.

8. Wolpe, *Healer*, 157.

Chapter 6. Micah and Isaiah: The Southern Prophets

1. Walter Brueggemann, *Texts That Linger, Words That Explode: Listening to Prophetic Voices* (Minneapolis: Fortress Press, 2000), 82.

2. See David J. Wolpe, *The Healer of Shattered Hearts: A Jewish View of God* (New York: Penguin, 1991), 74.

3. Ibid., 173.

4. See the footnotes to Isaiah 31 in the Christian Community Bible (17th ed., 1991).

5. For more on Josiah, see the chapter above on Jeremiah.

6. For this and the following, see Felicity Arbuthnot's article in *New Internationalist* (November 1998).

7. "Buy the Right Thing: Ben Cohen's Journey from Peace Pops to War Costs," *Lapis:* 21–24.

8. For information on Pax Christi USA and the American Catholic Peace Movement, see *www.paxchristiusa.org*.

Chapter 7. Lamentations and Ezekiel: The Pain and Hope of Exile

1. David J. Wolpe, *The Healer of Shattered Hearts: A Jewish View of God* (New York: Penguin, 1991), 135.

2. Ibid., 131.

3. A more detailed version of this story is found in "The Revelation of the *Shekhinah* by the Western Wall," in *Like a Hammer Shattering Rock*, 140–45.

4. Rubem Alves, *Tomorrow's Child: Imagination, Creativity, and the Rebirth of Culture* (New York: Harper & Row, 1972).

5. For the bishops' testimony and the other statements that follow, see the website of the United States Catholic Conference.

6. Texts available from the National Conference of Catholic Bishops and the United States Catholic Conference, Washington, D.C.

7. From Elie Wiesel, "The Refugee — Elie Wiesel," in *Sanctuary: A Resource Guide for Understanding and Participating in the Central American Refugees' Struggle,* ed. Gary MacEoin (New York: Harper & Row, 1985).

8. Ibid.

9. Ibid.

10. Rabindranath Tagore, *A Rich Harvest: The Complete Tagore/Elmhirst Correspondence and Other Writings,* ed. Kissoonsingh Hazareesingh (Stanley, Rose-Hill, Mauritius: Editions de l'Océan indien, 1992), 101–2.

Chapter 8. Second Isaiah

1. John Eaton, *Mysterious Messengers: A Course on Hebrew Prophecy from Amos Onwards* (Grand Rapids, Mich.: Eerdmans, 1997), 140–41.

2. David J. Wolpe, *The Healer of Shattered Hearts: A Jewish View of God* (New York: Penguin, 1991), 66–68.

3. Mary C. Grey, *The Outrageous Pursuit of Hope: Prophetic Dreams for the Twenty-First Century* (London: Darton, Longman & Todd, 2000), 104n.24.

4. See Winona LaDuke, *All Our Relations: Native Struggles for Land and Life* (Cambridge, Mass.: South End Press, 1999). Winona LaDuke is the program director of the Honor the Earth Fund, founding director of the White Earth Land Recovery Project, and Ralph Nader's running mate for the Green Party in the 2000 presidential campaign. See also *www.lbbs.org/sep/sep.htm.*

5. Pax Christi USA, 532 West Eighth Street, Erie, PA 16502; phone: 814-453-4955; fax: 814-452-4784; e-mail: *info@paxchristusa.org*; website: *www.nonviolence.org/pcusa.*

Chapter 9. *Third Isaiah, Haggai, Zechariah, and Malachi: The Prophets of the Return*

1. Another version of the story, cited above, is given in Nahum N. Glatzer, ed., *A Jewish Reader: In Time and Eternity* (New York: Schocken Books, n.d.); reprinted in *Parabola Magazine* (spring 1998): 45.

2. Martin Luther King Jr., "Our God Is Marching On!" March 25, 1965, Montgomery, Alabama.

3. Quoted in David J. Zucker, *Israel's Prophets: An Introduction for Christians and Jews* (New York: Paulist Press, 1994), 160.

4. Quoted in ibid., 183–84.

5. *Peacework* (June 2000): 5.

6. Marc Girard, *Haggai, a Prophet for Our Times: Everything Must Be Built Anew* (Sherbrooke, Canada: Mediaspaul, 1996), 67–80.

7. Alexander Solzhenitsyn, quoted in Phil Cousineau, ed., *The Soul Aflame: A Modern Book of Hours* (Berkeley, Calif.: Conari Press, 2000), 56.

Chapter 10. *Nahum, Habakkuk, Obadiah, Jonah, Nehemiah, Ezra, Daniel, Joel: The Prophets Not Included*

1. Samuel Sandmel, *The Hebrew Scriptures* (New York: Knopf, 1963), 116.

2. See the footnotes to Nehemiah in the Christian Community Bible (17th ed., 1991), p. 465.

3. Daniel Berrigan, *Daniel: Under the Siege of the Divine* (Farmington, Pa.: Plough, 1998)

4. Hildegard of Bingen, *Scivias*, trans. Columba Hart and Jane Bishop (New York: Paulist Press, 1990), cited in Elizabeth Johnson, "Remembering Creator Spirit," in *Women's Spirituality: Resources for Christian Development*, ed. Joann Wolski Conn (New York: Paulist Press, 1996), 372.

5. For more background and some pastoral connections, see Daniel Berrigan, *Minor Prophets: Major Themes* (Freeman, S.Dak.: Pine Hill Press, 1995).

Chapter 11. *Contemporary Prophets: "Would That All Yahweh's People Were Prophets!" (Numbers 11:29)*

1. David J. Wolpe, *The Healer of Shattered Hearts: A Jewish View of God* (New York: Penguin, 1991), 2.

2. Robert Muller, "Earth to World Leaders," *Lapis* (summer 2000): 42.

3. John Ross, "Defending the Forest and Other Crimes," *Sierra* (July-August 2000): 66–71, 88.

4. Ibid., 71.

5. Ibid., 88.

6. Ibid.

7. Ibid., 71.

8. Ibid.

9. Write to Ambassador Jesus Reyes-Heroles, Embassy of Mexico, 1911 Pennsylvania Ave., N.W., Washington, DC 20006.

10. Phone: 202-675-6279; e-mail: *alejandro.queral@sierraclub.org*, or visit the Sierra Club website, *www.sierraclub/human-rights/Mexico/*.

11. *Sierra* (March-April 2000): 20.

12. Don Snow, "Meditation on the Kooskooskee," *Northern Lights* (spring 2000): 3.

13. Ibid.

14. For information on this issue, see "FISH: The Last Gasp," *New Internationalist* (July 2000): 325; the periodical can be obtained at P.O. Box 1143, Lewiston, NY 14092. This superb journal highlights a different global topic in each issue. Website: *www.newint.org*.

15. Cited in "Women and Terminator Technology," *Witness* (March 2000): 28.

16. From an e-mail report by Wes Veatch of the Whidbey Institute, Whidbey Island, Washington.

17. More information is available through the Whidbey Institute in Washington State (*whidbeyinstitute.org*) or through Danny Martin at the Sokoni Project at *DANANN0305@aol.com*.

18. For more information, see Irene Dankelman and Joan Davidson, eds., *Women and the Environment in the Third World: Alliance for the Future* (London: Earthscan Publications, 1988), 49ff.

19. *The Plough* 55 (spring 1998): 13–14.

20. Ibid., 14.

21. Quoted in Gary MacEoin, "Seeds of the Word," *National Catholic Reporter*, February 18, 2000, 10–14.

22. Ibid., 10.

23. Ibid.

24. Quoted in Gary MacEoin's "Samuel Ruíz, Voice of the Voiceless," *CrossCurrents* (fall 1996): 364.

25. Ibid., 365.

26. Ibid., 368.

27. Quoted in María López Vigil, *Oscar Romero: Memories in Mosaic* (Washington, D.C.: EPICA, 2000). See also *epica@igc.org*.

28. Adapted from a commentary in "Learn Torah With," *Shabbat*, July 19, 1997 (Torah Aura Productions).

29. David Hodges, *Songs from Solitude* (Caldey Island, Wales: The Abbey, 1999), 22.

30. *Arms for the Poor,* a documentary film.

31. "Marketing Mayhem: Arms Sales in the Post-nuclear World," *Shambhala Sun* (January 1999): 49.

32. Richard Woods, "The Seven Bowls of Wrath: An Ecological Parable," *Ecotheology* 7 (1999): 8–21.

33. Ibid.

34. Ibid.

35. Ibid.

36. Ibid.

37. Ibid.

38. Wendell Berry, "Manifesto: The Mad Farmer Liberation Front," in *The Country of Marriage* (New York: Harcourt Brace Jovanovich, 1975).

39. Oscar Romero, quoted in *Maryknoll Magazine* (November 2000): 27.

Bibliography

Achtemeier, Elizabeth. *Preaching from the Minor Prophets*. Grand Rapids, Mich.: Eerdmans, 1998.

Alfaro, Juan I., O.S.B. *Micah: Justice and Loyalty*. Grand Rapids, Mich.: Eerdmans, 1989.

Alves, Rubem. *Tomorrow's Child: Imagination, Creativity, and the Rebirth of Culture*. New York: Harper & Row, 1972.

Bellis, Alice Ogden, ed. *Many Voices: Multicultural Responses to the Minor Prophets*. Lanham, Md.: University Press of America, 1995.

Berrigan, Daniel. *Daniel: Under the Siege of the Divine*. Farmington, Pa.: Plough, 1998.

———. *Ezekiel: Vision in the Dust*. Maryknoll, N.Y.: Orbis Books, 1997.

———. *Isaiah: Spirit of Courage, Gift of Tears*. Minneapolis: Fortress Press, 1996.

———. *Jeremiah: The World, the Wound of God*. Minneapolis: Fortress Press, 1997.

———. *Minor Prophets: Major Themes*. Freeman, S.Dak.: Pine Hill Press, 1995.

Brueggemann, Walter. *Cadences of Home: Preaching among Exiles*. Louisville: Westminster/John Knox Press, 1997.

———. *Finally Comes the Poet: Daring Speech for Proclamation*. Philadelphia: Fortress Press, 1989.

———. *Hopeful Imagination: Prophetic Voices in Exile*. Philadelphia: Fortress Press, 1986.

———. *Isaiah 1–39 and Isaiah 40–66*. Louisville: Westminster/John Knox Press, 1998.

———. *The Land: Place as Gift, Promise, and Challenge in Biblical Faith*. Overtures to Biblical Scholarship. Philadelphia: Fortress Press, 1977.

———. *The Prophetic Imagination*. Philadelphia: Fortress Press, 1978.

———. *Texts That Linger, Words That Explode: Listening to Prophetic Voices*. Minneapolis: Fortress Press, 2000.

Buber, Martin. *The Prophetic Faith*. New York: Collier Books, 1949.

Ceresko, Anthony R., O.S.F.S. *Introduction to Old Testament Wisdom: A Spirituality for Liberation*. Maryknoll, N.Y.: Orbis Books, 1999.

Connolly, Sean. *Bede: On Tobit and on the Canticle of Habakkuk.* Dublin: Four
    Courts Press, 1997.
Coote, Robert B. *Amos among the Prophets: Composition and Theology.*
    Philadelphia: Fortress Press, 1981.
Eaton, John. *Mysterious Messengers: A Course on Hebrew Prophecy from
    Amos Onwards.* Grand Rapids, Mich.: Eerdmans, 1997.
Encyclopedia Judaica. New York: Macmillan, 1972.
Ginzberg, Louis, ed. *Legends of the Jews.* 7 vols. Philadelphia: Jewish Publica-
    tion Society, 1967.
Girard, Marc. *Haggai, a Prophet for Our Times: Everything Must Be Built
    Anew.* Sherbrooke, Canada: Mediaspaul, 1996.
Gowan, Donald E. *Theology of the Prophetic Books: The Death and Resurrec-
    tion of Israel.* Louisville: Westminster/John Knox Press, 1998.
Graffy, Adrian. *Alive and Active: The Old Testament beyond 2000.* Dublin:
    Columba Press, 1999.
Grey, Mary C. *The Outrageous Pursuit of Hope: Prophetic Dreams for the
    Twenty-First Century.* London: Darton, Longman & Todd, 2000.
Heschel, Abraham Joshua. *The Prophets: An Introduction.* Vols. 1 and 2. New
    York: Harper & Row, 1962.
Isaacs, Ronald H. *Messengers of God: A Jewish Prophets' Who's Who.*
    Northvale, N.J.: Jason Aronson, 1998.
Jacobs, Louis. *A Jewish Theology.* London: Darton, Longman & Todd, 1973.
Kaylor, R. David. *Jesus the Prophet: His Vision of the Kingdom on Earth.*
    Louisville: Westminster/John Knox Press, 1994.
Kirsch, Jonathan. *Moses: A Life.* New York: Ballantine Books, 1998.
Kodell, Jerome, O.S.B. *Lamentations, Haggai, Zechariah, Malachi, Obadiah,
    Joel, Second Zechariah, Baruch.* Old Testament Message Commentary 14.
    Wilmington, Del.: Michael Glazier, 1982.
Mays, James Luther, and Paul J. Achtemeier, eds. *Interpreting the Prophets.*
    Philadelphia: Fortress Press, 1987.
The Midrash [*Midrash Rabbah*]. New York: Soncino, 1877. (Includes: *Genesis
    Rabbah, Exodus Rabbah, Leviticus Rabbah, Numbers Rabbah, Deuteron-
    omy Rabbah, Ecclesiastes Rabbah, Song of Songs Rabbah, Ruth Rabbah*).
Nakanose, Shigeyuki. *Josiah's Passover: Sociology and the Liberating Bible.*
    Maryknoll, N.Y.: Orbis Books, 1993.
Pearl, Chaim. *Theology in Rabbinic Stories.* Peabody, Mass.: Hendrickson,
    1997.
Pesikta de Rav Kahana. R. Kahana's Compilation of Discourses for Shab-
    bat and Festal Dates. Trans. William G. Braude and Israel J. Kapstein.
    Philadelphia: Jewish Publication Society, 1975.
Religious Life Digest: Prophets and Martyrs. Quezon City, Philippines: Clare-
    tian Publications, 1987.
Sobosan, Jeffrey G. *Christian Commitment: Prophetic Living.* Mystic, Conn.:
    Twenty-Third Publications, 1986.

Sölle, Dorothee. *Suffering*. Philadelphia: Fortress Press, 1974.

Stuhlmueller, Carroll, C.P. *The Prophets and the Word of God*. Notre Dame, Ind.: Fides Publications, 1964.

Tanakh [Torah, Nevi'Im, Keutvim]: The Holy Scriptures. Philadelphia: Jewish Publication Society, 1985.

Visotzky, Burton. *The Road to Redemption: Lessons from Exodus on Leadership and Community*. New York: Crown, 1998.

von Rad, Gerhard. *The Message of the Prophets*. New York: Harper & Row, 1965.

Von Speyr, Adrienne. *The Mission of the Prophets*. San Francisco: Ignatius Press, 1966.

Wolpe, David J. *The Healer of Shattered Hearts: A Jewish View of God*. New York: Penguin, 1991.

Zucker, David J. *Israel's Prophets: An Introduction for Christians and Jews*. New York: Paulist Press, 1994.